Baldur's Gate 3: The Complete Walkthrough and Guide

LAVERNE SMITH

CONTENTS

Introduction

Baldur's Gate 3 stretches player opportunity to the outright edge. That unmatched degree of opportunity can be tracked down in essentially every part of the game, from its personality creation to battle, and after two full playthroughs and twelve continuous missions, I've still scarcely started to expose what's underneath. No two encounters are indistinguishable, and each character I've made feels interesting. While the game can't necessarily stay aware of the immediacy of a genuine Prison Expert, it figures out how to offer a lot of organization while likewise guaranteeing that its immense, web-like story is convincing beginning to end.

Baldur's Gate 3 starts in the stomach of a Nautiloid, a Lovecraftian spaceship guided by a squid-like race known as illithids. After you make your symbol and pick a class, you are contaminated with a parasite that gradually (and horrendously) transforms its host into an arm embellished mind flayer. You and the other impacted individuals from your party should figure out how to eliminate the parasites before the change is finished. A magnificently dim arrangement permits Larian Studios to arrange a diverse group of characters with a wide exhibit of convictions, demeanors, and foundations and give them a shared objective. These characters aren't adventuring together out of kinship (generally), however need. By and large it's an uncomfortable allyship overflowing with interior show and struggle.

Baldur's Gate 3 routinely puts its characters first, and it's better for it. While the story isn't exactly fascinating all alone and essentially sums to "cleanse the parasite and save the world," the different cast of characters works everything out such considerably more significant by making an additional layer of subtlety that grounds the whole involvement in additional individual stakes. Karlach is a hot-headed tiefling savage with an endearing personality, Astarion is a vainglorious and showy rebel with barely sufficient appeal to prevail upon you, and Lae'zel is a fight solidified champion that puts an intriguing twist on the lost soul model. There are 10 potential party individuals altogether, and every one is upheld by sharp composition, flawless acting, and lively activitys.

What's most amazing is the manner by which these characters respond and develop to your choices all through the game. How you play your personality factors into your relationship with your party. For instance, Astarion can be cruel and eager for power, and you can either support those dull inclinations or deftly attempt to control him away from them. This permits Astarion to go about as a sensational foil to a prude character or an evil partner to a more tumultuous person. Regardless of how you decide to play your personality, you will get to know a few characters and make foes with others, and in the event that you conflict with a party part a lot of they can leave you through and through. This is essential for what causes Baldur's Gate 3 to feel so receptive. Albeit the story and the arrangement continues as before across different playthroughs, the party elements and character connections keep on amazing on each resulting playthrough.

What likewise keeps the characters and collaborations new is the game's funny bone. Baldur's Gate 3 is entertaining and, assuming that you incline toward the idiocy, it tends to be humorous. The satire functions admirably in light of the fact that it originates from your bombed dice rolls, unfortunate choices, and flighty battle connections. This implies that these snapshots of levity feel special to you and your party. Of course, there are some composed into the content, such as persuading a troll to kowtow to you in Act 1, yet the most entertaining minutes feel unplanned. For instance, my personality had a wonderfully composed honest conversation with Lae'zel as she came to see the value in a dawn she once disdained. Notwithstanding, I neglected to wash off some comedian cosmetics I bought at a bazaar, so the second was to some degree subverted by my look.

These scenes and connections are upheld by a firm show. For a game with such countless factors, each discussion feels high quality because of the realistic methodology Larian Studios took with exchange. Each line other than your own is completely voiced, characters are expressive, and the camera cuts flawlessly between the activity. While this approach isn't novel, scarcely any games, if any, have done it to the size of Baldur's Gate 3. Show isn't all that matters, yet in that frame of mind of Baldur's Gate 3, it makes each playthrough, regardless of how absurd, feel composed and deliberate.

This amazing degree of reactivity stretches out to battle. While battle depends on D&D's fifth release ruleset, Larian Studios took a few freedoms to make it more receptive in a virtual setting. The outcome is a rich, layered battle framework that plays out like a turn-based strategic RPG. At first, every person has one activity and one reward activity. Assaults and spells normally require an activity while optional abilities like hopping or utilizing a thing require a reward activity. There are exemptions, yet by and large, the majority of your harm managing moves require an activity. Battle itself is determined through secret dice rolls. Like D&D, this adds a touch of vulnerability to the situation.

Where Baldur's Gate 3 separates itself from other strategic RPGs, however, is the manner by which adaptable its battle mechanics are. The game once in a while, if at any point, tells you "no," even in a portion of the more basic battles. As a matter of fact, the more you step up, the more ludicrous and capricious battle gets. For instance, I transformed an especially difficult supervisor into a goat utilizing a polymorph spell, and had our tiefling goddess Karlach kick him into a void. In Act 3, the companions I was playing with discovered that the Legend's Banquet spell makes the whole party safe to harm until the following extended rest. This implied that our wizard could project Cloudkill anyplace while our warrior and paladin-warlock could wipe up the stifling enemies, all while overlooking the spell's destructive impacts. Indeed, even something as straightforward as projecting Scurry and Activity Flood on a level 11 contender so they can go after multiple times (10 assuming they have a reward activity assault) in one turn wants to twist the principles to execute a shrewd play that can emphatically move the tide of fight, however the game supports it.

The battle is so adaptable, particularly close to the end, that a very much streamlined party can decimate even probably the hardest enemies in the game. However in any event, when the fights begin to feel all in all too simple, they never become repetition. Each spell connection, natural snare, or shrewd move feels like a stroke of splendor that main you and your party might have evoked. During one battle, a small bunch of traps were regurgitating smoke powder bombs that would detonate after a turn and send anybody in the impact range flying. The conspicuous game-plan is cripple the snares or avoid the bombs. Notwithstanding, since the bombs didn't explode right away, I put down a Mass of Fire with my magician, and the remainder of my party individuals decisively heaved the planned bombs to send off my enemies into the blast. Was it effective? Likely not. Was it viable? Totally. The way that Baldur's Gate 3 permitted me to mess with this large number of factors and compensated my inventiveness addresses how much innovativeness the battle can empower.

Contingent upon your decisions, each feature of Baldur's Gate 3 works pair to convey a climactic third demonstration. The story works to a troublesome last decision, key battle experiences are fittingly epic, and everything happens in the thick city of Baldur's Gate. However great as the initial two demonstrations may be, it truly feels like Baldur's Gate 3 holds back something special for later. The goal of character bends specifically truly sticks out. In my experience, Karlach's story wrapped up with a self-contradicting, genuine second that nearly carried me to tears. In the mean time, I figured out how to "fix" Astarion's more obscure propensities by uncovering a portion of his injury. While various, the two circular segments felt similarly fulfilling and fulfilling.

Yet, your choices can likewise prompt an iron deficient third demonstration that comes up short on profound result at all. In an extremely tumultuous center mission, my party and I killed as well as irritated essentially every significant person. Your mission log actually drives you to some of Act 3's critical set pieces, however a large portion of them felt exposed without characters like Shadowheart and Astarion to ground the experience. It's an unusual issue to have, on the grounds that most games basically wouldn't allow you to kill off characters that are this fundamental to the story, yet Baldur's Gate 3 lets you, and there are ramifications. Is it Larian Studios' liability to guarantee that each and every journey, plotline, and character circular segment is fulfilling assuming those characters are never again near? I have to take a hard pass, and on account of Baldur's Gate 3, that proud player opportunity is undeniably more vital to the general insight. You get what you really ask for, and in some cases what you sow is a miserable and desolate end.

Regardless, that sort of result shows that the game's degree of opportunity reaches out past a performance experience to center, where the factors are muddled further by having other human-controlled swashbucklers. Up to four players can make their own personality and play through the whole mission together. Shockingly, the center is almost indistinguishable from the single-player experience. It has a few idiosyncrasies, however any player can push the story forward, pursue significant choices, and aggro NPCs without any other person knowing. It's enabling (and somewhat startling) realizing that you might actually sink a whole questline or character curve in view of a choice you make that the remainder of your party could miss.

In my center run I chose to play as the Dim Desire, an adjustable pre-made character that has a propensity for homicide. To appropriately pretend this person, I chose to pick all of the Dim Urge-explicit discourse choices. This implied I gnawed off Hurricane's arm at every turn and we at no point ever saw him in the future; his whole questline and character curve dissipated speedier than my personality could swallow his cut off arm. In another example, one of my party individuals was attempting to de-raise what is happening between the druids of Emerald Woods and some tiefling exiles. As he was attempting to quiet everybody down, I got excessively near their golden calf and aggroed the whole town. It was entertaining at the time, however since we concluded right off the bat that we wouldn't save filth, this implied we bombed a whole questline on the grounds that I was excessively restless.

Regardless of whether your party plays it straight, it very well may be challenging to follow buddy missions, particularly with three or four dynamic players. Now and again just certain players can converse with explicit party individuals, discussions are frequently rehashed, and the game can't necessarily follow who expressed what to whom. To make things more troublesome, in the event that you really do have a four-player crusade going, you will be unable to take party individuals along for their particular journeys. Shadowheart, for instance, deserted our party since we didn't have space for her during a significant snapshot of her circular segment. There are strategies for getting around this, for example, picking a beginning person toward the start of the mission or by trading party individuals on the fly. Notwithstanding, picking a beginning person restricts your customization choices, and trading party individuals on the fly just works with a gathering of a few players.

When my party had come to the third demonstration, Shadowheart had deserted us, Hurricane had disappeared after I gnawed off his hand, Wyll had passed on during the Emerald Forest disaster, Karlach had wouldn't go along with us due the Emerald Woods disaster, Minthara had gone after us in light of the fact that a party part attempted to guess what she might be thinking expeditiously after a sexual experience, and I had killed Astarion since I could have done without the manner in which he treated me. Our main enduring party part was Lae'zel who, wonderfully, was determined by our (for the most part my) silly viciousness. This brought about an empty and divided last venture that constrained us to fill in the spaces. By and by, this issue is established in Baldur's Gate 3's tremendous degree of opportunity. Without a doubt, Larian Studios might have set up security rails so we might have had the "legitimate" insight, however that would come at the expense of the opportunity that is so center to the game, particularly in a helpful setting where each player ought to feel like a legend unto themselves.

The protection of outright opportunity in center additionally raises the all around magnificent battle. With up to four players, each controlling a person, the speed of engagements eases back to cause it to feel more key. As your party opens new spells and capacities, correspondence becomes essential. Once in a while this can be to execute undeniable level combos and systems, different times it tends to be to just try not to be burned or lost a precipice by your companions. One way or the other, center battle turns into a strained and profoundly fulfilling issue that rewards cooperation and coordination.

I spent approximately 20 of my 200 hours of recess on PlayStation 5. In light of my involvement with Acts 1 and 3 of the control center variant, the presentation was unshakable. Battle, investigation, and discourse moved along as expected, and because of its cross-save usefulness, I had the option to take up where I left out on PS5, Steam Deck, and PC. While I favor mouse and console for a game like this, the DualSense functions admirably for Baldur's Gate 3. The majority of the truly difficult work is finished through outspread menus. Whenever you can pull up your activity menu and cycle through adjustable spiral menus that house your activities, assaults, spells, and things. Stock administration can get a piece unpredictable, however, particularly in the event that you are playing solo and moving things between each of the four party individuals. It tends to be somewhat overpowering, particularly right off the bat, however I can't envision another way Larian Studios might have packed that large number of connections into a regulator. Furthermore, regardless, I favored straightforwardly controlling my personality and the camera with simple sticks over clicking around on a guide.

PlayStation 5 additionally takes into account two-player split-screen center. A decent expansion is nearly essentially as vigorous as online center. In any case, gathering the HUD and all that relevant data into two separate longwise boards is not even close to exquisite. I did likewise run into some minor sound bugs, especially when it came to discourse not continuously setting off.

Despite the fact that PlayStation 5 isn't the most ideal way to encounter Baldur's Gate 3, it's actually certainly worth your time assuming that is your main choice. There may be a few developing torments with regards to the collaboration haggle, yet everything feels unimportant when you consider the extension and desire of a game like this.

According to close to the furthest limit of Baldur's Gate 3, a person, "A lot of opportunity can be terrifying." It's a strong line inside the setting of the story, yet it likewise addresses Baldur's Gate 3 on a more profound level. The opportunity that it offers is phenomenal, and it takes a short time to see the extent of how that affects the game, as a matter of fact. On occasion, the sheer number of decisions and results can overpower. However, in a little while, it becomes evident that Baldur's Gate 3 permits players to be the creators of their own fates in a manner no other game has previously. It's that opportunity and reactivity matched with incredible show and phenomenal characters truly put Baldur's Gate 3 aside, it's the reason following 200 hours I'm actually returning to it. A lot of opportunity can be startling, however Larian confides in its players to capitalize on it, for better or in negative ways.

Game Guide

General Guide

Tips and tricks

You will track down a bunch of tips for fledglings for Baldur's Gate 3. We've arranged different tips and deceives on, for example battle and investigation of the game world. Things recorded there ought to assist you during the main hours with BG3.

Save your progress as often as possible

In Baldur's Gate 3 you can save without limitations and you ought to utilize this. You can do manual, quick, and auto saves. Save the game:

- Prior to inspecting an obscure gadget or having a discussion with a significant NPC. There is dependably the chance of a few significant decisions or one of a kind choices.

- Prior to endeavoring to pass an expertise check. In the event that the endeavor falls flat, you will not have the option to rehash it.

- Prior to stirring up some dust. This will permit you to test various approaches to getting ready for a fight and to surprise the foes. You can likewise utilize the recoveries to keep away from battles.

- At the point when you are in the battle. You can save the game in each turn and after each move. This will permit you, for instance, to drop a terrible move or rehash a missed assault.

Examine opponents by checking the cards with information about them

Baldur's Gate 3 permits you to show data about your adversaries and any remaining characters free of charge. To do this, you want to move the cursor over a given person, press the right mouse button, and select the choice to show the person card.

You can learn, for example about the quantity of their wellbeing focuses, protective layer class, protection from various sorts of assaults and spells, speed of development, capability, or drive. This information will assist you with deciding if you will actually want to effortlessly overcome this person, as well as better plan to go after it (for example picking assaults and spells related with its shortcomings).

Try to place your party members in such a way that would give you an advantage over enemies

You can and ought to get ready for some battles by putting your characters close to adversaries before the battle begins. Use covertness mode to try not to be recognized too early. You can change the arrangement of party individuals when the battle starts - foes will respond to your choices. Recall to:

- Place party individuals battling a good ways off (utilizing sorcery or went weapons) on higher landscape. The thought is to give them the level benefit that builds the possibilities of effective assaults.

- Attempt to situate characters battling with light scuffle weapons behind adversaries' backs. Back assaults bargain more harm. This is especially significant while controlling a person having a place with the Officer class.

Environmental hazards can be a hindrance or advantage

The combat zones in Baldur's Gate 3 are intuitive - you need to consider this while arranging assaults and courses for your party individuals. Contingent upon the conditions, ecological dangers might assist you with disposing of adversaries or represent extra dangers to your party. Here are a few hints for them:

- Attempt to check the war zone before you stir something up, or do this in the principal turn. By moving the cursor over intelligent items or components of the ground, you can see data about their qualities.

- Search for chances to debilitate adversaries utilizing natural dangers, for example by setting dangerous articles ablaze or exploding them, or by dropping weighty freight on adversaries.

- Stay away from contact with expected risks, for example, fire or elusive surfaces that can slow or debilitate your party individuals.

Not all fights are mandatory

Baldur's Gate 3 is a sort of game where numerous missions and individual showdowns can be finished in different ways. Some of them let you keep away from battles. This can be especially useful when you can be compelled to battle serious areas of strength for an or a gathering. Recall the accompanying:

- You can begin a fight by settling on unambiguous decisions during the discussion, for example, picking a discourse choice that sets off a battle or falling flat a skillcheck. Make sure to save the game before each experience.

- A few battles can be kept away from by not drawing near to rivals noticeable somewhere out there. For instance, you can attempt to sneak past them or search for something else altogether to your objective.

Choose those skillchecks where you have the best chance of success

A more prominent likelihood of coming out on top in a skillcheck gives you extra focuses to the worth you got from a dice roll (in the model in the image over, this reward is 3). You can get a reward if the skillcheck is connected to an expertise wherein the person has accomplished capability, or to a characteristic that the individual has grown adequately. Attempt to search for these skillchecks, particularly in the event that there are a few distinct ones to browse during a solitary scene or discussion. Two significant things to recollect here:

- A skillcheck is constantly finished by the legend who started it. In the event that you can pick the individual to play out a given movement, pick the legend who will get the most elevated reward.

- The progress of the skillcheck, even with the likely reward, relies vigorously upon karma. We unequivocally encourage you to make a fast save prior to taking any skillcheck-a bombed test can't be rehashed.

Search all locations thoroughly

In Baldur's Gate 3, there is a lot of plunder ready to be found the areas you visit. You can track down it in two principal ways:

- By holding the ALT key in each new area. This will feature a portion of the intelligent components nearby, like cadavers or chests. You can then look at them looking for treasure.

- By moving the cursor over every one of the extraordinary components of the climate. This will assist you with finding those items or chests that were not set apart with the ALT key. These holders may likewise conceal a few fortunes.

Look for optional locations and paths

Each significant area in BG3 contains discretionary entries and minor areas that can hold novel fortunes or elective ways to regions related with missions. Here are a few vital clues for them:

- You can leap to certain spots. Search for racks and stages that are apparently out of reach. You can continuously check in the event that they're inside bouncing reach.

- You can stack things and climb them. This is one more strategy for arriving at areas that are distant from the beginning.

- The hoodlum's instruments allow you an opportunity to open a locked entryway. Make sure to pick a legend with enough places in Skillful deception.

Recruit companions as soon as possible after completing the prologue

After the preface on board the Nautiloid, your personality awakens alone on an ocean side. Luckily, you will not be separated from everyone else for a really long time. By investigating the region you can rapidly select the main sidekicks. For instance, right close to the ocean side, you will run over a shut access to the remnants - a minister named Shadowheart stands close by. Selecting her will give you admittance to numerous valuable spells.

Hosting additional gathering individuals will be exceptionally useful in winning the underlying fights. This likewise gives you more noteworthy flexibility, both on the combat zone and in groupings that expect, for instance, utilizing characters' abilities to build the possibility passing skillchecks.

Analyze the queue of moves during fights

While battling, the line of the moves is constantly shown in the upper left corner of the screen, in which colleagues and partners (green boundary) and rivals (red line) are incorporated. You can utilize that information and attempt to dispense with, debilitate or deaden more grounded rivals before their turn. Essentially, you can likewise recuperate, reinforce or force favors on those partners who will before long take their actions.

Be sure to defuse the traps

Traps in Baldur's Gate 3 can immediately kill one or even all of the colleagues. So it's ideal to pay special attention to them while investigating a wide range of prisons, graves and different areas with significant fortunes. Traps can be recognized through effective discernment tests.

Subsequent to finding a snare, you most certainly attempt to kill it by utilizing a person with deft hands and a set to incapacitate the snares. Prior to any such activity, save the game, on the grounds that a bombed endeavor can prompt the deficiency of instruments, yet additionally to the setting off of the snare. In the event that you can't incapacitate the snare, it's ideal to leave it for some other time, get back with more insight.

Push enemies off high ledges

There's a reward activity called Push, and it's accessible for all characters no matter what the addressed class. You can pick this activity from the blue bar to one side of the person's thumbnail at the lower part of the screen.

With Push, you can truly debilitate or kill rivals. Attempt to utilize this activity on foes remaining on high stone retires or close to a gap. While arranging a Push, you will see the rival's likely "direction" (model in the image). Foes tumbling from more prominent levels will get more harm. In outrageous cases, the pushed adversary might pass on.

Difficulty levels

In Baldur's Gate 3 there are a great deal of choices to modify the interactivity, and this likewise applies to the degree of challenge. On this page of our aide, we make sense of the distinctions between 3 principal trouble levels - Voyager, Adjusted and Strategist. This will assist you with picking a diffculty level that will give the best insight and accommodated your capability in RPG games, particularly turn-based ones. We likewise answer whether a relaxed "story mode" dificulty level exists.

List of difficulty levels

In Baldurs Gate 3, there are 3 essential trouble levels accessible:

- Explorer - This is the least trouble level present. It permits the player to zero in chiefly on the story, putting less accentuation on right person improvement and bad-to-the-bone tactical turn-based interactivity. Extra highlights of this setting are more troublesome killing of cordial NPCs (bringing down their possibilities of inadvertent demise), 20% better costs from traders, and a beginning +2 reward to Proficiencies for party individuals.

- Balanced - This is the default proposed typical trouble level. Picking this setting will require more thoughtfulness regarding character improvement and party piece, and requires getting ready for fights and giving right orders. Nonetheless, there ought not be a situation where some part of the game is very troublesome and difficult to finish. This is the suggested decision for a first playthrough.

- Tactical - this is the most elevated conceivable trouble level, which is a likeness conventional "extremely high" setting. Each off-base choice connected with character improvement, group determination and strategies during fights can prompt a fast passing. This mode builds the number and insights of adversaries, including their capacity set and their man-made consciousness. Also, the quantity of traps and other potential risks might increment.

Does BG3 have a story mode?

- Numerous contemporary creations offer a story mode that permits you to zero in exclusively on following the plot without stressing over dealing with a group or giving right orders in fights.

- In BG3, you won't see as a conventional "story" trouble level, yet with Explorer picked, the game ought to be perceptibly more straightforward than at default trouble setting. By and by, you can't totally overlook strategies in fight or the subject of fostering the capacities and hardware of the legends. Explorer doesn't need point by point diving into insights or seeing more complicated ongoing interaction mechanics.

Lockpicking

On this page of our game manual for Baldurs Gate 3 we make sense of how the lockpicking framework functions in the game. You can utilize lockpicks to open shut entries and get close enough to the items in locked chests and holders. You'll likewise figure out how to save lockpicks and not to lose criminal's tools time after time.

As the game advances, you might experience many locked entryways and chests. Locked entryways might obstruct admittance to additional areas and locked chests might keep you from stealing from them to get important fortunes that are being put away in them. You can act in two ways like clockwork:

- Search for a key that matches the lock.

- Utilize the Thieves' Tools to incapacitate the lock.

You can track down the Thieves' Tools with other plunder by investigating the game world, or get them from merchants. They are sold by, for example Mattis and Arron in the Druid Forest. Mattis ought to offer you less expensive costs for lockpicks.

The viability of the Thieves' Tools relies upon the level of the Skillful deception ability of specific legend. Thus, it is ideal to pass the tools to one of the colleagues who has capability in the Skillful deception expertise. For instance, Astarion the maverick ought to have this capability. He can join the group in the space which you investigate soon after finishing the preamble of the game.

Giving the tools to a person that is great in lockpicking is vital, as a bombed endeavor of opening a lock will make the Thieves' Tools vanish from the stock. Nonetheless, on the off chance that your lockpicking endeavor was effective, the tools will not vanish and you can utilize them in the future later on.

To set up the Thieves' Tools for use, finding them in the stock and utilize the Add to Hotbar option is ideal.

As the possibilities incapacitating a specific lock are reliant upon karma, we unequivocally prescribe to make a fast save each time prior to utilizing the Thieves' Tools. In the event that you have neglected to open the lock and lost the tools, you can stack the game and attempt once more. Along these lines, you will not need to abandon opening a particular way or stealing from a chest. Additionally, you will not need to search for another Thieves' Tools.

Classes

Fighter

Guide

In this BG3 guide, you will track down fundamental data on the most proficient method to make the best Fighter. We make sense of which race, subclass, and foundation to decide and how to convey expertise focuses. At the lower part of the page, we've recorded the best forms for the Fighter, contingent upon battle style.

Best background for Fighter

While picking Fighter's experience, you ought to match proficiencies connected with the essential capacities of this class, specifically with Strength and Constitution. The best foundation for a Fighter is:

- Outlander - capable in Games and Endurance.

- Soldier - capable in Games and Terrorizing.

Best race for Fighter

The main capacities of a Fighter are Strength and Constitution, so the best races for this class are:

- Shield Dwarf with +2 Strength and +2 Constitution.

- Githyanki with +2 Strength and +1 Knowledge.

- Human who has a +1 reward for each detail.

Best combat style for Fighter

While making a Fighter character, you can pick 1 of 6 battling styles, which give different detached rewards.

- **Archery** - +2 to attacks with ranged weapon.

- **Defence** - +1 bonus to Armour Class wearing armour.

- **Dueling** - +2 bonus to damage rolls with a weapon and an increased chance of dealing heavy damage when the character is equipped with only one weapon and the other hand remains empty.

- **Great Weapon Fighting** - when a damage roll for a two-handed weapon results 1 or 2, the roll is repeated.

- **Protection** - when a character has a shield, it imposes a disadvantage on the enemy who attacks one of your allies. Works within a 1.5 m radius.

- **Two-Weapon Fighting Style** - when a character attacks with the second hand, you can add your ability modifier to the damage of the offhand attack.

The decision of battling style relies upon what sort of Fighter you might want to play as. In the event that you're searching for an immense person blade, the Incomparable Weapon Battling has an exceptionally fascinating choice of rerolling ominous harm rolls. A Fighter who picks the Two Weapon Battling bargains the most harm. Likewise worth adding subsequent to arriving at the fifth level, the Fighter gets an extra assault each turn.

Fighter'ss ability points

- Strength is the main measurement of, an entirely in one-on-one Fighter on-one battles. An elevated degree of Solidarity will be helpful for protective tosses.

- The second most significant element of this class is Constitution, which gives extra hit focuses.

Best Fighter subclass

After arriving at Level 3, the Fighter will actually want to pick 1 out of 2 subclasses.

- **Battle Master - has Superiority Dice**, which allows you to draw 3 out of 4 options: **Menacing Attack** deals Piercing damage and can frighten target; **Pushing Attack** deals Piercing damage and can push the target back; **Rally**, which enhances hit points of a creature; **Riposte**, which when missed attack, allow the Fighter use Superiority Dice to execute a counterattack and inflict a certain amount of Piercing damage.

- **Eldritch Knight** has many cantrips and spells. They can use, among others, Magic Missile, Witch Bolt, Thunderwave, Mage Armour, or Poison Spray.

Every one of these subclasses has its assets. In the event that You like playing areas of strength for a with mysterious capacities, pick the Eldritch Knight subclass. In the event that you like to have a bigger number of strong assaults, pick the Battle Master.

Best Fighter class actions

- **Second Wind** is additional action that recovers hit points.

- Using **Action Surge** you can perform extra action, which can be used for Attacks or casting a Spell or Cantrip.

Best Fighter build

Ready build for a Fighter fighting with a two-handed weapon:

- **Race:** Shield Dwarf

- **Background**: Outlander

- **Subclass**: Battle Master

- **Fighting Style**: Great Weapon Fighting

- **Abilities**: Strength 17, Dexterity 16, Constitution 16, Wisdom 11-12, Intelligence and Charisma 9-10.

- **Weapon:** Everburn Blade

- **Armour:** Splint Armour

The best build for a Fighter using two weapons:

- **Race**: Githyanki

- **Background:** Soldier

- **Subclass**: Battle Master

- **Fighting Style**: Two-Weapon Fighting Style

- **Abilities**: Strength 17, Dexterity 13, Constitution 14, Wisdom 12, Intelligence and Charisma between 8-10.

- **Weapon**: Morningstar and Rapier

- **Armour:** Splint Armour

The following build is prepared for a Fighter with a weapon and shield:

- Race: Human

- Background: Outlander

- Subclass: Eldritch Knight

- Fighting Style: Protection or Defence

- Abilities: Strength 16, Dexterity 14, Constitution 15, Wisdom 13, Intelligence and Charisma 10.

- Weapon: Shortsword of First Blood

- Armour: Splint Armour

- Shield: Absolute's Warboard

Build

Fighter is quite possibly of the most general class in Baldur's Gate 3. A Fighter can battle in close battle, a good ways off and even has an enchanted subclass. In this aide, we will uncover the best and the most grounded work for a Fighter in Baldur's Gate 3, because of which no foe will be really difficult for you.

Character creation wizard

The best race for a Fighter is a Half-Orc. This is because of his racial capacities. One of them permits you to get basic hits on rolls of 19-20 and the subsequent one truly intends that on the off chance that your HP dips under zero once during an extended rest, you won't kick the bucket yet be left with 1 HP.

This expertise will prove to be useful while standing up to adversaries, particularly when you consider the way that the Fighter will most frequently be taking most of the blows.

Taking everything into account, the most ideal decision would be Soldier because of their capability in Games and Terrorizing.

Class progression

- At level 1, you pick the fighting style - pick Two-Handed Weapons Fighting, as this form centers around precisely that sort of weapons.

- Your primary battle circle will be the Action Surge gained at the subsequent level and a brief reprieve just after it. On account of this, you will actually want to overcome a foe in a productive manner.

- At level 3, pick Battle Master as your subclass - this model offers the most flexible abilities and simultaneously the greatest lift in harm that anyone could hope to find. For moves, pick Precision Attack, Disarming Strike and Riposte.

- At level 4, you get the chance to take an accomplishment or increment the attributes reward. Pick +2 for Strength, so as of now you ought to as of now have 20 Strength focuses, which will give you +5 harm from the Attribute Modifier alone.

- In the accompanying areas, you will figure out how to acquire the missing 1 assuming that you actually have 19 Strength focuses at level 4.

- Level 5 involves a reward attack, which duplicates your battle productivity.

- Level 6 brings a reward accomplishment. You can reassign it to attribute improvement, despite the fact that getting the Incomparable Weapon Master include is a superior thought, as it permits you to take a - 5 punishment while the harm increments by 10. Joined with 20 in Strength and Precision Attack, it altogether builds the possibility managing extra harm.

- At level 7, you gain a subclass capacity, in which case you pick another move. You can pick, for instance, Repulsing Impact.

- Level 8 brings another accomplishment and, very much like previously, you can expand your attributes - Constitution is suggested increment the quantity of HP. On the other hand, you can choose the Charge highlight, which builds your versatility, or Vigilant, which guarantees that you will not get amazed and adds +5 Drive.

- At level 9, you get a significant capacity that gives you a re-roll on a bombed saving toss.

- Level 10 involves more moves. At this stage, you can pick what you see as generally helpful.

- At level 11, you will get another attack (and you'll be the main class to get it). Right now, you have 3 attacks - in the event that you consolidate them with Action Surge, you can proceed upwards of six attacks for every round!

- At the last level, you pick between highlights. You can take Weighty Reinforcement Master or Intense, which builds your HP.

Ilithild Powers

Don't be afraid to **unlock and use these skills** - focus especially on **Cull the Weak, Repulsor** and **Black Hole**. Unleashing the full power of Ilithild Powers doesn't affect the character negatively, so leave all tadpoles for yourself.

Party members - their skills and spells

To get the a large portion of your group, right party sythesis and abilities are an unquestionable requirement. Due to their abilities, the best arrangement is to have a Minister, a Wizard or a Troubadour in your group.

The Priest can recuperate your Fighter and furnishes them with helpful buffs, for example, Shield of Confidence, which builds AC by 2. On the other hand, they can draw a portion of the hits onto themselves, make your weapon mysterious and cast a very valuable Favor. Shadowheart fits this job impeccably.

The Wizard has one of the most remarkable spells available to them, to be specific Flurry. This spell flips around a Fighter and transforms them into a relentless killing machine, as it speeds up, your AC and awards you a reward action. Assuming you join this with Action Surge at level 5, you will get six attacks, perhaps seven when joined with the Savage Attacker accomplishment. Storm will function admirably as this sort of a person.

At long last, the Poet is likewise incredibly valuable - because of their Motivation, they can expand your hit opportunity as well as mysteriously reinforce you. Minstrel consolidates the two previously mentioned choices, yet since no sidekick is a Versifier, you should change someone into one.

Equipment and bonuses from it

There are a few fascinating things to get in Act I. The most grounded ones are recorded beneath:

Not long before the finish of the preface, Ilithid will battle one of the devils. Kill the devil and afterward the Psyche Flayer to get a thing that is very strong at this stage - a two-handed sword that bargains an extra 1d4 fire harm.

In the Myconid State Thullia will give you boots that permit you to Run as an Extra Action. At a similar area, the vendor Derryth can sell you an amuletthat permits you to project mending.

While moving toward the finish of the Underdark missions, you will have the potential chance to utilize the Grymforge. Manufacture plate protection and a head protector. The covering diminishes the damageyou get and concedes you a detached capacity on account of which you can't be fundamentally hit. The head protector will give you admittance to the Tracker's Imprint: a spell that adds 1d6 harm to every one of your attacks.

In the troll camp, subsequent to killing Razglin, you will track down gloves on a heap of fortune. They make things simpler in skirmish battle when you are encircled by two foes. In a similar area, search for Smasher - kill him or burglarize him to get a ring that speeds up by 3m.

Concerning inactive rewards, the main one can be acquired while going up against Aunt Ethel. At the point when her wellbeing level dips under roughly 20 HP, a cutscene will set off in which she offers you strength and power in return for getting by. Consent to this and you will get 1 to your picked attribute - for this situation, pick Strength.

In Act III, attempt to get Balduran's Giantslayer on the off chance that you are into scuffle battle. This strong two-handed blade pairs your Solidarity reward while managing harm. To expand your guarded abilities, you ought to get Helldusk Protective layer dropped in the wake of killing Raphael and Viconia's Strolling Post, which you will get subsequent to overcoming Viconi DeVir.

Consumables

Below you will find a list of consumables that will make your Fighter even stronger.

- **Oil of Accuracy** - provides +2 to Attack Rolls.

- **Elixir of Heroism** - gives +10 temporary HP and grants the Bless status.

- **Potion of Flying** - additional mobility is something that is always needed.

- **Potion of Hill Giant Strength** - perfect if you don't have 20 Strength yet.

- **Elixir of Vigilance** - provides +5 to Initiative, make sure to drink it before tougher battles.

Wizard

Guide

Wizards are strong spellcasters who have committed as long as they can remember to concentrating on the regulations and standards of wizardry. This is the most prototype of the relative multitude of sorcery based classes in Baldur's Gate 3, furnished with an unbelievably wide stockpile of spells and supernatural impacts, which will demonstrate very valuable in the risky universe of the Forgotten Realms.

Best race for Wizard

In the full arrival of Baldur's Gate 3, the engineers have eliminated selective racial rewards. From here onward, while picking a race, you can add +2 and +1 rewards to any detail you'd like. Regardless of this, a few racial capacities prove to be useful for specific classes.

- High Elf - This race receives 1 bonus Cantrip, which you can add to your arsenal of known spells.

- High Half-Elf - Similar to the previous race, it offers a bonus Cantrip.

Ability Points

When distributing skill points for a Wizard, **prioritize a high Intelligence coefficient first and foremost**. You should also invest into:

- **Dexterity**, which will grant some valuable **Armor Class** to fragile, armorless Wizards.

- **Constitution** provides a few extra **Hit Points** and helps maintain concentration when casting **concentration spells**.

Best background for Wizard

Some of the best backgrounds for Wizards include:

- **Acolyte** - proficiency in **Insight** and Intelligence-based **Religion** both complete the image of a well-read Wizard, proving rather useful during your adventure.

- **Sage** - proficiency in two Intelligence-based skills, **Arcana** and **History**, fits Wizards rather well.

Arcane Recovery

A class capacity, that allows Wizards to utilize an action to recapture a portion of their pre-owned spell spaces, however their complete level can't surpass half of the Wizard's. For instance:

- a Level 2 Wizard can recover a solitary Level 1 spell opening.

- a Level 4 Wizard can recover a solitary Level 2 spell openings or two Level 1 spell spaces.

Obscure Recuperation must be utilized beyond battle.

Best spells

Wizards are strong spellcasters ready to utilize lots of various hostile, protective and utility spells. Like Druids and Priests, Wizards can set up a portion of their known spells consistently, keeping this rundown until their next extended rest.

With how wide their spell program is, choosing only a couple of them is troublesome. On a different page of the aide, Best Wizard spells, we've recorded the best spells of all schools and levels.

Cantrips:

- **Light** and **Dancing Lights** - both spells create **sources of bright light**. Useful for characters without Darkvision.

- **Ray of Frost** - deals **1d8** cold damage to a single target and reduces their **speed**.

- **Shocking Grasp** - a melee spell that deals **1d8** damage. Has **advantage** against targets wearing **metal armor**.

Spells:

- **Mage Armour** - changes an unarmored target's Armor Class to **13 plus their Dexterity modifier**.

- **Magic Missile** - fires **three projectiles** which deal **1d4+1** damage each, are guaranteed to hit and have **18 meters** of range.

- **Sleep** - nearby enemies whose total amount of **hit points** doesn't exceed **24** fall into a magical slumber. The target wakes up when receiving damage.

- **Ray of Sickness** - deals **2d8** poison damage and can inflict the **Poisoned** status on the target.

- **Find Familiar** - the Wizard summons a **small creature** (cats, frogs, rats, etc.) as a familiar. It can help you during exploration or in combat.

- **Cloud of Daggers** - covers an area with sharp blades, which deal **4d4** damage every turn.

- **Web** - a **Level 2** spell that covers an area with a sticky, flammable substance.

- **Scorching Ray** - fires **three rays of scorching light**, dealing **2d6** damage each.

- **Counterspell** - **interrupts and dispells** a different spell as it's being cast. The higher the spell's level, the more difficult it is to counter.

- **Fireball** - an iconic **Level 3** spell that deals **8d6** area damage.

Best subclass for Wizard

Wizard subclasses focus on **Spell Schools**, which represent a certain area of arcane knowledge. The base game is to have **eight Schools**, but the Early Access version features only **two**. These are:

- **Evocation School** - a subclass focused on evoking powerful, **elemental** arcane effects. **Evocation Savant** reduces the cost of learning Evocation spells from scrolls by half. **Sculpt Spells** lets the Wizard create **invlunerability areas** for their allies while casting, within which they automatically pass checks and saving throws against Evocation spells cast by them.

- **Abjuration School** - Abjuration Wizards are masters of **defensive magic**. Their wide range of defensive spells makes them invaluable allies in combat. **Abjuration Savant** works similar to the other schools' Savant abilities, cutting the cost of learning the school's spells by half. **Arcane Ward** is a powerful ability, that lets the Wizard create a special barrier once per day - this barrier **absorbs some enemy attacks**. The barrier regains hit points with each Abjuration spell its holder casts.

- **Illusion School** - a subclass based on creating illusions to deceive foes. The **Improved Minor Illusion** ability available from level 2 will allow you to cast this Cantrip as a **bonus action**. Additionally, you can create a distracting image **even in hiding**, and even when being **Silenced**.

- **Necromancy School** - a school ruling over life and death, letting the caster control undead. The **Grim Harvest** ability available from level 2, allows you to **recover some Health Points** when **you deliver a mortal blow to a creature when using a spell**. The amount of points recovered is equal **to twice the level of the spell used to cause death, or even three times if the spell used was from the Necromancy School**.

- **Transmutation School** - based on manipulating matter, transforming items and creatures. The **Experimental Alchemy** ability means that from now on, **your Wizard will create 2 alchemical products instead of 1 when working with reagents. To do so, however, you must pass a Medicine skill check with level 15 difficulty**. The **Transmuter's Stone** available at later levels, also allows you to store the selected transmutation ability within a physical object.

- **Conjuration School** - Conjurers are adept at creating objects and effects out of nothing. Over time, they also learn how to instantly cover huge distances. Available from level 2 **Minor Conjuration: Create Water** allows the Wizard to **summon rain in the selected area**. The action can be performed after a short rest and **does not consume a spell slot**. At later levels, a Wizard using the Conjuration School can also **teleport**.

- **Enchantment School** - based on affecting the enemies' minds and bending their will. **Hypnotic Gaze** allows you to bend your opponent's will so that they **stop performing their actions**. The skills available later will also allow you to change the direction of a charging enemy's attack.

- **Divination School** - based on predicting future events and preventing them. The **Portent**ability gives you access to **2 random dice roll each long rest**. The Divination Wizard **may replace any attack roll or saving throw on a different one**. The ability resets after a long rest.

Best build for Wizard

As a summary, this is an example build for a Level 3 Wizard:

- **Race**: Stone Gnome

- **Subclass**: Conjuration School

- **Background**: Sage

- **Ability Scores**: Intelligence around 16/17, Dexterity and Constitution around 16/14, Wisdom around 12, Charisma and Strength around 10/8.

Spells

From this section of the manual for Baldurs Gate 3, you will realize what are the spells accessible for the Wizard - one of the classes accessible in the game.

The Wizards are masters of enchantment and they approach a larger number of spells than some other person classes accessible in Baldurs Gate 3. The spells that can be found on your personality are partitioned into levels, and that implies that you can get to additional strong spells whenever you have acquired a specific degree of involvement.

Spells - Level 1

The table beneath addresses generally level 1 Wizard spells accessible while making another person in Baldurs Gate 3.

> **Witch Bolt**
> **Effect**: the hero summons a beam of energy that causes 1d12 Lightning damage and connects to the target with an electric arc.
> **Range**: 18 meters.
> **Concentration**: required
> **Additional information**: you can activate the arc of lightning in each round to automatically inflict 1d12 electrical injuries.

> **True Strike**
> **Effect**: detect the target's defensive properties to have an easier time when attacking it.
> **Range**: 18 meters.
> **Concentration**: required

Thunderwave

Effect: the hero unleashes a wave of deafening power that causes 2d8 Thunder damage and kickbacks creatures and objects.

Range: 5 meters.

Sleep

Effect: magically put the creatures with a total of 24 health points to sleep.

Range: 18 meters.

Additional information: sleeping creatures will wake up if injured.

Shocking Grasp

Effect: lightning fires from your hero's hands, causing 1d8 Lightning damage and prevents the target from reacting.

Range: 1.5 meters.

Ray of Sickness

Effect: the hero summons a beam of toxic energy that inflicts 2d8 Poison damage and can cause the target to be poisoned.

Range: 18 meters.

Ray Of Frost

Effect: the hero summons an icy ray of pale blue light that causes 1d8 Cold damage and reduces the target's speed by 3 metres.

Range: 18 meters.

Protection from Evil and Good

Effect: protect the benevolent being from aberrations, celestial, elementals, fey, fiends, and undead.

Range: 1.5 meters.

Concentration: required

Other information: the attacks of the above creatures against this target are at disadvantage and they cannot charm, frighten or possess it.

Poison Spray

Effect: project a puff of noxious gas that deals 1d12 Poison.

Range: 3 feet.

Magic Missile

Effect: create three darts of magical force, each dealing 1d4+1 Force to its target.

Range: 18 meters.

Mage Hand

Effect: create a spectral hand that can manipulate and interact with objects.

Range: 18 meters.

Concentration: required

Mage Armour

Effect: surround the creature with magical energy to enhance its armor class by 3.

Range: 1.5 meters.

Requirements: no armor.

Longstrider

Effect: touch a creature to increase its speed by 3 feet.

Range: 1.5 meters.

Light

Effect: Infuse an object with an aura of light.

Range: 1.5 meters.

Jump

Effect: touch a creature to triple its jumping range.

Range: 1.5 meters.

Grease

Effect: cover the selected area with fat, making it difficult terrain, and the creatures found on it can be knocked down.

Range: 18 meters.

Friends

Effect: enchant a non-hostile creature to gain advantage on Charisma checks against it.

Range: 9 meters.

Concentration: required

Fog Cloud

Effect: you create a cloud of thick fog. The beings residing in the area of operation of this spell are Heavily Obscured and Blinded.

Range: 18 meters.

Concentration: required

Fire Bolt

Effect: you throw a fireball that causes 1d6 Fire damage and creates a flammable surface.

Range: 18 meters.

Find Familiar

Effect: Gain the service of a familiar, a fey spirit that assumes the role of an animal of your choosing.

Range: 18 meters.

Additional information: you can summon the following animals - Spider, Crow, Rat, Frog, Crab and Cat. Each has a different skill.

Feather Fall

Effect: the hero can slow down the falling speed of allied heroes/creatures, resulting in immunity from fall damage.

Range: 9 meters.

False Life

Effect: the hero can use this spell to strengthen himself with the necromantic facsimile of life and gain 5 temporary life points.

Expeditionary Retreat

Effect: turn Sprint into an extra action allowing the character to move at extraordinary speed.

Concentration: required

Disguise Self

Effect: magically change all aspects of your appearance.

Dancing Lights

Effect: create wisps of light that illuminate in a 12m radius.

Range: 18 meters.

Concentration: required

Colour Spray

Effect: creates a dazzling array of flashing, colored lights that Blind creatures up to a combined 33 hit points.

Range: 5 meters.

Chill Touch

Effect: assail a creature with the chill of the grave. The target receives 1d8

Necrotic and cannot regain hit points. Undead creatures also get disadvantage on attack rolls.

Range: 18 meters.

Charm Person

Effect: Magically charm a humanoid in your field of vision.

Range: 18 meters.

Additional information: a charmed character can't hurt a character casting the spell.

Burning Hands

Effect: fire shoots from your outstretched fingers. It ignites anything flammable and deals 3d6 Fire.

Range: 5 meters.

Additional information: after a successful defense throw the target receives only half of the damage.

Blade Ward

Effect: you gain immunity to Bludgeoning, Piercing, and Slashing injuries caused by weapon attacks.

Acid Splash

Effect: hurl a bubble of acid that deals 1d6 Acid to each creature it hits.

Range: 18 meters, 2 meters blast radius.

Spells - Level 2

The table beneath presents level 2 Wizard spells. Your personality will get close enough to them once the individual in question arrives at third experience level.

Blindness

Effect: magically Blind an enemy creature.

Range: 18 meters.

Additional information: the blinded creature may try to recover from this condition at the end of each tour.

Blur

Effect: the body of your character becomes blurred, making it harder for your enemies to attack him or her.

Concentration: required

Darkness

Effect: a character creates a cloud of magic darkness that will hide and blind creatures inside it. Darkness makes it impossible to perform ranged attacks.

Range: 18 meters.

Concentration: required

Darkvision

Effect: enables a creature to see in the darkness for up to 18 meters.

Range: 1.5 meters.

Detect Thoughts

Effect: focus to read thoughts of some creatures while speaking with them.

Concentration: required

Hold Person

Effect: paralyze a humanoid.

Range: 18 meters.

Concentration: required

Additional information: at the end of each round, the creature may try to free itself.

Invisibility

Effect: touch a creature to make it invisible.

Range: 1.5 meters.

Concentration: required

Additional information: the spell ends prematurely if a creature attacks or uses magic.

Melf's Acid Arrow

Effect: shoot a green arrow that sprays acid and deals 4d4 instant Acid damage and 2d4 additional Acid damage once the turn ends.

Range: 18 meters.

Additional information: after a successful defense test, the target receives only half of the initial damage.

Mirror Image

Effect: the character creates three illusory doppelgangers that will distract the opponents. Each copy increases the Hero's KP by 3.

Additional information: one of the illusions will disappear whenever you successfully dodge an attack.

Misty Step
Effect: the character becomes surrounded by a dark mist and he or she teleports to a free spot in his or hers sight.
Range: 18 meters.

Ray of Enfeeblement
Effect: the character shots a ray of weakening energy from his or hers hand. Target that is hit can deal half damage of Strength-based weapon attacks.
Range: 18 meters.
Concentration: required

Scorching Ray
Effect: fire three streams of fire, and each one deals 2d6 Fire damage.
Range: 18 meters.

Shatter
Effect: cause an intense, painful noise that deals 3d8 Thunder damage for creatures and items.
Range: 18 meters.
Additional information: after a successful defense test, the target receives only half of the initial damage. Inorganic creatures build from materials like rocks will have their defense throws harder.

Web
Effect: cover an area with a thick, flammable web that can tangle creatures within it.
Range: 18 meters.
Concentration: required
Additional information: tangled enemy or ally can use his or hers action to try to break the web.

Races

From this part of the manual for Baldurs Gate 3 you will realize which races accessible in the game are the most ideal for a Wizard.

Assuming you choose to play as a Wizard in Baldur's Gate 3, you ought to check out races that have reward to Knowledge, Constitution, or even Smoothness. Likewise, there are extra abilities presented by individual races, which can additionally advance your personality's playing style.

Elf

Elves are one of the more popular races available in *Baldurs Gate 3* because they greatly fit Wizard's traits, especially with the High Elf sub-class.

- **Race Bonus**: +2 to dexterity;

- **High-Elf sub-class**: +1 to Intelligence;

- **Keen Senses**: the hero is proficient in Perception;

- **Fey Ancestry**: the hero will have an advantage during saving throws against charms, and the magic can't put them to sleep;

- **Darkvision**: the hero can see in the dark within a radius of 12 meters.

Half-Elf

Halfelfs join the most desirable characteristics of Mythical people and humans, and hence they truly do well in the job of Mage.

- **Race Bonus**: +2 to Charisma;

- **Race Bonus**: 2 additional trait points to divide. Up to one point can be added to one trait. You should pick 1 to intelligence and 1 to constitution;

- **Darkvision**: the character can see in the dark within a radius of 12 meters;

- **Fey Ancestry**: the character will have advantage in defense tests against charms and magic won't be able to put him or her to sleep.

Tiefling

Tiefling is another race accessible in Baldurs Gate 3 that fits the Wizard class well because of its Knowledge reward and exceptionally helpful uninvolved capacities.

- **Race bonus:** +1 to Intelligence, +2 to Charisma;

- **Hellish Resistance:** the character gains fire resistance - all received fire damage is halved;

- **Darkvision:** the hero can see in the dark within a radius of 12 meters.

Human

Humans are probably the most versatile race available in *Baldurs Gate 3* so it will work well as a warrior. Human receives a +1 bonus to every attribute available in the game.

Build

This section of the Baldur's Gate 3 aide depicts a prepared Wizard fabricate. We propose which race works best as a Wizard, how to best spend capacity focuses, what hardware and spells to pick, and what abilities to choose.

Wizard is one of the most impressive person classes accessible in Baldurs Gate 3. Wizards bargain huge harm to one objective or potentially a bigger gathering of rivals all at once at the expense of low defensive layer class and few lifepoints. In the introduced Wizard construct, we center around the Evocation specialization (subclass), which permits your legend to employ the energy of strong components.

Race

While picking the right race for the Wizard class, it is certainly worth picking the High Mythical being. The following is a rundown of all the critical rewards your personality will get.

- **1 to Intelligence**: an ability allowing the Wizard to cast spells;

- **2 to Dexterity**: a useful auxiliary ability;

- **Keen Senses**: the hero is proficient in Perception;

- **Base race speed**: the distance you can travel in each round is 9 metres;

- **Fey Ancestry**: the hero will have an advantage during saving throws against charms, and the magic can't put them to sleep;

- **Darkvision**: the hero can see in the dark within a radius of 12 meters. As a result, the character will not receive penalty when attacked in a dark room.

From all the High Mythical people's cantrips accessible, we propose picking Dancing Lights.

> Dancing Lights
>
> **Effect**: create wisps of light that illuminate in a 12m radius.
>
> **Range**: 18 meters.
>
> **Concentration**: required
>
> **Additional information**: characters who do not have the Darkvision skill receive penalty to attack when fighting in a dark room. With the Dancing Lights spell, you'll be able to light up the darkness, help your team, and affect their chances of hitting the target.

If for some reason you don't want to play as a High Elf you can also opt for the Half-Elf or a Tiefling race. It should be noted, however, that you will then have to additionally develop Charisma.

Background

While picking the foundation for your Wizard, worth picking between choices benefit from the created Knowledge, and keeping away from those that ensure abilities connected with Allure, which we will not foster here.

- **Sage**: proficiency in Arcana (Intelligence) and History (Intelligence);

- **Hermit**: Religion proficiency (Intelligence), Medicine proficiency (Wisdom).

Concentration

A few Wizard's spells are sufficiently muddled to require fixation so their impact isn't intruded. Sadly, focus is certainly not an enduring impact and can be intruded on in more than one way.

- By casting another spell that requires concentration;

- After receiving damage while maintaining concentration, the Wizard must perform a defensive dice roll (Constitution) to ensure the effect is not interrupted.

As Wizards must maintain concentration when casting certain spells, we invest some points in the Constitution.

Skills

While picking abilities for your Wizard, give specific consideration to those that will benefit most from his most evolved capacities, like Insight and Smoothness.

Contingent upon the foundation you pick, decide on any of the accompanying choices:

- **Investigation**: a skill associated with Intelligence;

- **Nature**: a skill associated with Intelligence;

- **History:** a skill associated with Intelligence;

- **Religion**: a skill associated with Intelligence;

- **Arcana**: a skill associated with Intelligence;

- **Acrobatics**: a skill associated with Dexterity;

- **Stealth:** a skill associated with Dexterity;

Abilities

While fostering Wizard's capacities, one must initially zero in on Knowledge as the capacity liable for Spellcasting. Then, at that point, it merits allocating focuses to Constitution and Adroitness.

We propose to allocate the ability points for your Wizard as follows:

- Intelligence: 16 points;

- Constitution: 15 points;

- Dexterity: 15 points;

- Strength: 10 points;

- Wisdom: 10 points;

- Charisma: 10 points;

Learning Spells from Scrolls

The Wizards gain their insight into spells from many sources, one of which is the parchments you will find while investigating the tremendous universe of Baldurs Gate 3. At the point when you find a spell look over that you don't have the foggiest idea yet and you need to learn it, simply click on it and pick the spell learning choice which will cost 50 gold pieces.

Cantrips

By making a Wizard-class character in Baldur's Gate 3, you will actually want to pick 3 Cantrips that your personality will actually want to utilize. While taking a gander at the rundown of accessible spells, we especially suggest Ray of Frost, Fire Bolt, and Poison Spray.

Ray Of Frost

Effect: the hero summons an icy ray of pale blue light that causes 1d8 Cold damage and reduces the target's speed by 3 metres.

Range: 18 meters.

Fire Bolt

Effect: you throw a fireball that causes 1d6 Fire damage and creates a flammable surface.

Range: 18 meters.

Poison Spray

Effect: project a puff of noxious gas that deals 1d12 Poison.

Range: 3 feet.

Additional information: in the later stages of the game, you will find the Poisoner's robe, which will have synergy with the Poison damage spells.

Because of the way that Cantrips can be utilized in each round without any impediments, you ought to choose ones that you will utilize. Attack spells are a decent decision since you will actually want to ceaselessly harm your rivals without losing your spell openings.

Level 1 spells

Wizards have the biggest pool of spells of the relative multitude of characters accessible in the game, and during character creation you can pick the ones that your personality will have toward the start of the game. We especially suggest Enchantment Rocket as a very valuable attack spell, Mage Reinforcement that will significantly improve your legend's protection, and Rest as a helpful control device.

Magic Missile
Effect: you create three magical arrows, each one dealing 1d4 1 Force damage.
Range: 18 meters.
Additional information: the opponent cannot protect himself from this spell, and your hero cannot miss so he will always hit the target. You can choose up to 3 targets that the Wizard will hit at the same time.

Mage Armour
Effect: surround the creature with magical energy to enhance its armor class by 3.
Range: 1.5 meters.
Requirements: no armor.
Additional information: after casting this spell, its effect lasts until a long rest in the camp.

Thunderwave
Effect: the hero unleashes a wave of deafening power that causes 2d8 Thunder damage and kickbacks creatures and objects.
Range: 5 meters.
Additional information: it is worth knowing that creatures thrown off from a high altitude receive a lot of damage from falling, so this is an ideal way to quickly eliminate stronger opponents.

Sleep
Effect: magically put the creatures with a total of 24 health points to sleep.

Range: 18 meters.

Additional information: an excellent control tool that does not require concentration. With this spell, you can completely disable an inconvenient opponent from the fight. Because in *Baldurs Gate 3* you see how many health points your opponent has, you don't have to wonder if the spell will be effective. Sleeping creatures will wake up if injured.

Ray of Sickness

Effect: the hero summons a beam of toxic energy that inflicts 2d8 Poison damage and can cause the target to be poisoned.

Range: 18 meters.

Additional information: poisoning is a great way for dealing with Wizards, because every turn they will have to make a defensive dice roll to maintain concentration - provided they use such spells. In the later stages of the game, you will find the Poisoner's robe, which will have synergy with the Poison damage spells.

Witch Bolt

Effect: the hero summons a beam of energy that causes 1d12 Lightning damage and connects to the target with an electric arc.

Range: 18 meters.

Concentration: required

Additional information: you can activate the arc of lightning in each round to automatically inflict 1d12 electrical injuries.

Not at all like the recently depicted Cantrips, spells utilize an opening while being projected which implies they can't be utilized endlessly. You recharge your enchanted openings after an extended rest in the camp.

Level 2 spells

In the wake of arriving at experience Level 3 Wizards get sufficiently close to Even out 2 spells and two spell spaces for this sort of spells. Subsequent to arriving at experience level 4, you will actually want to choose 2 extra Level 2 spells, so you will have 4 of them altogether. We especially suggest Misty Step, Scorching Flame, Melf's Acid Arrow and Shutter.

Misty Step

Effect: your hero is surrounded by a black mist and teleported to a vacant spot in his field of vision.

Range: 18 meters.

Additional information: This spell is included as an additional action, so you can use it to quickly teleport your hero to a place, which will give you the High Ground advantage over your opponent.

Scorching Ray

Effect: fire three streams of fire, and each one deals 2d6 Fire damage.

Range: 18 meters.

Melf's Acid Arrow

Effect: shoot a green arrow that sprays acid and deals 4d4 instant Acid damage and 2d4 additional Acid damage once the turn ends.

Range: 18 meters.

Additional information: after a successful defense test, the target receives only half of the initial damage.

Shatter

Effect: cause an intense, painful noise that deals 3d8 Thunder damage for creatures and items.

Range: 18 meters.

Additional information: after a successful defense test, the target receives only half of the initial damage. Inorganic creatures build from materials like rocks will have their defense throws harder.

Arcane Recovery - an important action

All along, a Wizard approaches a unique action that he can utilize one time each day.

Because of the way that Obscure Recuperation is essential for the action, attempt to utilize this capacity prior to stirring something up so as not to lose a turn wherein you can play out an attack to recapture the spell spaces.

Arcane Recovery

Effect: once a day, while not in combat, you can regenerate used spell slots.

Additional information: the hero can recover two Level 1 spell slots or one level 2 slot cell.

Equipment

A Wizard is a person class who depends on spells to bargain harm to rivals in each conceivable circumstance. Wizard utilizes post weapons (stick, staff), which frequently furnishes him with extra properties and rewards. Your Wizard ought to wear Robes so you can in any case utilize the Mage Protective layer spell.

Specialization (Subclass)

In the wake of arriving at level 2, a Wizard should pick one of two specializations (subclasses). Assuming you pick the Evocation School, your personality will actually want to utilize spells that center the energy of strong elementals. The Evocation School is an ideal decision for Wizards who like to zero in on causing however much harm as could reasonably be expected. By picking this way you will likewise get an extra detached capacity.

- Shape Spells: Wizard makes a wellbeing pocket for the Evocation School spells. Partnered animals will naturally breeze through guard assessments effectively and they will not get harm from these spells.

Upgrading abilities

In the wake of arriving at experience level 4, you will actually want to work on your Officer's capacities by spending extra 2 focuses on picked capacities. This is the best chance to build the worth of the Knowledge capacity to 18 places.

General tips

Before you play as a Wizard in Baldurs Gate 3, you ought to know a couple of key tips that will bring you considerably nearer to this class and essentially influence your legend's viability during battle.

- Key position advantage: if conceivable, consistently attempt to take a situation over your rival prior to stirring up some dust (on a slope, rooftop, steps, gallery, and so on), to acquire the Strategic position advantage. If fundamental, feel free to the Misty Step spell;

- Spell openings: a portion of the spell spaces you use can be reestablished with Arcaner Recuperation. All the spell spaces utilized will be recuperated after an extended rest in the camp;

41

- Scrolls: Wizards can gain extra spells from scrolls you find as you meander through the game's tremendous world. Assuming that you go over a spell that your legend doesn't have any idea, he can continuously learn it.;

- Mage protection: attempt to keep the impact of the mage reinforcement spell on the legend to expand his guard.

Rogue

Guide

On this page of our aide you'll find a pre-made Rogue work for BG3. We've recorded the best races and encouraged on which subclass to pick. Our tips will assist you with appropriately circulating your Capacity Scores and pick a fitting foundation.

Best background for Rogue

When choosing a Rogue background, aim for **Dexterity or Intelligence** proficiencies. Some backgrounds worth your time are:

- **Urchin**, granting proficiency in Sleight of Hand and Stealth.

- **Criminal**, granting proficiency in Stealth and Deception.

- **Charlatan**, granting proficiency in Deception and Sleight of Hand.

Best race for Rogue

The main Rogue attributes are Dexterity and Intelligence. A few races conceding rewards to them are:

- **Elf**, with +2 Dexterity and +1 Intelligence or Wisdom, depending on the subrace.

- **Drow**, with +2 to Dexterity and +1 to Charisma.

- **Halfling**, with +2 to Dexterity and +1 to Charisma or Constitution, depending on the subrace.

- **Gnome**, with +2 to Intelligence and +1 to Dexterity or Constitution, depending on the subrace.

Rogue's Ability Scores

- • Dexterity is each Rogue's essential detail. It influences both your precision and weapon harm. It likewise builds your Drive and Protective layer Class.

- • Rogues are capable in Intelligence Saving Tosses. High Intelligence will keep them sharp, assist them with tracking down signs and investigate. Rogues can without much of a stretch spot traps, stowed away items and perceive wounds. High Intelligence is particularly significant for the Little known Prankster subclass, which awards spellcasting and a wide program of spells.

- High Constitution will allow you more hit focuses with each step up.

Best subclass for Rogue

- When your Rogue arrives at Level 3, you'll have two subclasses to browse:

- Obscure Comedian is a spell caster and realizes the Mage Hand cantrip, which makes an imperceptible ghastly hand that can be utilized to play out certain undertakings securely. The accessible spells incorporate Enchantment Rocket, Acid Sprinkle, Rest, Stunning Handle and numerous others.

- Criminal has two inactive capacities and can play out extra actions on their turn. Quick Hands awards them an extra reward action each turn, while Second-Story Workprevents fall harm.

Best Rogue class actions

- **Sneak Attack Melee** - deals additional 1d6 damage on melee attacks.

- **Sneak Ranged Attack** - deals additional 1d6 damage on ranged attacks.

- **Cunning Action Dash** - doubles movement speed during the current turn.

- **Cunning Action Disengage** - movement during the current turn doesn't trigger Opportunity Attacks.

Best build for Rogue

- **Race:** High Elf

- **Background:** Urchin

- **Subclass:** Arcane Trickster

- **Ability Scores:** Strength 8, Dexterity 17, Stamina 14, Intelligence 14, Wisdom 12, Charisma 10

- **Melee weapon:** Rapier +1

- **Ranged weapon:** The Joltshooter

- **Armor:** Studded Leather Armour +1

Races

From this section of the aide you will figure out which races accessible in Baldurs Gate 3are most appropriate to Rogue class.

While choosing to play as a Rogue in Baldur's Gate 3, you ought to focus on races that have rewards to attributes like Dexterity, Shrewdness, and Constitution. Likewise, there are extra abilities presented by individual races, which can additionally improve your personality's playing style.

Elf

Elves are always a good choice for all character classes based on agility and dexterity.

- **Race Bonus:** +2 to dexterity;

- **Keen Senses:** the hero is proficient in Perception;

- **Fey Ancestry:** the hero will have an advantage during saving throws against charms, and the magic can't put them to sleep;

- **Darkvision**: the hero can see in the dark within a radius of 12 meters.

- Depending on the subrase you choose, you can augment your Rogue even better.

- **High-Elf subrace**: You can travel 9 meters per Turn, +1 to Intelligence;

- **Wood-Elf subrace**: basic walking speed 10.5 meters, proficient in Stealth, +1 to Wisdom.

Halfling

Halfling is another good choice if you want to roll Rogue in *Baldur's Gate 3*, especially with Lightfoot Halfling subrace.

- **Race Bonus**: +2 to dexterity;

- **Lucky**: when you throw 1 for an attack roll, ability check or saving throw you can reroll the dice and must use the new roll;

- **Lightfoot Halfling**: the Naturally Stealthy ability ensures your hero's proficiency in concealment, giving you an advantage during Stealth Checks, and +1 to Charisma.

Drow

Drow is another race in *Baldurs Gate 3* that is worth noting when creating a Rogue.

- **Racial bonus**: +2 Dexterity, 1+ Charisma;

- **Fey Ancestry**: you have an advantage on saving throws against Charmed, and magic can't put you to sleep.

- **Superior Darkvision**: the protagonist can see in the dark within 24 meters.

- **Dancing lights**: a clever spell that creates wisps of light that illuminate a 12m radius.

Human

Humans are presumably the most flexible race that anyone could hope to find in Baldurs Gate 3 - they are additionally fit to Rogues. Human gets a +1 reward to each attribute accessible in the game.

Build

Rogue is perhaps of the most general class in Baldur's Gate 3. Because of their numerous abilities, they can address the different difficulties presented by the game. Their class capacities, for example, Sneak Attack permit them to be a flexible and successful harm seller. In this aide, you will figure out how to make the best Rogue fabricate.

Character creation wizard

The best race for a Rogue is a **Lightfoot Halfling** due to their natural ability making **Stealth checks** easier. Additionally, you don't have to worry about rolling a 1, as this race has **the ability to reroll a critical failure**. Alternatively, you can choose a **Wood Elf**, who grants **long bow proficiency** and **increases movement speed**.

As far as the **background** is concerned, you should focus on playing off your greatest feats. **Orphan** or **Criminal** are good options - the former provides access to **Stealth** and **Sleight of Hand**, while the latter to **Stealth** and **Deception**.

Class progression

- At level 1, you get your main damage-boosting skill, **Sneak Attack**. Additionally, you receive **Expertise** - you choose **two skills** and double your proficiency bonus for them.

- Level 2 unlocks the following actions as part of a **bonus action: Hide, Dash** and **Disengage**.

- At level 3, choose **Thief** - it'll provide you with an **additional bonus action**, which translates into an additional attack in the case of fighting with two types of weapons. In addition, your Sneak Attack damage increases by 1d6.

- At level 4, you choose a feat - choose Two-Weapon Fighting, which will allow you to use a Dexterity bonus for attacks with the second weapon.

- Level 5 brings another damage dice for Sneak Attacks and the Uncanny Dodge ability, which reduces the damage taken by half (once per turn).

- Level 6 means another expertise.

- At level 7, your Sneak Attack damage dice increases. You also gain the Evasion ability - it reduces damage from area effects and spells by half.

- Level 8 means another feat. In this case, it is worth choosing to increase the attribute.

- Level 9 gives you another Sneak Attack damage dice and the Invisibility ability.

- Level 10 brings another feat. At this stage of the game, follow your own instinct and choose what you consider most useful.

- At level 11, you get a new increase to your Sneak Attack damage dice and an ability that allows you to treat all skill check scores below 10 as a 10.

- The last level is a feat - again, follow your instincts.

Ilithild Powers

Feel free to open and utilize these abilities - center particularly around Winnow the Weak, Repulsor and Black Hole. Releasing the full force of Ilithild Powers doesn't influence the person adversely, so leave all fledglings for yourself.

Equipment and bonuses from it

Tragically, on account of Act 1, the Rogue class doesn't have such a large number of good things that they could utilize.

You ought to create a blade; you will get a mission for it in the produce during your most memorable experience with the trolls in the Blighted

Village. Then again, while investigating the Underdark, you will track down Phalar Aluve - a very decent one-handed sword giving great rewards to the whole group.

Taking everything into account, in the wake of killing Razglin, you will find gloves on the fortune heap, which give a benefit in skirmish battle when encircled by two adversaries. In a similar area, search for Smasher - kill him or loot him to get a ring that speeds up by 3m. Moreover, in the Underdark you will track down the Shadow of Menzoberranzan - a hood that permits you to become undetectable.

At long last, towards the finish of Act 1, while investigating the Githyanki territory, you will actually want to find the Gloves of Dexterity, which help it to 18 and award you a +1 attack reward.

In Act 3, the situation is completely different. One of the main antagonists (**Orin**) will drop two fantastic weapons upon being killed - **Crimson Mischief** and **Bloodthirst**. The first one is a short sword that deals **extra damage for attacks with Advantage**. The second one **reduces the number you need to roll for a critical hit by 1** and it allows to launch a **riposte** after an unsuccessful attack by the enemy.

Additionally, in Act 3 you should acquire the **Bhaalist Armour**, which creates an aura with a radius of two meters, in which enemies **are vulnerable to piercing damage**.

Party members - their skills and spells

If you want to get the most of your class, you will need **your allies' support**. The best solution is to have a **Fighter/Paladin/Druid**, a **Cleric**, and a **Wizard** on the team because of their skills.

The Cleric is able **to heal** your hero and provides you with useful buffs such as **Shield of Faith**, which **increases AC by 2**. Alternatively, they can soak some of the damage by targeting it on themselves, **imbue your weapons** and cast an extremely useful **Bless**. Shadowheart fits this role perfectly.

A **Fighter/Paladin/Druid** will also be extremely useful. These three classes are listed together because each of them are naturally **predisposed to tank damage** - especially **the Druid**, who can take an exceptionally large amount. Fortunately, during the game you have the opportunity to recruit Halsin and Jaheira, who can fulfill this role.

Consumables

Below you will find a list of consumables that will make your Rogue even stronger.

- **Oil of Accuracy** - provides +2 to Attack Rolls.

- **Elixir of Heroism** - gives additional 10HP temporarily and applies "Blessed" status.

- **Potion of Flying** - additional mobility is something that is always needed.

- **Potion of Hill Giant Strength** - perfect if you don't have 20 Strength yet.

- **Elixir of Vigilance** - provides +5 to Initiative, make sure to drink it before tougher battles.

Ranger

Guide

Could it be said that you considering foundation and competition to decide for your Officer in BG3? On this page you'll find out about the Officer's best subclass and most valuable spells. We'll make sense of which details to focus on, and what would it be advisable for you pick for your Inclined toward Adversaries and Normal Explorer characteristics.

Best background for Ranger

Your Ranger's background should complement the class' two primary abilities, **Dexterity and Wisdom**, which is why some good choices include:

- **Urchin**, granting proficiency in Sleight of Hand and Stealth.

- **Criminal,** granting proficiency in Stealth and Deception.

- **Charlatan,** granting proficiency in Deception and Sleight of Hand.

Best race for Ranger

When choosing a race for your Ranger, **aim for extra points to Dexterity and Wisdom**. This means mechanically the best choices are:

- **Wood Elf,** with +2 Dexterity and +1 Wisdom.

- **Drow,** with +2 Dexterity and +1 Charisma.

- **Strongheart Halfling,** with +2 Dexterity and +1 Constitution.

- **Human,** with +1 to every ability.

Best subclass for Ranger

Once your **Ranger reaches Level 3**, you'll have two subclasses to choose from:

- **Hunter** grants you the **Horde Breaker** feature, letting you aim at two creatures standing next to each other. When choosing this subclass, you'll also have one of two additional features to choose from: **Colossus Slayer**, which lets you deal additional damage on an attack once per turn; or **Giant Killer**, which gives you reactions when you're being attacked by a larger creature.

- **Beastmaster** can summon an animal companion to help in infiltration and combat. There are some available companions to choose from: a bear, a boar, a giant spider, a raven or a wolf.

Both Ranger subclasses have their own assets. In the event that you'd like a person who can easily deal with gatherings or bigger foes, pick the Tracker. Assuming you'd prefer work close by a creature sidekick, pick the Beastmaster.

Favored Enemies

While making a Ranger, you'll have to pick one of these choices, which award proficiency or open spells:

- **Bounty Hunter** - grants proficiency in Investigation and the Ensnaring Strike skill, which gives disadvantage on saving throws to creatures attacked by the Ranger.

- **Keeper of the Veil** - grants proficiency in Arcana and knows the spell Protection from Good and Evil.

- **Mage Breaker** - grants proficiency in Arcana and the True Strike cantrip.

- **Ranger Knight** - grants proficiency in History and heavy armor.

- **Sanctified Stalker** - grants proficiency in Religion and the Sacred Flame cantrip.

Natural Explorer

While making a Ranger, you should pick one of the accompanying Natural Explorer types, conceding you new capacities:

- **Beast Tamer** - knows the Find Familiar spell.

- **Urban Tracker** - grants proficiency in Sleight of Hand.

- **Westland Wanderer** - grants one of three different resistances: to fire, cold or poison.

Ranger's Ability Scores

While appropriating the Ranger's Capacity Scores, you ought to change them to your arranged subclass at Level 3, as well regarding your Natural Explorer and Leaned toward Adversaries decisions.

- **Dexterity is the most important attribute for all Rangers**, affecting how well you handle ranged weapons and some melee weapons. It will let you strike first in combat and increase your Armor Class.

- **Rangers are proficient in Strength Saving Throws**, so their Strength shouldn't be lower than 11.

- The secondary important stat for Rangers is **Wisdom, which they use to cast spells**. Wisdom also increases their Animal Handling, Medicine

51

and Survival. It will let them recognize the environment and determine the true intentions of encountered creatures.

Best spells for Ranger

Spells unlocked at Ranger Level 2:

- **Animal Friendship** - prevents beasts with 3 or less Intelligence from attacking the Ranger for 10 turns.

- **Cure Wounds** - heals 1d8 hit points.

- **Goodberry** - creates four magical berries for the Ranger and their allies. One berry heals 1d4 hit points. The berries disappear after a Long Rest.

- **Speak with Animal** - uses an action to talk to animals.

- **Hail of Thorns** - creates an explosion of thorns on a weapon hit, dealing additional 1d10 piercing damage.

- **Hunter's Mark** - a concentration spell which marks the creature, letting the Ranger deal additional 1d6 damage on each attack against them. If the target dies before the spell ends, the Ranger can mark another creature without expending a new spell slot.

- **Spells unlocked at Ranger Level 5:**

- **Barkskin** - on touch, increases a creature's Armor Class to 16.

- **Darkvision** - gives a creature Darkvision for up to 12 meters.

- **Silence** - creates a soundproof sphere no creature within which can cast spells. Additionally, everyone inside the sphere is immune to thunder damage.

- **Spike Growth** - creates spikes on the ground, dealing 2d4 piercing damage to anyone who moves through them.

- **Pass Without Trace** - creates a shadow veil, giving the Ranger and their allies +10 to Stealth checks.

Best fighting style for Ranger

Upon reaching level 2, your Ranger can choose between four fighting styles:

- **Archery** - grants +2 to ranged weapon accuracy rolls.

- **Defense** - grants +1 to Armor Class.

- **Dueling** - grants additional damage when holding a single one-handed weapon.

- **Two-Weapon Fighting** - increases damage dealt with an off-hand weapon.

Best build for Ranger

- Background: Urchin

- Race: Wood Elf

- Favored Enemies: Bounty Hunter

- Natural Explorer: Beast Tamer

- Ability Scores: Strength 12, Dexterity 17, Constitution 13, Intelligence 8, Wisdom 15, Charisma 10

- Subclass: Hunter

- Fighting style: Archery

- Weapon: Steelforged Sword

- Ranged weapon: Crossbow +1

- Armor: Githyanki Half Plate

Spells

From this part of the Baldurs Gate 3 aide, you will realize which spells are accessible to Ranger - one of the person classes accessible in the game.

After arriving at level 2, your legend will get close enough to Spell Projecting ability that will permit him to utilize Level 1 spells. At this level, you may have the option to pick two spells that will be utilized in undertakings ahead. On level 3, there will be three spell spaces, and afterward every two continuous levels the legend will be given admittance to another opening. Expecting that the most extreme level of the person that can be reached in Baldurs Gate 3 is level 10, when this limit is reached, you will have 6 spots for spells.

Spells - Level 1

Since in Early Admittance to Baldurs Gate 3 you can arrive at level 4, you will actually want to gain proficiency with a limit of 3 first level spells.

Animal Friendship

Effect: you can charm a Beast and convince it that you don't want to hurt it.

Range: 18 meters.

Condition: the beast cannot have an intelligence of 4 or higher. The spell stops when you or one of your companions attacks the enchanted beast.

Cure Wounds

Effect: the affected creature recovers 1d8+2 health points.

Range: 1.5 meters.

Additional information: the spell does not work on undead and constructs.

Ensnaring Strike

Effect: the hero's attack summons thorny vines, which inflicts 1d6+3 Piercing damage and can immobilize the target.

Range: 18 meters.

Concentration: Required

Additional information: injuries are inflicted at the beginning of each round. The creature or an ally of the trapped target can use their action to try to tear the vines apart.

Fog Cloud

Effect: you create a cloud of thick fog. The beings residing in the area of operation of this spell are Heavily Obscured and Blinded.

Range: 18 meters.

Concentration: required

Hail of Thorns

Effect: you fire a volley of thorns that inflict 1d6+3 Piercing damage and explode, inflicting 1D10 Piercing damage on the main target and the creatures around it.

Range: 18 meters, 2 meters of explosion range.

Additional information: after a successful Save Throw, targets receive only half of the damage from the blast.

Hunter's Mark

Effect: mark a creature with the Hunter's Mark to inflict an additional 1d6 Piercing damage every time you hit it with an attack.

Range: 18 meters.

Concentration: required

Additional information: if the marked target dies before the spell is over, you can use an additional action to mark another being.

Jump

Effect: touch a creature to triple its jumping range.

Range: 1.5 meters.

Longstrider

Effect: touch a creature to increase its speed by 10 feet.

Range: 1.5 meters.

Speak with Animals

Effect: you gain the ability to understand and communicate verbally with animals.

Concentration: Required

Races

From this section of the aide you will figure out what races accessible in Baldurs Gate 3 are best fit for the Ranger class.

While choosing to play Ranger in Baldur's Gate 3, you ought to focus on the races that have a reward to specific Ranger-helpful attributes, like Dexterity, Shrewdness and Constitution. Likewise, there are extra abilities offered by individual races, which can additionally improve your personality's playing style.

Elf

Elves are certainly the right race for Ranger and probably the first to come into your head when creating this character.

- **Race Bonus:** +2 to dexterity;

- **Keen Senses:** the hero is proficient in Perception;

- **Fey Ancestry:** the hero will have an advantage during saving throws against charms, and the magic can't put them to sleep;

- **Darkvision:** the hero can see in the dark within a radius of 12 meters.

- Depending on the subrace you choose, you can affect your Ranger even more.

- **High-Elf subrace:** You can travel 9 meters per Turn, +1 to Intelligence;

- **Wood-Elf subrace:** basic walking speed 10.5 meters, proficient in Stealth, +1 to Wisdom.

Halfling

Halfling is another good choice if you want to roll Ranger in *Baldur's Gate 3*, especially with Lightfoot Halfling subrace.

- **Race Bonus:** +2 to dexterity;

- **Lucky:** when you throw 1 for an attack roll, ability check or saving throw you can reroll the dice and must use the new roll;

- **Lightfoot Halfling:** the Naturally Stealthy ability ensures your hero's proficiency in concealment, giving you an advantage during Stealth Checks, and +1 to Charisma.

Human

Humans are presumably the most flexible race that anyone could hope to find in Baldurs Gate 3 so Ranger additionally works. Human gets a +1 reward to each attribute accessible in the game.

Build

Ranger is one more very general class in Baldur's Gate 3, permitting you to battle both in close battle and a good ways off. This guide makes sense of how for make a Ranger zeroed in on went battle, which attributes to zero in on the most and which accomplishments to pick.

Character creation wizard

The best race for a Ranger is a **Wood Elf**. Thanks to the increased movement speed, natural proficiency in **Stealth**, resistance to certain crowd control effects, and **Darkvision**, this race allows for effective playthrough with a class of our interest.

Drow can be an alternative here, although the only significant advantage is **better Darkvision** (a difference of 12m) and the spell **Faerie Fire**.

As far as the origin is concerned, the best choice will be the **Outlander** - proficiency in **Survival** and **Athletics** will definitely be needed.

Class progression

- At level 1, you choose a **Favoured Enemy** and **Natural Explorer**. Both of these skills add certain bonuses to your class. In the case of the first one, we recommend choosing **Bounty Hunter** and for the second one - **Beast Tamer**.

- Level 2 is the choice of **fighting style** - in this case, choose **Archery**. In addition, you receive two spells - choose **Hunter's Mark** and **Cure Wounds**.

- Level 3 is the choice of **subclass** - this build is based on **Hunter**. Choose **Colossus Slayer** - this ability will allow you to deal **an additional 1d8 damage** every turn.

- Level 4 lets you pick a **feat** - the recommended choice is **Sharpshooter**, which will allow for a penalty of **-5 hit points** to add **+10 to the damage dealt**.

- Level 5 is primarily an **additional attack** and **additional spells**. Choose **Spiked Growth**and **Pass without Trace**.

- At level 6, again, you get to choose a Favored Enemyand Natural Explorer. Choose Wasteland Wanderer (one of the available variants) and Ranger Knight.

- Level 7 includes additional spells and defensive tactics. Choose Multiattack Defense.

- Level 8 brings another feat - in this case, choose to increase the attribute (ultimately +2 to Dexterity). Additionally, you gain a the Land's Stride ability, which prevents difficult terrain from slowing you down.

- At level 9, you receive additional spells - you can choose Conjure Barrage and Lightning Arrow.

- Level 10 brings another choice in the Favoured Enemy and Natural Explorer categories. At this stage, follow your intuition and choose what you feel you miss the most.

- Level 11 doesn't bring any feats.

- The last level is an additional feat. You can choose to increase the attribute to have 20 Dexterity.

Ilithild Powers

Make sure to open and utilize these abilities - center particularly around Winnow the Weak, Repulsor and Black Hole. Releasing the full force of Ilithild Powers doesn't influence the person adversely, so leave all fledglings for yourself.

Party members - their skills and spells

Regarding buddies, pick Astarion, Lae'zel and Shadowheart without changing their classes. Lae'zel will be areas of strength for a, Astarion will open each lock and arrangement the perfect proportion of harm when important. Shadowheart, then again, will actually want to recuperate you and take care of numerous issues with the assistance of wizardry.

Equipment and bonuses from it

In Act I, there are several intriguing items to acquire. The strongest ones are listed below:

Try to get the Titanstring Bow, which allows you to add a Strength modifier to your damage. Besides, create a medium armor in the Grymforge.

Additionally, items like Disintegrating Night Walkers that you get in the Underdark or the Crusher's Ring from the Goblin Camp are items that increase your mobility.

In Act III, focus on obtaining items such as Gontr Mael, which is a legendary bow. You'll obtain it after killing the Steel Watcher Titan in the Steel Watch Foundry. Additionally, Helm of Balduran is an item that increases your persistence and defensive abilities. Finally, Bloodthirst is an item that reduces the number you need to roll get a critical hit by +1. You get it after killing Orin.

Consumables

Below you will find a list of consumables that will make your Ranger even stronger:

- Oil of Accuracy - provides +2 to Attack Rolls.

- Elixir of Heroism - gives additional 10HP temporarily and applies "Blessed" status.

- Potion of Flying - additional mobility is something that is always needed.

- Potion of Hill Giant Strength - perfect if you don't have 20 Strength yet.

- Elixir of Vigilance - provides +5 to Initiative, make sure to drink it before tougher battles.

Cleric
Guide

Clerics are profound champions committed to a god. Despite the fact that they generally act as the party's primary healer, their real scope of capacities and spells is a lot more extensive. This page makes sense of about Clerics.

Best race for Cleric

In the full arrival of Baldur's Gate 3, the engineers have taken out elite racial rewards. From this point forward, while picking a race, you can add +2 and +1 rewards to any detail you'd like. Notwithstanding this, a few racial capacities prove to be useful for specific classes.

- • Drow - dim mythical beings get helpful spells at Level 3 and Level 5: Faerie Fire and Murkiness. The race additionally has Darkvision, which demonstrates valuable during battle in dim regions.

- Gold Dwarf - this subrace awards +1 HP each level. It's extremely helpful while making sturdy Cleric tanks.

Ability Points

As mentioned in the previous paragraph, the Cleric's primary stat responsible for the power of their spells is **Wisdom**. Other than that, when distributing points you should also consider:

- **Constitution** - high Constitution will grant you more health, useful for healers and for **tank Clerics**.

- **Dexterity** or **Strength** - choose one of these stats to determine the kind of Cleric you'll play as. If you'd like to use **light or medium armor** and stay in the backline, choose Dexterity. If you want to be a **tank Cleric, wielding heavy weapons and armor**, invest into Strength.

Best background for Cleric

The usefulness of a Cleric's background depends on the role they are to play in the party. Some interesting choices include:

- **Urchin** - especially useful for **Trickery Domain Clercis** with high **Dexterity**. Gives proficiency in **Sleight of Hand** and **Stealth**.

- **Sailor** - will appeal to a frontline Cleric with high Strength. **Athletics** and **Perception** will come in handy during your journey through the Sword Coast.

- **Acolyte** - proficiency in **Insight** and **Religion** complements the Cleric's skillset.

Channel Divinity

Cleric's class ability. From Level 2 onwards, your character can summon divine energyand channel it as a special effect. All Clerics share the Turn Undead effect, which comes in handy against the undead. Further effects are exclusive to subclasses (Domains).

The higher level you are, the **more uses of Channel Divinity you'll get**. Ability slots are restored during **Short and Long Rests**.

Destroy Undead

From **Level 5** onward, all undead enemies affected by Turn Undead receive **4d6 radiant damage**.

Best spells

Because of huge assortment in playstyles between Cleric subclasses, we'll zero in on a couple of spells generally supportive to each form. Clerics of various Spaces often get admittance to elite spells, which they generally have arranged.

Cantrips:

- Sacred Flame - a ranged offensive spell dealing 1d8 radiant damage.

- Thaumaturgy - a simple cantrip granting a bonus during Performance and Intimidationchecks.

- Guidance - a useful spell providing allies with +1d4 during skill checks.

- Spells:

- Bane - inflict up to 3 simultaneous targets with a -1d4 penalty on their attack rolls and saving throws.

- Shield of Faith - grant +2 to the target's Armor Class.

- Guiding Bolt - a projectile dealing 4d6 radiant damage and granting advantage on the next attack roll against the target.

- Inflict Wounds - a touch spell inflicting a massive 3d10 necrotic damage.

- Command - force the target to stop, get closer, run away, go prone or drop their weapon.

- Healing Word and Cure Wounds - basic Cleric healing spells.

- Bless - provide up to 3 simultaneous targets with a +1d4 bonus on their attack rollsand saving throws.

- Prayer of Healing - a Level 2 spell which heals the entire party, only outside of combat.

- Revivify - a Level 3 spell which revives a dead ally. The target comes back to life with 1 hit point.

- Spirit Guardians - summons four spirits which deal 3d8 damage to nearby enemies every turn while halving their movement speed.

Best subclass for Cleric

The Cleric's subclass relies upon the divinity they love. You should pick your subclass at Level 1, so consider cautiously. The Early Access rendition highlights three Cleric Areas, while the full delivery is because of add another four. These are:

Life Area - zeroed in on recuperating and skirmish battle. Life Clerics are proficient with weighty covering, while their Supporter of Fundamental ability enables their mending spells, giving a 2 + spell level reward with the impact of each recuperating spell. While Directing Heavenly nature they can utilize Save Life to reestablish their partners' wellbeing, the worth equivalent to multiple times the Cleric's level.

Light Area - humble workers of the light, employing strong spells and represent considerable authority in fighting undead. Their Warding Flare capacity allows them to utilize their reaction to incur weakness for adversary attacks against them. Their Channel Godliness, Brilliance of the Day break, disperses all haziness and arrangements 2d10 + Cleric level of harm to all adversaries inside 9 meters. A spells selective to this Space are:

- **Faerie Fire** - reveals hidden enemies and grants advantage on attacks against them.

- Burning Hands - deals 3d6 fire damage at a short distance.

- Fireball - a ranged spell inflicting 8d6 area damage.

Trickery Domain - followers of gods embodying deceit, manipulation and pranks. Their ability is Blessing of the Trickster, granting the target advantage on Stealth checks. Their Channel Divinity, Invoke Duplicity, lets the Cleric summon an illusory copy of themselves. This subclass' exlusive spells include:

- **Pass** without Trace - the party gains a +10 bonus to Stealth checks.

- Mirror Image - creates three illusory copies of the Cleric to distract enemies. Each copy gives +3 to Armor Class.

Tempest Domain - Clerics channeling electricity and wind to sow havoc among enemy forces. The Wrath of the Storm ability grants a Reaction which forces each attacking enemy within 1.5m to make a Dexterity saving throw. This enemy takes 2d8 damage on a fail. Their Channel Divinity, Destructive Wrath, lets them inflict maximum damage when using Lightning and Thunder effects. Some spells exclusive to this Domain are:

- Fog Cloud - obscures an area of choice with fog, making it difficult to see in.

- Gust of Wind - a powerful gale moves creatures by 5 meters and staggers enemies.

Nature Domain - friends to plants and animals. Their skills are heavily tied to controlling fauna and flora. Acolyte of Nature, unlocked on Level 1, lets the Cleric learn a single Druid cantrip and grants proficiency in Animal Handling, Nature or Survival. Charm Animals and Plants is their unique Channel Divinity, letting them Charm the aforementioned creatures. Some spells exclusive to this domain are:

- Speak with Animals - the character can speak to and understand animals.

- Spike Growth - covers the area with sharp thorns. Creatures moving through the area take 2d4 damage every 1.5 meters.

Knowledge Domain - Clerics devoted to knowledge and science. Skills revolve around gaining temporary proficiency and controlling enemies during combat. Blessings of Knowledge lets them learn two additional languages and grants proficiency in two skills chosen from the pool below:

- Arcana;

- History;

- Religion;

- Nature.

The proficiency bonus applied to the chosen skills is doubled. Their Channel Divinity is Knowledge of the Ages, granting proficiency in a chosen skill until the next Long Rest.

War Domain - battle-hardened Clerics ideal as frontline combatants. Apart from proficiency in heavy armor and martial weapons, War Clerics gain the War Priestability, granting a number of charges equal to their Wisdom modifier. This charge can be used to make an extra attack as a bonus action. Their Channel Divinity, Guided Strike, grants a massive +10 to attack rolls. Some spells exclusive to this Domain are:

- **Divine Favour** - this spell grants the Cleric +1d4 to damage rolls when using weapon attacks.

- Magic Weapon - turns a weapon magical, giving it +1 to attack rolls and damage **rolls**.

Best build for Cleric

Here is a sample build for a Level 3 Cleric:

- **Race**: Gold Dwarf

- **Subclass**: Life Domain

- **Background**: Sailor

- **Ability Scores**: Wisdom about 16, Constitution and Strength about 14, Charisma about 12, Dexterity and Intelligence about 10.

Spells

Though most players associate Clerics with healers, the class' **wide range of spells**makes them much more versatile than that. Below we've listed some of the most universally useful spells.

Best offensive Cleric spells

Cantrips:

- **Sacred Flame** - a simple, offensive spell dealing **1d8 radiant damage** on hit.

Level 1 spells:

- Guiding Bolt - a bolt of divine energy that deals 4d6 radiant damage. On hit, gives advantage on the next attack against the target. The spell can be upcast using higher level spell slots to increase its damage.

- Inflict Wounds - a powerful spell inflicting a massive 3d10 necrotic damage. Its biggest flaw is it range, as it only works on touch.

- Burning Hands - a cone of flame dealing 3d6 fire area damage for up to 5 meters. This spell is exclusive to Light Domain Clerics.

Level 2 spells:

- Flaming Sphere - summons a 2-meters wide burning sphere, dealing 2d6 fire damageto nearby units and shedding light around itself The sphere lasts for 10 turns or until the Cleric's concentration is broken. This spell is exclusive to Light Domain Clerics.

- Scorching Ray - just like the previous spell, this one is also exclusive to Light Domain. Fires three rays of fire dealing 2d6 **damage each**.

Level 3 spells:

- **Warding Glyph** - a powerful spell triggering the chosen magical effect. Can deal up to **5d8 area damage** of a chosen type.

- **Fireball** - an iconic Level 3 spell that deals **8d6 area damage**. Exclusive to **Light Domain Clerics**.

Best defensive and support Cleric spells

Cantrips:

- **Resistance** - gives the target **+1d4 to saving throws**.

Level 1 spells:

- **Shield of Faith** - gives the target **+2 Armor Class**. Increases a tank's tanking capabilities and a spellcaster's survivability.

- **Bane** - inflicts up to **three simultaneous targets with a -1d4 penalty on their attack rolls and saving throws**.

- **Bless** - an exact opposite to the previous spell. **Gives three targets +1d4 to attack rolls and saving throws**.

- **Healing Word** and **Cure Wounds** - basic Cleric healing spells. The former is particularly useful, as it lets you heal unconscious allies **from a distance**.

- **Command** - if the target fails their saving throw, they must **run away, get closer, stop or drop their weapon**.

Level 2 spells:

- **Blindness** - blinds the target for **10 turns**. Crucially, this spell **does not require concentration**.

- **Hold Person** - **paralyzes** the target if they fail their Wisdom saving throw.

- **Prayer of Healing** - heals **2d8 hit points** to all allies within line of sight. Only available **outside of combat**.

- **Aid** - healing effects always restore **the maximum amount of health possible** when used on targets affected by **Aid**.

Level 3 spells:

- Revivify - revives a dead ally and restores them to 1 hit point.

- Spirit Guardians - summons helpful spirits around the Cleric, dealing damage to nearby enemies (3d8) and slowing them down.

- Beacon of Hope - healing effects restore the maximum amount of health possible to affected allies and grants the same allies advantage on Wisdom saving throws.

Best utility Cleric spells

Cantrips:

- **Thaumaturgy** - a simple cantrip granting advantage on **Intimidation** and **Performance**checls.

- **Level 1 spells:**

- **Disguise Self** - a **Trickery Domain** spell that temporarily **changes the character's appearance** to outwit other creatures.

- **Create or Destroy Water** - the caster summons **rain or dries up an area**. Keep in mind **wet enemies become vulnerable to cold and lightning damage**. Though a situational spell, it could potentially prove useful outside of combat too.

Level 2 spells:

- **Enhance Ability** - gives the target **advantage on checks tied to a chosen stat**. Useful during crucial rolls, when you especially want to reduce the possibility of failure.

- **Pass without Trace** - a utility spell exclusive to **Trickery Domain Clerics**, granting them and their nearby allies **+10 to Stealth checks**.

Level 3 spells:

Animate Dead - transforms a corpse into an **undead minion**.

Races

This part of the aide depicts which races accessible in Baldurs Gate 3 best fit the Cleric class.

While choosing to play as Cleric in Baldur's Gate 3, you ought to focus on the races that have a reward to the important characteristics, like Insight, Constitution, even Strength or Dexterity. Likewise, there are extra abilities offered by individual races, which can additionally advance your personality's playing style.

Dwarf

The dwarf is an ideal race for a Cleric in Baldurs Gate 3, as he is extremely durable and provides this class with additional valuable bonuses, especially as a Gold Dwarf subrace.

- **Race Bonus**: Constitution 2;

- **Gold Dwarf subrace**: +1 Wisdom ;

- **Dwarven Toughness**: your hero's maximum health points increase by 1 and will increase by 1 with each experience level unlocked;

- **Dwarven Resilience**: the character is given the opportunity to defend himself against Poison and gains immunity to poison;

- **Darkvision**: the character can see in the dark within a radius of 12 meters;

Elf

Elves are one of the most popular races available in *Baldurs Gate 3* and fit perfectly with the Cleric character class, especially with the Wood Elf subclass.

- **Race Bonus**: +2 to dexterity;

- **Wood Elf subrace**: +1 Wisdom;

- **Fleet of Foot**: your hero's base walking speed is 10.5 metres;

- **Mask Of The Wild**: proficiency in sneaking;

- **Keen Senses**: the hero is proficient in Perception;

- **Fey Ancestry**: the hero will have an advantage during saving throws against charms, and the magic can't put them to sleep;

- **Darkvision**: the hero can see in the dark within a radius of 12 meters.

Half-Elf

Half-elves combine the best qualities of Elves and humans, and it is for this reason that they do well as Clerics.

- **Race Bonus**: +2 to Charisma;

- **Race Bonus**: 2 additional trait points to divide. Up to one point can be added to one trait. Best pick 1 to wisdom and 1 for constitution;

- **Darkvision**: the character can see in the dark within a radius of 12 meters;

- **Fey Ancestry**: the character will have advantage in defense tests against charms and magic won't be able to put him or her to sleep.

Human

Humans are probably the most versatile race available in *Baldurs Gate 3* so they will work well as Clerics. Human receives a +1 bonus to every attribute available in the game.

Build

This section of the Baldur's Gate 3 aide depicts a prepared Cleric fabricate. We propose which race works best as a Cleric, how to best spend capacity focuses, what gear and spells to pick, and what abilities to choose.

Cleric in Baldurs Gate 3 can be created in various ways: a mixture of a skirmish fighter and a supporting person, a normal legend who helps the group with recuperating and reinforcing spells, or will utilize any conceivable spell that arrangements harm. We offer another choice, to be specific a supporting person fighting a ways off with a Long bow. With this arrangement, Cleric will actually want to remain nearby colleagues to fortify them with his spells, as well as attack successfully from a good ways and arrangement serious harm without gambling with the deficiency of wellbeing focuses.

Race

When choosing the right race for the Cleric class, **it is definitely worth choosing the Wood Elf.** Below is a list of bonuses your character will receive.

- 2 to Dexterity;

- 1 to Wisdom - the ability allowing Clerics to cast spells;

- Keen Senses: the hero is proficient in Perception;

- Base race speed: the distance you can travel in each round is 9 metres;

- Mask of the Wild: the character is proficient at Sneaking.

- Fey Ancestry: the hero will have an advantage during saving throws against charms, and the magic can't put them to sleep;

- Darkvision: the character can see in the dark within a radius of 12 meters;

- Long Bow proficiency: with this build it will be the Cleric's main weapon;

- Short Bow proficiency.

- Short Sword proficiency: one of the best auxiliary weapons;

- Long Swords Proficiency

On the off chance that you like to zero in on a standard Cleric construct that may be founded on spells, you can choose a very strong race of Dwarves, coordinated Half-Mythical people or flexible humans.

Background

While picking the foundation for your Cleric, worth picking between choices benefit from created Dexterity, and staying away from those that give abilities connected with Intelligence, as Clerics don't foster it.

- **Folk Hero:** Speak with Animals proficiency (Wisdom), Survival proficiency (Wisdom);

- Urchin: Sleight of Hands proficiency (Dexterity), Sneaking proficiency (Dexterity).

Specialization (Subclass)

As one of only a handful of exceptional person classes accessible in Baldur's Gate 3, Cleric can pick his specialization (subclass) as soon as during the person creation. The proposed construct shines on the Light Space subclass as the legend gains admittance to the helpful Faerie Firespell and Warding Flare that give the Cleric extra security.

- **Warding Flare:** react and shield yourself with divine light to hinder your opponent's attack, which may entirely miss you.

Subclass properties - Level 1

In the wake of choosing the Light Area, your Cleric will quickly gain admittance to 2 attack spells you don't have to plan (Burning Hands, Faerie Fire) and one cantrip (Light).

Burning Hands
Effect: fire shoots from your outstretched fingers. It ignites anything flammable and deals 3d6 Fire.

Range: 5 meters.

Additional information: after a successful defense throw the target receives only half of the damage. Because the cleric will attack from a distance using a bow, this spell will be used in specific situations where, for example, something needs to be set on fire.

Faerie Fire
Effect: enfold one or more targets with a colorful glow to make them visible. Attack tests against them become easier.

Range: 18 meters.

Concentration: required

Additional information: as the opponent or opponents are tagged all the characters in the team will have easier attack throws against them which will translate into the frequency of hitting the target.

Light

Effect: Infuse an object with an aura of light.

Range: 1.5 meters.

Spell type: cantrip.

Subclass properties - Level 2

Upon reaching experience level 2, you will get access to another spell closely related to the Light Domain (Radiance of the Dawn) and one that all Clerics, regardless of their chosen specialty, receive (Turn Dead).

Radiance of the Dawn

Effect: use the power of the sun to disperse the darkness and deal 2d10 x (X - depending on the character level) Radiance damage to all hostile creatures.

Range: 9 meters.

Restrictions: you can use it once a day.

Additional information: after a successful defense throw the target receives only half of the damage. Use this spell when you can hit at least 2 or 3 targets at once.

Turn Undead

Effect: all the undead who see or hear you are forced to flee from you.

Range: 9 meters.

Subclass properties - Level 3

As a Cleric with the Light Domain subclass, after reaching experience Level 3 you will gain access to 4 additional level 2 spells. **We particularly recommend Scorching Ray, help and Darkvision.**

Scorching Ray

Effect: fire three streams of fire, and each one deals 2d6 Fire damage.

Range: 18 meters.

Additional information: with this spell, you can attack 3 targets simultaneously or focus on one opponent.

Darkvision

Effect: enables a creature to see in the darkness for up to 18 meters.

Range: 1.5 meters.

Additional information: if one of the party members does not have the Darkvision ability and the fight takes place in a dark place, they receive negative status during the attack. With this skill, you can lighten the darkness and help your ally.

Aid

Effect: strengthen your allies' strength and determination by treating them and increasing the maximum number of health points by 5.

Range: 9 meters.

Lesser Restoration

Effect: remove one disease or condition that afflicts the creature.

Range: 1.5 meters.

Concentration

A few Clerics' spells are sufficiently confounded to require fixation with the goal that their impact isn't intruded. Sadly, focus is definitely not an enduring impact and can be intruded on in more ways than one.

- By projecting another spell that requires focus;

- In the wake of getting harm while keeping up with fixation, the Cleric should play out a cautious dice roll (Constitution) to guarantee the impact isn't hindered.

Skills

While picking abilities for your Cleric, give specific consideration to those that will benefit most from his most evolved capacities, like Insight and Dexterity.

Contingent upon the foundation you pick, settle on any of the accompanying choices:

- **Insight**: a skill associated with Wisdom;

- **Medicine**: a skill associated with Wisdom;

- **Animal Handling** - a skill associated with Wisdom.

- **Perception**: a skill associated with Wisdom;

- **Survival**: a skill associated with Wisdom;

- **Acrobatics**: a skill associated with Dexterity;

- **Sleight of Hands**: a skill associated with Dexterity;

- **Stealth:** a skill associated with Dexterity;

Abilities

When developing Cleric's abilities, one must first focus on Wisdom as the ability responsible for Spellcasting. It is then worth assigning points to Dexterity and fitness Constitution.

We propose to allocate the ability points for your Cleric as follows:

- **Wisdom**: 16 points;

- **Dexterity**: 16 points;

- **Constitution**: 14 points;

- **Strength**: 10 points;

- **Charisma:** 10 points;

- **Intelligence:** 8 points;

Cantrips

While making a Cleric-class character in Baldur's Gate 3, you will actually want to pick 3 cantrips that your personality will actually want to utilize. You can pick between 4 spells, and we suggest the set beneath.

Resistance

Effect: magically strengthen the creature's defense to assign its D4 bonus to the defensive throws.

Range: 1.5 meters.

Concentration: required

Guidance

Effect: give guidance to a creature - it receives a d4 bonus to their chosen trait test.

Range: 1.5 meters.

Concentration: required

Additional information: this spell is useful when you want to perform a specific action, such as stealing or opening a closed door.

Sacred Flame

Effect: summon a fiery glow that causes 1d8 Radiant damage.

Range: 18 meters.

Additional information: this spell can often be nullified by the opponent because the defensive dice roll against it is based on Dexterity. Still, it's worth having this spell at hand, because it can be used when you can't hit the target from the bow (no visibility).

Level 1 spells

Clerics have a foreordained spell pool toward the beginning, yet they will begin a game with the individuals who are chosen for the classification of arranged spells. To get ready different spells, a person should be beyond battle, open their book of spells (default K), recognize spells the individual in question would rather not use, and pick others all things being equal. For the start of the game, we enthusiastically suggest the Directing Bolt as a very helpful offensive spell, Soothing Word, Bane, and Bless.

Guiding Bolt

Effect: summon a beam of light that will cause 4d6 Radiant damage and allow for the next attack against the chosen target.

Range: 18 meters.

Additional information: a spell can deal between 4 and 24 damage points, but they must be cast from a further distance. When a character is standing too close to the target it will be much harder for him or her to hit the opponent.

Soothing Word

Effect: a creature in your hero's field of vision recovers 1d4 X (X - depending on the character's level) health points.

Range: 18 meters.

Additional information: with this spell you can revive a fallen ally. What's more, Soothing Word counts as a Bonus action so it can be used in a single round along with the attack.

Bane

Effect: target a maximum of 3 creatures that will receive a D4 penalty to attack and defensive rolls.

Range: 9 meters.

Concentration: required

Bless

Effect: bless up to 3 creatures who will receive a D4 bonus to attack and defensive rolls.

Range: 9 meters.

Concentration: required

Additional information: this spell is counted as an action so make sure it is cast just before the fight starts.

Not at all like the recently portrayed Cantrips, spells utilize a space while being projected which implies they can't be utilized endlessly. You reestablish your enchanted spaces after an extended rest in the camp.

Level 2 spells

In the wake of opening experience Level 3, every Cleric (no matter what the subclass) gains admittance to a few new level 2 spells. Particularly valuable will be the Mending Word by which the Cleric can recuperate the whole group simultaneously.

Blindness

Effect: magically Blind an enemy creature.

Range: 18 meters.

Additional information: the blinded creature may try to recover from this condition at the end of each tour.

Hold Person

Effect: paralyze a humanoid.

Range: 18 meters.

Concentration: required

Additional information: at the end of each round, the creature may try to free itself.

Prayer of Healing

Effect: all allied creatures in your character's field of vision regain 2d8 x (X - depending on the character's level) health points.

Range: 9 meters.

Additional information: this spell has no effect on the undead and constructs. It can't be used in combat.

Silence

Effect: the protagonist creates a soundproof sphere. Creatures and objects within the sphere are silenced and unaffected by Thunder.

Range: 18 meters.

Concentration: required

Equipment

This form is very flighty, as your Cleric's principal weapon will be a longbow that can be utilized proficiently by the Mythical people, and this influences the viability of the legend's attacks. As a second arrangement of weapons, it merits deciding on Dexterity-subordinate weapons (a short sword) and a shield that builds the person's Protection Class. Your Cleric ought to wear light protective layer, which gives a Dexterity reward.

Since changing your weapon set isn't included as an action in Baldurs Gate 3, change your weapon set to a short sword with a shield to reinforce your Cleric's Protection Class. Subsequent to beginning the following round, you can change to the bow, play out an attack and return to the protective design, and so on.

Upgrading abilities

In the wake of arriving at experience level 4, you will actually want to work on your Cleric's capacities by spending extra 2 focuses on picked capacities.

This is the best chance to expand the worth of the Widsom capacity to 18 places.

General tips

Before you play as a Cleric in Baldurs Gate 3, you ought to know a couple of key tips that will bring you considerably nearer to this class and fundamentally influence your legend's viability during battle.

- High Ground advantage: if conceivable, consistently attempt to take a situation over your rival prior to stirring up some dust (on a slope, roof, steps, gallery, and so forth), to acquire the High Ground advantage. This extraordinarily builds the legend's possibility hitting an objective while utilizing a bow or the Directing Bolt spell;

- Spell slots: Clerics recuperate utilized spell slots after an extended rest in the camp. Brief reprieves just reestablish some wellbeing;

- Concentration: prior to utilizing a spell that requires concentration, ensure you don't interfere with another impact;

- Healing: recollect that the Cleric has healing spells that can keep partners alive. Some of the time spending the action in healing a colleague than on attacking the target is better.;

- Darkvision: recall that the Light Space gives the Cleric a spell with which the person can concede a partnered animal the capacity to find in obscurity. This is valuable while fighting in dim rooms and utilized on characters whose race doesn't give this property, like human or Githyanki.

Warlock

Guide

Warlocks are spellcasters who have made a settlement with a strong element to acquire their powers. Employing many strong spells and capacities, they make for extremely supportive sidekicks.

Best race for Warlock

In the full arrival of Baldur's Gate 3, the engineers have taken out selective racial rewards. From this point forward, while picking a race, you can add

+2 and +1 rewards to any detail you'd like. Regardless of this, a few racial capacities prove to be useful for specific classes.

- **Tiefling** - each subrace innately knows a different, useful spell.

- **Drow** - dark elves at level 3 and level 5 gain access to useful spells: Faerie Fire and Darkness. They also have Darkvision.

Ability Points

When distributing stat points for a Warlock, prioritize Charisma. Your secondary stats should be:

- **Constitution** - it will grant some extra **hit points** and help with passing **concentration**checks.

- **Dexterity** - high Dex will increase your Armor Class when wearing **light armor**.

Best background for Warlock

Among all available backgrounds, Warlocks can especially benefit from:

- **Charlatan** - grants proficiency in **Deception** and **Sleight of Hand**, nicely complementing a high Dexterity build.

- **Criminal** - just as useful as Charlatan, though granting **Stealth** instead of Sleight of Hand.

Eldritch Invocations

The Warlock's class ability, available from **Level 2** onwards. They gain bonuses thanks to the pact they made. Among available invocations we especially recommend:

- **Agonizing Blast** - Damage dealt by the **Eldritch Blast** cantrip is increased by the Warlock's Charisma modifier.

- **Repelling Blast** - creatures hit with Eldritch Blast are pushed back by **3 meters**. Nicely synergises with the previous invocation.

- **Mask of Many Faces** - lets you cast **Disguise Self** without using a spell slot.

- **Devil's Sight** - lets the Warlock see up to 24 meters in regular or magical darkness. Especially useful to races without innate Darkvision, such as Humans.

Pact boon

At Level 3, the Warlock receives a **boon** from their benefactor, granting additional abilities.

- **Pact of the Chain** - the Warlock gains the ability to summon a Familiar, which can take one of several forms: an imp, a quasit or an animal. Each has different traits and can help you in combat. The familiar's form can be freely modified.

- **Pact of the Blade** - the Warlock can summon a **chosen melee weapon** as an action. It can be drawn or hidden, but must be equipped by the Warlock. The Warlock is always **proficient** in using it.

- **Pact of the Tome** - the Warlock receives a special grimoire from their patron. It lets them learn **three Cantrips** from any class. Having this book, the Warlock can cast these cantrips at will.

Best spells

The Warlock has not many spell slots, however it's remunerated by how these slots are generally the highest accessible level. Furthermore, Warlocks reestablish their spell slots on brief reprieves, while most different casters require extended reprieves.

Cantrips:

- **Eldritch Blast** - the Warlock's signature cantrip, dealing a huge **1d10** damage. The damage scales as you level up, while the **Agonizing Blast** invocation makes it an extremely formidable attack.

- **Chill Touch** - **1d8** damage and an additional effect preventing your foes from restoring health.

- **Minor Illusion** - creates an illusory object to distract nearby creatures.

- **Spells:**

- **Armor of Agathys** - the Warlock gains **+5 AC** and deals **5 cold damage** to each enemy who attacks them in melee.

- **Hex** - the target receives **1d6 damage**, takes bonus damage on subsequent attacks and has **disadvantage on selected ability rolls**.

- **Arms of Hadar** - the target takes **2d6 necrotic damage** and can no longer use reactions.

- **Expeditious Retreat** - the caster can **Dash as a bonus action**.

- **Protection from Evil and Good** - protects the target from **fiends, fey, celestials, aberrations and elementals**. These types of enemies can no longer **charm, frighten** or **possess** the target. They also have **disadvantage** on attacks against the target.

- **Witch Bolt** - the target takes **1d12 damage**. Every turn, the caster can remotely trigger the arc connecting them to the target to deal **1d12 damage again**.

- **Misty Step** - a Level 2 spell which lets the caster teleport to a chosen, visible location.

- **Hold Person** - paralyzes a humanoid target, preventing them from moving or taking actions.

- **Hunger of Hadar** - a Level 3 spell which creates a nightmarish sphere. Creatures inside the sphere take **2d6 damage**. Ending a turn inside the sphere deals another **2d6 damage**. The sphere counts as **difficult terrain** and all creatures within are **blinded** until they leave it.

Best subclass for Warlock

Warlock Subclasses are characterized by the being they've made a settlement with. Each strong supporter awards different capacities and select spells.

The Fiend - the character has made a pact with an evil Fiend from another plane of existence. The **Dark One's Blessing** ability lets the Warlock **restore hit points**, equal to their Charisma modifier, whenever they reduce an enemy to 0 HP. This subclass' exclusive spells include:

- **Burning Hands** - deals **3d6** fire damage.

- **Command** - forces the target to stop, get closer, run away, go prone or drop their weapon.

The Great Old One - the character has made a pact with an ancient eldritch being. The Mortal Reminder ability frightens nearby enemies for a turn whenever the Warlock crits. This subclass' exclusive spells include:

- Dissonant Whispers - alarms the objective for 2 turns and arrangements 3d6 harm.

- Phantasmal Force - a Level 2 spell which makes an illusion in the objective's psyche, managing 1d6 harm each turn for 10 turns.

Archfey -the person has made a settlement with a strong Fey, abilities to acquire spinning around swarm control and status infirmities. Fey Presence is an action driving close by animals to make an Insight saving toss. Whenever fizzled, the animal is enchanted or terrified. Accessible later on, Misty Break allows the Warlock to become undetectable in the wake of being hit and cast the Misty Step spell. This subclass' restrictive spells incorporate:

- Faerie Fire - reveals hidden enemies and grants advantage on attacks against affected foes.

- Phantasmal Force - the target's mind has an illusion implanted in it, dealing 1d6 physical damage each turn (spell lasts for up to 10 turns). When the affected target receives damage from a different source, the Phantasmal Force damage type also changes. Similarly to the previous spell, it requires maintaining concentration.

Best build for Warlock

Here's an example of a Warlock build, to sum up all knowledge provided on this page:

- **Race**: Drow

- **Subclass**: The Great Old One

- **Background**: Charlatan

- **Ability Scores**: Charisma around 16, Constitution and Dexterity around 14, Intelligence around 13/12, Wisdom and Strength around 10/8.

Spells

From this section of the manual for Baldur's Gate 3, you will become familiar with the spells accessible for the Warlock - one of the classes accessible in the game.

Warlocks, limited by a settlement with an almighty benefactor, get the capacity to employ dull and perilous wizardry. The spells that can be found on your personality are partitioned into levels, and that implies that you can get to additional strong spells whenever you have acquired a specific degree of involvement.

Spells - Level 1

The table beneath shows the Warlock's all's spells from the primary level that are accessible while making another person in Baldur's Gate 3.

Eldritch Blast

Effect: summon an energy ray that will cause 1D10 Force damage.

Range: 18 meters.

Blade Ward

Effect: you gain immunity to Bludgeoning, Piercing, and Slashing injuries caused by weapon attacks.

Chill Touch

Effect: assail a creature with the chill of the grave. The target receives 1d8 Necrotic and cannot regain hit points. Undead creatures also get disadvantage on attack rolls.

Range: 18 meters.

Friends

Effect: enchant a non-hostile creature to gain advantage on Charisma checks against it.

Range: 9 meters.

Concentration: required

Mage Hand

Effect: create a spectral hand that can manipulate and interact with objects.

Range: 18 meters.

Concentration: required

Poison Spray

Effect: project a puff of noxious gas that deals 1d12 Poison.

Range: 3 feet.

True Strike

Effect: detect the target's defensive properties to have an easier time when attacking it.

Range: 18 meters.

Concentration: required

Armour of Agathys

Effect: the hero is covered in frost and gains 5 temporary health points. In addition, the hero causes 5 Cold damage to all creatures that attack them with a melee attack.

Arms of Hadar

Effect: summon the dark energy. Targets receive 2d6 Necrotic damage and cannot respond.

Range: 3 feet.

Additional information: after a successful defense throw the target receives only half of the damage.

Charm Person

Effect: Magically charm a humanoid in your field of vision.

Range: 18 meters.

Additional information: a charmed creature can't hurt a character casting a spell.

Expeditionary Retreat

Effect: turn Sprint into an extra action allowing the character to move at extraordinary speed.

Concentration: required

Hellish Rebuke

Effect: the next time your hero gets injured, they will unleash infernal flames, which cause 2d10 Fire damage to the enemy attacking them.

Additional information: after a successful defense throw the target receives only half of the damage.

Protection from Evil and Good

Effect: protect the benevolent being from aberrations, celestial, elementals, fey, fiends, and undead.

Range: 1.5 meters.

Concentration: required

Other information: the attacks of the creatures listed above aimed at this target are hindered and they cannot inflict Charm, Frightened or Possessed statuses.

Hex

Effect: cast a curse on an enemy to inflict additional 1d6 Necrotic damage with each attack ending with a hit. The target also has difficulties with passing skillchecks for an attribute of your choice.

Range: 18 meters.

Concentration: required

Witch Bolt

Effect: the hero summons a beam of energy that causes 1d12 Lightning damage and connects to the target with an electric arc.

Range: 18 meters.

Concentration: required

Additional information: you can activate the arc of lightning in each round to automatically inflict 1d12 electrical injuries.

Spells - Level 2

The table beneath shows Warlock's level two spells. Your legend will gain admittance to them subsequent to arriving at experience Level 3 no matter what the picked specialization (subclass).

Blindness
Effect: magically Blind an enemy creature.
Range: 18 meters.
Additional information: the blinded creature may try to recover from this condition at the end of each tour.

Hold Person
Effect: paralyze a humanoid.
Range: 18 meters.
Concentration: required
Additional information: at the end of each round, the creature may try to free itself.

Ray of Enfeeblement
Effect: the character shots a ray of weakening energy from his or hers hand. Target that is hit can deal half damage of Strength-based weapon attacks.
Range: 18 meters.
Concentration: required

Darkness
Effect: a character creates a cloud of magic darkness that will hide and blind creatures inside it. Darkness makes it impossible to perform ranged attacks.
Range: 18 meters.
Concentration: required

Burning Hands
Effect: fire shoots from your outstretched fingers. It ignites anything flammable and deals 3d6 Fire.
Range: 5 meters.
Additional information: after a successful defense throw the target receives only half of the damage.

Misty Step
Effect: the character becomes surrounded by a dark mist and he or she teleports to a free spot in his or hers sight.
Range: 18 meters.

Shatter

Effect: cause an intense, painful noise that deals 3d8 Thunder damage for creatures and items.

Range: 18 meters.

Additional information: after a successful defense test, the target receives only half of the initial damage. Inorganic creatures build from materials like rocks will have their defense throws harder.

Invisibility

Effect: touch a creature to make it invisible.

Range: 1.5 meters.

Concentration: required

Additional information: the spell ends prematurely if a creature attacks or uses magic.

Races

This section of the aide depicts which races accessible in Baldurs Gate 3 best fit the Warlock class.

Assuming you choose to play as a Warlock in Baldur's Gate 3, you ought to check out races that have rewards to Charisma, Constitution, or even Dexterity. Likewise, there are extra abilities offered by individual races, which can additionally enhance your personality's playing style.

Half-Elf

Half-elves combine the best qualities of Elves and humans and are the best possible choice for the Warlock class.

- **Race Bonus**: +2 to Charisma;

- **Race Bonus**: 2 additional trait points to divide. Up to one point can be added to one trait. Best to choose +1 to Constitution and 1 for Dexterity;

- **Darkvision**: the character can see in the dark within a radius of 12 meters;

- **Fey Ancestry**: the character will have advantage in defense tests against charms and magic won't be able to put him or her to sleep.

Tiefling

Tiefling is another race available in *Baldurs Gate 3*, which fits well with the Warlock class due to the bonus to Charisma and very useful passive abilities.

- **Racial bonus**: +2 to Charisma, +1 to Intelligence;

- **Hellish Resistance:** the character gains fire resistance - all received fire damage is halved;

- **Darkvision**: the hero can see in the dark within a radius of 12 meters.

Drow

Drow is another race in *Baldurs Gate 3* that is worth noting when creating a Warlock class character.

- **Racial bonus**: +1 to Charisma, +2 to Dexterity;

- **Fey Ancestry**: you have an advantage on saving throws against Charmed, and magic can't put you to sleep.

- **Superior Darkvision**: the protagonist can see in the dark within 24 meters.

- **Dancing lights**: a clever spell that creates wisps of light that illuminate a 12m radius.

Human

Humans are likely the most adaptable race that anyone could hope to find in Baldurs Gate 3 so they will function admirably as Warlocks. Human gets a +1 reward to each attribute accessible in the game.

Build

Warlocks are another class zeroing in on went battle utilizing supernatural spells. These understudies of dull expressions base their power on an extraordinary settlement that they make with one of three every strong benefactor. On this page of our aide, you can find tips and fabricate thoughts that will help while endeavoring to play as a Warlock.

Character creation wizard

On this page we detail a form in view of the Monster subclass. Creating different paradigms might vary marginally from what we arranged beneath.

While picking a race for your Warlock, we suggest looking at Tieflings and Drows. Both of these races are described by their natural wizardry potential which appears through learning an extra Cantrip or spell. This choice will definitely carry an assortment to your enchanted munitions stockpile, particularly in the start of the experience.

Class progression

- Warlocks choose **a subclass** at level 1. By choosing **The Fiend**, you'll receive access to **Dark One's Blessing** class feature. With it, **when you bring enemy HP to 0**, you'll receive **temporary health points**. This feature thus promotes an **aggressive style of gameplay**based on **finishing off opponents**. When choosing initial spells, make sure to learn the **Eldritch Blast** Cantrip. This is the most powerful offensive Cantrip available in the game, increasing your combat potential immensely. Besides Eldritch Blast, consider choosing the following spells: **True Strike, Bone Chill, Armour of Agathys, Hex**, and **Witch Bolt**.

- At level 2, you'll have to choose **2 Eldritch Invocations**, which are a unique class feature of Warlocks. We especially recommend **Agonizing Blast, Repelling Blast**, and **Armour of Shadows**.

- After reaching level 3, you'll stand before the choice of 1 of 3 available **Pact Boons**. Although all of them offer useful bonuses, we recommend choosing between **Pact of the Chain** and **Pact of the Blade**. When it comes to choosing level 2 spells, we recommend **Scorching Ray, Cloud of Daggers**, and **MIsty Step**.

- On level 4, you'll have to decide on your first **Feat**. Same as with other spellcasting classes, a good choice may be **Ability Improvements** spent on **Charisma**. A better Charisma modifier **will make your spells more powerful**, and positively affect the bonus damage from **Agonizing Blast**.

- On level 5, you can choose the next **Eldritch Invocation**. It may be a good idea to choose the other ones mentioned earlier, or **Sign of Ill Omen** if you're looking to unlock an additional spell. From level 5 spells, consider **Fireball**, **Counterspell**, or **Hunger of Hadar**.

- Level 6 means **a new subclass feature. Dark One's Own Luck** allows adding **1d10** to any **Ability Check**. This skill can be used once per **short rest**.

- At level 7, you can choose another **Eldritch Invocation**. We recommend **Book of Ancient Secrets** which unlocks spells such as **Ray of Sickness, Chromatic Orb**, and **Silence**. These spells **can be cast once per long rest** and don't use a spell slot. When it comes to level 4 spells, consider **Wall of Fire** and **Banishment**.

- Level 8 means choosing another **Feat**. Once again, you can choose **Ability Improvements (Charisma)**, or go on a different path and go for **War Caster** or **Lucky**.

- Among the **Eldritch Invocations** available on level 9, we recommend **Minions of Chaos**. This skill can conjure **elementals** fighting on your side. When it comes to level 5 spells, we recommend **Flame Strike** and **Cone of Cold**.

- Level 10 means access to another class feature - **Fiendish Resilience**. With it, after each short rest, you will be able to determine **the type of damage** to which you will become **Resistant**. To get the most out of the ability, strategically plan your breaks and choose resistances based the type of enemies you will soon have to fight.

- At level 11, you learn **Mystic Arcanum**, which **is a level 6 spell** that you can cast **without spending a spell slot**. When it comes to the choice of spell, we recommend choosing **Circle of Death** or **Eyebite**.

- Level 12 means choosing the final **Eldritch Invocation**. We recommend **Lifedrinker**, which will add Necrotic damage **to your every melee attack**, or one of the Invocations unlocking **an additional spell.** You'll also get to choose a final Feat - consider the aforementioned **War Caster** or **Moderately Armoured** which will allow you **to wear medium armor.**

Ilithild Powers

If you decide to utilize Ilithild Powers, consider **Shield of Thralls**, **Charm**, and **Cull the Weak** as your choices. These will increase the battle potential of your Warlock, and unlock new tactical options.

Party members - their skills and spells

Despite his undeniable potential, a finishing Warlock won't last long in battle without help. Make sure your team has a **supporting** character such as **a Cleric**, **Druid**, or **Bard**. The last choice may be especially useful. His **Song of Rest** skill will allow you to quickly regenerate most of Warlock class skills.

If the battle transforms into a melee onslaught, it would be good to have someone to watch your back. **Paladin** or **Fighter** will work great as tanks that distract and mitigate damage that may have been directed at your Warlock.

Equipment and bonuses from it

At the end of Act 1, in Myconid Colony in Underdark you can find Cinder Shoes, a footwear that gives Heat whenever you burn an enemy, and this item will be perfect for the fire-oriented repertoire of Fiend Warlock.

In later stages of the game, focus on getting items that increase magical power and defensive potential of the hero. Similarly to Bard or Sorcerer, consider getting Potent Robe that gives a choice of bonuses scaling with Charisma. If you prefer something with more protection and are proficient in medium armor, a good choice will definitely be Adamantine Scale Mail (you can forge it).

Consumables

Here are some useful potions and elixirs which every Warlock should keep handy:

- **Elixir of Vigilance** - provides a +5 bonus to Initiative, thanks to which your allies will receive support during combat faster.

- **All kinds of healing potions** - will quickly allow you to regenerate lost HP.

- **Potion of Flying** - a mobility boost that will allow you to take a strategic position on the battlefield.

- **Elixir of Heroism** - gives +10 temporary HP and grants the Bless status. It will help you prepare for an encounter with the enemy.

Paladin

Guide

To capitalize on your Paladin in BG3, you want to pick the sufficient background and race. This is only the initial step - for the Paladin to be essentially as strong as conceivable you should allocate Capacity focuses accurately and pick the best Spells and Actions for the person - we will assist with that. We likewise clarify the thought behind and how for utilize Divine Destroy and help in picking a sub-class from 4 accessible. At long last, in the base piece of the page, you can discover the absolute best and suggested Paladin constructs.

Best origin for a Paladin

While picking a history for Paladin, attempt to pick one that builds up Abilities that you will use as a delegate of this class. On account of the Paladin, we suggest the accompanying:

- **Outlander** - bonus to Athletics and Survival.

- **Guild Artisan** - bonus to Intuition and Persuasion.

- **Folk Hero** - bonus to Animal Handling and Survival.

Best race for a Paladin

Paladins are characterized by great strength, high constitution, and charisma, therefore the best races for this class are:

- **Half-elves** - +2 to Charisma and +2 to chosen Abilities (you can only add one point to one attribute, and only to Strength, Dexterity, or Constitution)

- **Dwarves - Shield Dwarf is especially recommended,** which receives +2 to Constitution and +2 to Strength.

- **Tieflings** receive +1 to Strength and +2 to Charisma as a racial bonus.

- **Githyanki** receive +2 to Strength and +1 to Intelligence.

- **Humans** receive +1 to all Abilities.

Paladin's ability points

- The essential attribute depicting a Paladin is Strength, which takes into consideration all the more impressive skirmish attacks. While picking a race like Half-mythical person and Dwarf, you'll start with 16-17 Strength, getting 3 modifiers of this attribute. High Charisma empowers the Paladin to project spells effectively. Paladin's most remarkable enchantment abilities expect you to land a scuffle attack first, so these two Attributes ought to be created however much as could be expected.

- Furthermore, additional focuses to Constitution will work on the solidness of the person, and a higher modifier of this Capacity will cause your Paladin to support Concentration spells better.

- With regards to Shrewdness, ensure you have something like 10 of it, as this Attribute assumes a part during guard rolls.

Best spells and actions for Paladin

- **Lay on Hands** - an Action accessible from level 1 of the person that recharges wellbeing and eliminates infections and poisons.

- **Bless** - a level 1 Concentration spell that applies a Blessing to up to 3 partners. With Blessed status, the impacted characters get a 1d4 reward to attack and safeguard rolls. The spell goes on for 10 turns.

- **Heroism** -a level 1 Concentration spell building up either the Paladin or a partner of another class. With Valor, the impacted legend can't become Unnerved and gets a reward to base wellbeing focuses (+5) with each turn. The spell goes on for 10 turns.

- **Shield of Faith** - a Concentration spell accessible from level 1 that encompasses a partner with a defensive enchantment obstruction adding +2 to shield class.

- **Thunderous Smite** - a level 1 Concentration spell. After an attack with a saturated weapon, the adversary is pushed 3 meters and gets 2d6 thunder harm. Also, the adversary might be wrecked.

- **Divine Favour** - a level 1 Concentration spell that when applied, adds additional harm to scuffle attacks (extra 1d4 harm from light) - the impact endures 10 turns.

- **Aid** - a level 2 spell that reinforces allies and increases their base Constitution up to the time of longer rest.

- **Branding Smite** - a level 2 Concentration spell that imbues the Paladin's weapon with astral glow that marks the target with light once struck and prevents them from becoming Invisible. The effect lasts for 10 turns.

- **Magic Weapon** - a level 2 Concentration spell that imbues the weapon with magic energy. This results with a 1+ bonus to attack and defense rolls.

Best subclass for Paladin

In Baldur's Gate 3, a Paladin can pursue one of two specializations:

- **Oath of Devotion** - unlocks Holy Rebuke skill. This spell creates an aura around an ally which deals 1d4 light damage to every being that attacks them in melee range. The effect lasts for 2 turns. **At level 3 of this specialization**, the Paladin receives **a spell called Sacred Weapon** which counts his Charisma modifier to attack rolls with held weapon and **Turn the Unholy spell** that can be cast on monster or undead groups. If Turn the Unholy hits its target, the enemies will be pushed to a certain distance and won't be able to perform any attacks or reactions for 3 turns. Aside from the above, you also receive access to two spells - **Protection from Evil and Good and Sanctuary**. Sanctuary protects an ally from damage up to 10 turns provided they don't perform any attacks on their own. **A perfect spell for protecting weak party members or NPCs.**

- **Oath of the Ancients** - this specialization unlocks Healing Radiance, a spell that heals all allies in a 3-meter radius. **At level 3 of the specialization, the Paladin receives Nature's Wrath**, a spell that immobilizes an enemy for 10 turns and reduces their attack and defense, and **Turn the Faithless**, a spell useful against tieflings and fairies. If Turn the Faithless reaches its target, it will make enemies stand at a certain distance and make them unable to perform any moves for 3 turns.

Best fighting style for Paladin

Upon reaching level 2, Paladin can choose 1 fighting style from 4 available:

- **Defense** - the Paladin receives a +1 bonus to armor class while wearing an armor.

- **Dueling** - when equipped with a melee weapon and a shield, the hero receives +2 bonus to attack rolls with the held weapon, increasing the chances of dealing heavy damage.

- **Great Weapon Fighting** - when Paladin lands 1 or 2 on the dice when attacking with a two-handed weapon, he can reroll the dice.

- **Protection** - when a monster in a 1.5-meter radius from the Paladin starts attacking a different target, he can impose Disadvantage on this enemy.

Paladins are perfect with weighty covering and two-handed weapons, which makes Extraordinary Weapon Fighting a truly suitable decision. Rerolling the dice in the event of a terrible toss will doubtlessly end up being valuable in basic circumstances.

Oathbreaker

Oathbreaker is the third Subclass available for Paladin. If Paladin kills an innocent NPC or lies too often in discoursed, he will break his oath, and lose all spells and abilities of his Subclass.

In the event that you break your pledge, the following time you visit the camp you will meet a Paladin who will offer you to recover your vow for 2000 gold. You can either acknowledge this offer or enter the Oathbreaker way.

At level 5, Oathbreaker Paladin receives 3 spells:

- **Spiteful Suffering** - deals 1d4 3 necrotic damage to a single target for 3 turns, additionally weakening his defense.

- **Control Undead** - all undead on a lower level than your Paladin will start following the hero and attack his enemies. Additionally, these beings will remain with him up to a long rest.

- **Dreadful Aspect** - casts an aura with a radius of 9 meters. All struck entities that fail the Wisdom roll will be Frigthened for 10 turns making them immobilized. Additonally, their attack and skill rolls will be weakened.

Divine Smite

Upon reaching level 2, the Paladin receives Divine Smite, an active spell **that deals light damage after each performed melee attack.** At level 5, this may mean even up to 3d8 additional damage.

Divine Smite is always prepared. You can **set up an automatic casting of this spell after a melee attack or only for critical strikes.** You can also set up a pop-up questions before using an automatic Divine Smite.

Best Paladin build

If you want your Paladin to use two-handed weapons, choose the following:

- **Race**: Zariel Tiefling

- **Subclass**: Oath of the Ancients

- **Abilities**: Strength and Charisma minimum 16, Constitution 13, Dexterity 12, Wisdom 10, Intelligence 8

- **Fighting style**: Great Weapon Fighting

- **Weapon**: Sussar Greatsword

- **Armor:** Chain Mail Armour

If you would like a Paladin that uses sword and shield in battle, choose:

- **Race:** Shield Dwarf

- **Subclass:** Oath of Devotion

- **Abilities**: Strength 17, Charisma 14, Constitution 14, Dexterity 13, Wisdom 10, Intelligence 8

- **Fighting style**: Duelling

- **Weapon**: Faithbreaker

- **Armor:** Slippery Chain Shirt

- **Shield:** Absolute's Warboard

Build

Paladin is a class that is predominantly centered around close battle. An appropriately evolved fabricate permits your personality to get through a ton of harm and arrangement a lot of it. From this aide, you will figure out how to utilize class capacities, which accomplishments to purchase, and which subclass to decide to make your Paladin the most grounded in the game.

Character creation wizard

Similarly as with the Hero and Brute, the best class for a Paladin is Half-Orc. His capacities are ideal for a person participated close by to-hand battle. Causing extra harm with a Basic Hit and recovering 1HP after being thumped down are too great abilities to skip.

On account of background, it merits considering Respectable, because of which you will acquire Proficiency in Influence that scales with your Charisma - one of the most fundamental attributes for a Paladin.

Class progression

- At the first level, unlike some classes, Paladin instantly chooses his **subclass** called **Oath**. This guide describes the build for the **Oath of Vengeance**, which is the strongest one available. Additionally, a Paladin at the first level receives a healing ability called **Lay on Hands**. You will also receive the **Divine Sense**, providing an advantage on attacks against **celestial, fiends,** and **undead** as a bonus action. **Inquisitor's Might** is an ability that causes a character's weapon to deal an additional **2 points of Radiant damage**.

- The second level involves choosing **spells, fighting style**, and the **Divine Smite** ability. As for the fighting style, choose **Great Weapon Fighting**, which provides higher damage when using **two-handed weapons**. In turn, **Divine Smite** allows you to deal **additional Radiant damage** if you hit an opponent in exchange for your **spell slot**.

- Level three gives you **another spell slot** for first-level spells, one additional **prepared spell**, a **Divine Health** ability that keeps your character **from getting sick,** and two subclass abilities - **Abjure Enemy** and **Vow of Enmity**. The first one is action allowing you to **frighten the opponent**. The second is a bonus action providing an advantage in the next attack.

- The fourth level is **Feat** and **another charge of Lay on Hands**. For feat, it is best to choose **ability improvement**, in this case, **Strength**.

- Level five will grant you **an additional attack** - an ability that will double your effectiveness in combat.

- On the sixth level, you will get **Aura of Protection**, which causes allies within a radius of three meters to gain a bonus **equal to your Charisma modifier** for **Saving Throws**.

- At level seven, you get the subclass feature - **Relentless Avenger**, which means that if you hit an opponent **with an Opportunity Attack**, you will receive **a speed bonus** of **4.5 m** in the next turn.

- The eighth level is another **Feat** - in this case, it is recommended to take **Great Weapon Master**, which will allow you to deal a bonus of **10 damage** in exchange for a penalty of **-5 to attack roll**.

- The ninth level is **bonus spells**.

- The tenth level provides another charge for **Lay on Hands** and **Aura of Courage** ability. It makes you and your allies immune to the effect of **Frightened** status.

- On the eleventh level, you receive an **Improved Divine Smite**, which makes your attacks deal **an additional 1d8 Radiant damage**.

- The last level is a **Feat** - you can take **Tough** for **an extra 24 HP** or **Savage Attacker** if you feel like you need to deal **more damage**.

Ilithild Powers

Don't be afraid to **unlock and use these skills** - focus especially on **Cull the Weak, Repulsor** and **Black Hole**. Unleashing the full power of Ilithild Powers doesn't affect the character negatively, so leave all tadpoles for yourself.

Party members - their skills and spells

As a Paladin, you can be a limited armed force, yet to build your group potential, add a Rogue or a Versifier to the party, because of which you will actually want to utilize the expertise Skillful deception. Also, Troubadour will give admittance to extraordinary help spells.

Then again, in the event that you really want more went harm, a Wizard, Magician, or Warlock will be reasonable for this undertaking.

On account of spells, during the game, you ought to zero in on three of them - Tracker's honest's Imprint, Shield, and Scramble. Tracker's Imprint is a reward action and expands the harm you bargain. The Shield of Confidence gives a reward of 2 to AC, and Scurry gives an extra action - notwithstanding, you just open these at the 10th level.

Equipment and bonuses from it

As a Paladin, you are intense and bargain a ton of harm, however one of the most concerning issues is the absence of portability. Make certain to get the Special necklace of Misty Step in the main demonstration in the Troll Camp.

Moreover, in the Underdark, at the Selunite Station, you will track down the Head protector of Destroying, and that implies that when you apply an impact with one of your Smites, you get reward HP as a Charisma reward.

Concerning weapons, complete the initial segment of the journey for Karlach to overcome the misleading paladins. One of them will have the Sword of Equity, which awards free utilization of the Shield of Confidence.

Toward the finish of the game, hold back nothing - an incredible two-handed sword that duplicates the reward from Solidarity to harm, and Helldusk Reinforcement, which gives a base 21AC, the capacity to fly, and protection from fire.

Consumables

Below you will find a list of consumables that will make your Paladin even stronger.

- **Oil of Accuracy** - provides +2 to Attack Rolls.

- **Elixir of Heroism** - gives additional 10HP temporarily and applies "Blessed" status.

- **Potion of Flying** - additional mobility is something that is always needed.

- **Potion of Hill Giant Strength** - perfect if you don't have 20 Strength yet.

- **Elixir of Vigilance** - provides +5 to Initiative, make sure to drink it before tougher battles.

Druid

Guide

Druids in the realm of Baldur's Gate 3 are mages who draw their power from an exceptional bond that interfaces them with the universe of nature. These persevering fighters can satisfy numerous jobs in the party: from being steady mages to merciless beasts crushing foes with their strong teeth and paws. The accompanying page presents a bunch of fundamental data that will assist you with figuring out what kind of Druid will be best for you.

Best race for a Druid

In the full arrival of Baldur's Gate 3, the engineers have taken out elite racial rewards. From here onward, while picking a race, you can add +2 and +1 rewards to any detail you'd like. Regardless of this, a few racial capacities prove to be useful for specific classes.

- **Wood Elf** - this subrace grants a useful **bow** proficiency and **higher base movement range**.

- **Drow** - this race grants **useful weapon proficiencies, Superior Dark Vision** and racial spells **Faerie Fire** and **Darkness**.

Ability Points

When assigning ability points, first pay attention to a high **Wisdom** indicator, as it is responsible for **the strength of the spells cast by the Druid**.

Secondly, focus on **Constitution** and **Dexterity**.

- **Constitution** will allow your Druid to endure a bit more during intense clashes, and will also make it easier for you to **stay focused** when casting spells that require concentration.

- High **Dexterity** will provide you with several additional armor class points when using medium and light armor - Druids are naturally proficient in using them.

The best origin for a Druid

While picking beginnings for your Druid, attempt to pick those that will give you proficiency in abilities in view of Astuteness. In a correlative manner, this will upgrade the qualities of your personality and permit you to effectively deal with dice rolls. Beginnings worth considering are among others. e.g.

- **Hermit** ensures proficiency in **medicine** and **religion**;

- **Folk Hero** will give you proficiency in **animal handling** and **survival**.

Wild Shape

After reaching **level 2**, the Druid gains access to their signature ability - **Wild Shape**. It allows them to transform into an **animal**. This option is available both during exploration and combat as well.

Turning into an animal has a number of consequences:

- Druid **gains new statistics**, armor class, and beast stamina points, but **keeps** his Intelligence, Wisdom, and Charisma.

- When the Druid's hit points in wild shape drop to 0, the Druid **returns** to their original form as it was before the transformation.

- You can use the ability **twice** before making a short rest.

The best form

Every creature structure enjoys its own benefits and detriments. Some of them will be more helpful in battle. Others will be useful during investigation. The following are a couple of fascinating instances of structures and their purposes:

- **Bear** - a powerful form useful in combat. Available **only for the Circle of the Moon subclass**.

- **Cat** - a rather useless form in combat. The cat's small size is useful in thorough exploration, while the ability to **meow** distracts the nearby NPCs.

- **Giant spider**- useful in combat, and with the ability of **long jump**, a form that allows you to get into hard-to-reach places.

Best spells for a Druid

The spells decision will to a great extent rely upon your play style and whether your Druid will be remaining on the cutting edge or maybe offering help until the end of the group, projecting spells from a remote place from the foes.

Here are a few spells worth considering:

Cantrips:

- **Guidance** - a useful cantrip providing the target with **1d4** to skill checks. Choose it if your party lacks a Cleric.

- **Shillelagh** - your **club or staff** becomes a magic weapon dealing bonus damage and using your Wisdom for attack rolls. Extremely useful if you want to use blunt weapons.

- **Thorn Whip** - the target hit receives **1d6** damage and is pulled 3 meters towards the Druid.

Spells:

- **Goodberry** - a classic Druid spell creating **4 fruits that restore 1d4 health points**. It can also serve as provisions when you are in a camp (provides one unit of Camp Supply).

- **Cure Wounds** and **Healing Word** - classic healing spells. The first restores **1d8** health through touch, the second **1d4** through eye contact.

- **Create or Destroy Water** - summons rain or removes water from a given area. Useful when paired with another magic user, because a wet **opponent will take extra damagefrom cold and electricity**.

- **Thunderwave** - a level 1 offensive spell. It deals **2d8 electric damage**, and pushes creatures and objects away.

- **Entangle** - a concentration spell that creates vines that wrap around the target and immobilize it.

- **Flame Blade** - level 2 spell. Creates a fiery saber that deals **3d6 fire damage**. The weapon also produces a blinding light. It can be holster and drawn by the caster.

- **Spike Growth** - Druid transforms the ground into sharp spikes. A creature moving through this area takes **2d4** damage for every 1.5 meters it walks.

- **Pass without Trace** - a practical spell granting the Druid and nearby companions a **+10to Stealth checks**.

- **Heat Metal** - a level 2 spell that allows you to heat an opponent's **metal weapon and armor**. Depending on the opponent's actions, they may discard the weapon, receive a penalty to attacks, or receive damage from fire.

- **Lesser Restoration** - a level 2 spell that **removes** negative effects and poisoning from its target.

Best subclass

Subsequent to arriving at level 2, the Druid picks supposed Circle addressing a subclass. In the early access form of Baldur's Gate 3, you can browse the Druid's two subclasses. The third Circle will be added after the send off:

Circle of the Land - a subclass zeroed in on projecting spells. By picking this class at level 2, you promptly gain admittance to an additional 1 cantrip. The druid likewise accesses Natural Recuperation. An expertise that permits you to recover a portion of your spell slots beyond battle. While arriving at level 3, you will actually want to pick the Spell Circle. It will furnish you with 2 extra spells, which from here on out will continuously be ready and prepared for your Druid to utilize. The decision of Spell Circle will eventually rely upon your play style, however it merits focusing on the accompanying gatherings:

- **Coast** - you will gain access to the spells Mirror Image and Misty Step. Useful for enemy spotting.

- Underdark - you will gain access to the spells Web and Misty Step. Spells useful in combat and for surprising enemies.

- Swamp - you will get access to the spells Acid Arrow and Darkness. This Circle will suit a more offensive style of play.

At level 5, you will get close enough to the following Circle. Notwithstanding, a couple of spells indistinguishable from those at level 3 will vary.

Circle of the Moon - a subclass zeroing in on the Wild Shape, which in this subclass you might enact during a reward action (Battle Wild Shape). Aside from the extra structure (bear), this Circle gives admittance to Lunar Repair beginning from level 2. This capacity permits the Druid in creature structure to utilize a spell opening to recuperate some wellbeing focuses. At level 4, a Druid utilizing Circle of the Moon likewise gets an extra crow formwhich will permit them to fly.

Circle of the Spores - a Circle zeroed in on using growths, molds, and spores to control living and dead creatures. The Corona of Spores capacity allows the Druid to deliver a cloud managing 1d4 necrotic harm. This harm can, significantly, be managed as a Reaction. It likewise functions admirably with Cooperative Element, which duplicates the harm of Radiance of Spores and gives additional 8 brief HP to a Druid from the Circle of the Spores.

Best build for a Druid

As a summary, below we present **2 exemplary builds** for a level 3 Druid using the above tips.

Druid as a mage:

- **Race:** Drow

- **Subclass:** Circle of the Land

- **Origin:** Hermit

- **Abilities:** Wisdom and Constitution 16, Intelligence around 14, Dexterity around 13/12, Strength around 10, Charisma around 8

- **Spells Circle:** Swamp

- Druid as a shape-shifter:

- **Race:** Wood Elf

- **Subclass:** Circle of the Moon

- **Origin:** Folk Hero

- **Abilities:** Wisdom and Constitution 16, Dexterity about 14, Intelligence about 12, Strength about 10, Charisma about 8

Spells

Druids are strong sorcery clients with a unique, cozy relationship with the powers of nature. This class accesses a wide collection of offensive, guarded, and utility spells. The accompanying rundown will assist you with picking the right spell for the right event.

The best offensive spells for the Druid

Cantrips:

- **Summon Flame (Produce Flame)** - The Druid creates a flickering flame that illuminates the space. You may then throw this type of projectile dealing **1d8 damage** on hit. An immediate throw after creation doesn't consume an action, but holding the flame for subsequent turns will require actions to throw it at enemies.

- **Shillelagh** - A useful spell that transforms the **club** or **staff** wielded by a Druid into a magical weapon dealing **1d8 2 damage**. Additionally, the ability responsible for casting spells in a Druid **(Wisdom)** is used **during attack rolls**. A mandatory part of the repertoire for a hero using blunt weapons.

- **Poison Spray** - a cantrip that deals impressive (especially in the early stages of the game) **1d12 poison damage**.

- **Thorn Whip** - the enemy takes **1d6 damage** on hit and is **pulled 3 meters** towards you. A skill that is useful for controlling the combat field in addition to forcing a specific set-up of the opponents.

Level 1 spells:

- **Thunderwave** - a powerful wave deals **2d8 damage** to enemies from sound and **pushes**them away from the hero. A useful spell when you need to force your opponent to extend the gap. Goals that pass the constitution test will still receive half damage.

Level 2 spells:

- Flaming Blade - A spell that creates a magical, burning saber dealing 3d6 damage upon hitting an enemy. Weapons can be freely taken up and holstered by the Druid and remain active until a long rest. This type of weapon may be useful when the Druid is forced fight directly.

- Flaming Sphere - an area-based, fiery zone dealing 2d6 fire damage. It can also be used to illuminate the darkness. The uninterrupted spell will last for 10 turns, but like many similar spells, Fireball requires the caster to maintain concentration.

- Moonbeam - Another area spell dealing up to 2d10 damage to creatures within. As part of the action, the Druid can move the zone by 18 meters.

Level 3 spells:

- Call of Lightning -an offensive spell that bargains 3d10 harm to focuses close enough. By keeping up with concentration, Druid can gather another destructive lightning bolt without utilizing another spell space. This spell is especially valuable against drenched rivals, as a wet objective gets twofold harm from power.

The best defensive and support spells for the Druid.

Level 1 spells:

- Entangle - the region of the spell's impact turns out to be thickly congested, which eases back downthe animals inside it. Adversaries who bomb their Dexterity saving roll become snared and immobilized.

- Faerie Fire - an enchanted light uncovers beforehand imperceptible foes and offers a benefit on attack rolls against them. Particularly helpful while confronting beasts that are difficult to see or in dim conditions.

- Healing Word -an essential healing that spell recuperates 1d4 wellbeing focuses. Its utility comes from the way that it works at a view distance, and can likewise be enacted in a reward action. Very valuable in a basic circumstance where the group's primary healer falls.

- Longstrider - A Druid or his ally receives a movement bonus (3 meters) until the next long rest.

- Create or Destroy Water - The Druid summons rain or dries up a certain area. It's worth remembering that wet enemies receive double damage from frost and electricity.

Level 2 spells:

- Immobilizing a person (Hold Person) - a creature that doesn't pass the saving throw on Wisdom becomes paralyzed, and cannot take actions or move. However, the spell requires the Druid to maintain concentration.

- Protection from Poison -the objective is in a flash relieved from the adverse consequences of dynamic poisons, gets a benefit on saving tosses against resulting poisonings, and furthermore gains protection from poison harm. The impact goes on until an extended rest.

- Mirror Image - creates 3 illusory copies of the Druid, which are distracting the opponent. Each duplicate increases Armor Class by 3. Available after selecting Circle of Mountain Spells at level 3 (sub-class of the Earth Circle).

Level 3 spells:

- Plant Growth - a picked region becomes covered with rich vegetation, and any units inside its reach move at 1/4 of their unique speed.

- Sleet Storm - An extreme tempest that quenches fires and makes an ice layer over a chose region. Animals close enough lose concentration. A spell valuable during experiences with other wizardry clients.

- Haste -the objective is sped up, acquiring an extra 2 defensive layer focuses, a benefit on Dexterity rolls, twofold development speed, and ready to make an extra move during their turn. Nonetheless, it ought to be recollected that when the spell stops having impact, the recently sped up unit becomes worn out - for 1 turn, and he can't move or make moves. A spell accessible for the Earth Circle Druid, who at level 5 picks the Cold Circle of Spells.

The best utility spells for the Druid

Cantrips:

- Guidance - the ally receives a 1d4 bonus on rolls related to the chosen ability.

Level 1 spells:

- Goodberry - The Druid creates 4 fruits that restore 1d4 health points. Berries can also serve as provisions while your party is in the camp (providing one unit of Camp Supply).

- Jump - the target's jump range is tripled. Useful when you want to get to a hard-to-reach place or during a fight for dynamic movement.

Level 2 spells:

- Pass without Trace - the hero and his companion gain a massive bonus of 10 to their Stealth rolls. Incredibly useful when you want to sneak somewhere unnoticed with the entire team.

- Enhance Ability - The target receives advantage on rolls related to the chosen trait. Useful during rolls when you want to reduce the probability of failure.

- Seeing in the Dark (Darkvision) - the creature receives the gift of seeing in the darkwithin a 12 meter range. A useful spell when a companion lacks the natural ability to see in the dark.

Level 3 spells:

- Daylight - a selected object is filled with burning light, which glow disperses darkness, including **the magical ones.**

Build

Nature-worshipping Druids are a unique caster class in Baldur's Gate 3. Their bond with forests and forest-living creatures gives them access to a variety of unique abilities including shapeshifting into animals. On this page, we provide tips on how to build a Druid correctly to make him formidable enough to travel the dangerous regions of Sword Coast.

Character creation wizard

On this page we center around building Druid under Circle of the Moon subclass. Creating different prime examples might contrast somewhat from what we arranged underneath.

At the point when in decision for a Druid-suitable race, we suggest Wood Mythical being. Their high base development speed, Darkvision expertise, proficiency with bows and Fey Family line element will clearly demonstrate helpful during battles.

Elective choices highlight Drows, with their natural magic potential, or Humans, who get an additional Proficiency of your choice.

While picking a Background, we recommend Individuals Legend or Maverick. These backgrounds give Proficiency in the primary limit with respect to Druid - Adroitness.

Class progression

- In case of Druid, on level 1, you only choose starting Cantrips and tier 1 spells. We recommend choosing the following Cantrips: Shillelagh, Thorn Whip, or Poison Spray, and when it comes to level 1 spells - Thunderwave, Healing Word, Speak with Animals, Goodberry, and Create or Destroy Water.

- After reaching level 2, you can choose a subclass. In this build, we chose to follow Circle of the Moon. Additionally, you receive access to the most important Druid skill - Wild Shape. It enables the Druid to shapeshift into a chosen animal. With Circle of the Moon, you receive an additional Shape (Bear) and unlock the ability to shapeshift under Bonus Action (Combat Wild Shape). Finally, after spending a Spell Slot, you'll be able to replenish a portion of your HP while still in animal form.

- Level 3 means access to level 2 spells. We recommend checking out Flaming Sphere, Spike Growth, Hold Person, and Moonbeam.

- With level 4, you receive access to two new Shapes, and unlock a Feat of your choice. The best pick here will be Ability Improvements and spending it on Wisdom.

- At level 5, you unlock Wild Strike, which allows you to perform an additional attack after an Unarmed Strike in Wild Shape. Among the available tier 3 spells, take an interest in Call Lightning, Plant Growth and Sleet Storm.

- Level 6 means two additional Shapes, as well as a Circle of the Moon-specific skill called Primal Strike that imbues your animal attacks with magic.

- With level 7, you can choose one tier 4 spell. We especially recommend Wall of Fire, Ice Storm, Conjure Woodland Beings, and Polymorph.

- On level 8, Druid under Circle of the Moon receives an additional Shape - Sabre-toothed Tiger. Additionally, on this level, you can choose a new Feat. Once again we recommend Ability Improvements spent on Wisdom.

- Level 9 means choosing first tier 5 spell. Consider Mass Cure Wounds, Insect Plague, or Conjure Elemental.

- At level 10, you unlock access to as many as 5 new Shapes, with four of them involving Myrmidons of different elements. Additionally, Improved Wild Strike will give you 2 additional attacks after an Unarmed Strike in animal form.

- On level 11, you can choose the first spell from the final tier. Among the available options, we recommend: Heroes' Feast, Heal or Sunbeam.

- At final level, you can choose next Feat. If you already have Wisdom maxed out, you can consider War Caster so you have an easier time maintaining concentration when casting spells.

Ilithid Powers

If you decide to harness Illithid Powers, consider **Charm, Shield of Thralls,** and **Luck of the Far Realms**. The universal nature of Ilithid Powers is that each skill broadens your tactical options immensely.

Party members - their skills and spells

Druid will not have the option to get by all alone during extreme battles - he really wants the help of his confidants. Despite the fact that a Druid has healing spells in his collection, smart is present another healing/support character to the party, like Cleric or Versifier. The subsequent option acquires extra help type of Tune of Rest that will renew your Wild Shape charges even busy investigating.

Moreover, consider enrolling the assistance a legend fighting with went weapons/spells. Rogue, Ranger, or a Wizard will unquestionably assist in battle with their capacity to give foes blasts of shots as well as spells.

At long last, a ton can be acquired in the event that you have a subsequent person fighting in scuffle range. This might be a Paladin, Fighter, or a Barbarian.

Equipment and bonuses from it

In beginning phases of the excursion, you can undoubtedly get Key of the People of yore - a headwear that gives a reward to Nature. You can additionally reinforce this impact by wearing Support Drifter Shield. This covering can be purchased from Arron in Druid Forest, and furthermore, it gives a reward to Dexterity Checks and Saving Tosses. Aside from the abovementioned, center around preparing things that increment your survivability and spell power.

In the later phases of the game, getting two things - Shapeshifter Cap and Protection of Moonbasking will be critical. Both the protective cap and the defensive layer give tremendous rewards to your Wild Shape capacity. The primary thing can be purchased from Helsik in Act 3 of the story. The second can be purchased in the sinkholes underneath the city.

Consumables

Here is a list of useful consumable items that a Druid should keep on hand:

- **Elixir of Vigilance** - gives +5 to Drive, on account of which you'll have the option to situate yourself on the battlefield before it reaches boiling point.

- A wide range of healing elixirs - they will rapidly permit you to recover lost wellbeing focuses.

- Oil of Accuracy - provides +2 to Attack Rolls.

- A wide range of obstruction mixtures - they will help you while fighting rivals who work in unambiguous kinds of attacks.

Monk

Guide

Monk is one of the 12 classes in BG3. Continue to peruse to figure out what beginning and race is best for a Monk. We clear up how for disseminate capacity focuses and which class actions and spells will be valuable in battle. We talk about the Monk's latent accomplishments, fighting style and subraces.

Best origin for a Monk

While picking beginnings for the Monk in BG3, try to pick proficiencies in abilities fitting for this class, to be specific those in view of Wisdom and Dexterity. The best origins for the Monk class are:

- **Acolyte** possessing proficiency in religion and intuition.

- **Folk Hero** whose specialization is animal care and survival.

- **Urchin** possessing sleight of hand and perception.

Best race for a Monk

In *BG3*, you will find several races with a **Dexterity bonus** like:

- **Wood Elf** with bonus +2 Dexterity and +1 Wisdom.

- Halfling with bonus +2 Dexterity and +1 to Charisma or Constitution, depending on the subrace.

- Human who has +1 to all abilities.

Ability points

- The most essential capacity of this class is Dexterity. A lithe Monk has a higher possibility incurring harm and trying not to be hit by the foe.

- You want to put more focuses Insight to project spells and read the goals of experienced animals. Shrewdness is likewise valuable in medication, discernment, and managing creatures.

- The Monk's Solidarity and Constitution ought not be under 11. A high degree of Solidarity will be helpful for guarded tosses. Constitution modifier is added to the protection class when the person isn't wearing covering.

Best spells and class actions for a Monk

- **Step of the Wind** is a class action that you can utilize both in battle and during investigation. Twofold your leap range.

- Flurry of Blows is a Monk's reward action during which you attack two times with uncovered hands.

- Patient Defense is a reward action thanks to which you can evade during your turn.

Best Monk subclass

Monk in *BG3* can have 1 of 3 subclasses below:

- **Way of the Four** Elements - Monk utilizes Ki focuses to project spells or conjure natural impacts. You can bargain up to 3 unarmed attacks and can make a water whip that either pulls an animal to you or wrecks it.

- Way of the Long Death - gives impermanent hit focuses in the wake of overcoming foes and can scare close by adversaries. This Monk can spend their Ki focuses and narrowly avoid the grave or move necrotic harm through touch.

- Way of the Shadow -This Monk subclass centers around secrecy and trickiness. It awards spells that cover the caster and magically transport him between shadows. They can project imperceptibility on themselves and utilize the rival's distraction to play out extra attacks.

Best combat style for Monk

Monks have **proficiency in using a shortsword** and any other simple weapon. They will perform perfectly without wearing armor.

Best Monk build

- Race: Wood Elf

- Subclass: Way of the Four Elements

- Origin: Acolyte

- Abilities: Dexterity and Wisdom 16, Strength and Constitution 11/12, Charisma and Intelligence around 8

- Weapon: Shortsword of First Blood

- Armor: None

Build

The Monk is a person fighting in skirmish range that when appropriately created can have colossal harm managing capacities. On this page of our aide, we highlight his most remarkable abilities, show what Accomplishments to pick, lastly, what things to prepare for greatest benefit.

Character creation wizard

The best base for a Monk is most certainly Wood Half-Mythical person. On account of his proficiencies in different kinds of weapon and sped up, you'll have the option to rapidly address different perils anticipating your party.

While picking a Background, pick Performer - this will bring about extra proficiency in Gymnastics and Execution.

Class progression

Playing a Monk in Baldur's Gate 3 is based on two main skills - Unarmoured Defenseand Unarmed Strike. The first of these skills offer a bonus to AC from Wisdom, provided you're not wearing armor. The second skill allows a Bonus Attack after performing the normal attack.

- As mentioned earlier, level 1 means Unarmoured Defense unlocked, as well as Unarmed Strike, but also the Ki mechanic, Dexterous Strike and Deft Strikes. Ki are special pool of points that can be spent to perform various special actions. The second allows using Dexterity for attack rolls, and the third increases Monk's minimum damage.

- With level 2, your movement is increased by 3 meters, and additionally, you receive the ability to use Step on the Wind: Dash and Step on the Wind: Disengage as a Bonus Action. You can invest one Ki point in Patient Defense, which will make all attacks directed at you harder to land.

- At level 3, you can choose a subclass - for the purpose of this build, we recommend Way ,of the Open Hand. The Flurry of Blows ability unlocked with this subclass chosen will allow you to Topple, Push, and Stagger opponents. Additionally, you can use Deflect Missiles to reflect projectiles back at opponents. Finally, your Hit Diceincreases to d6.

- On level 4, you choose a Feat - we recommend Tavern Brawler so your Monk **has his Strength modifier doubled when attacking with unarmed attacks**. Combined with **Potion of Hill Giant Strength**, the advantage is clearly visible.

- Level 5 comes with an Extra Attack, as well as the ability to stun opponents with Ki.

- With level 6, your movement speed is increased again, unarmed attacks count as magic attacks, and finally you can choose one of 3 manifestations which will add additional 1d6 damage to every attack. Finally, you receive a skill that allows receiving an additional Extra Action.

- Level 7 unlocks Evasion which reduces damage after a successful Dexterity Saving Throw by half or completely and Stillness of Mind that removes Charmed and Frightened statuses.

- On level 8, you choose another Feat, and at this stage we recommend Ability Improvement and adding to Dexterity. Additionally, your damage dice increases to d8.

- With level 9, difficult terrain tiles no longer slow you down. Additionally, you receive the ability to attack the opponent with Ki Resonation: Punch that **can be further detonated at any moment** - the ensuing explosion deals Force damage in a radius of **5 meters**.

- On level 10, you receive another bonus to movement speed, and become immune to Poison.

- Level 11 doesn't bring any advantages.

- On level 12, you can choose another Feat. Same as with other classes, rely on your instinct here and choose what you need the most.

Ilithild Powers

Don't hesitate for even a moment to open and utilize these abilities - center particularly around Winnow the Weak, Repulsor and Black Hole. Opening the powers doesn't influence the person adversely in any capacity, so there isn't anything forestalling your from taking all fledglings for yourself.

Party members - their skills and spells

To get the majority of your group, right party piece and abilities are an unquestionable necessity. The best arrangement is to have both Cleric and Mage in the party following their adaptable abilities.

The cleric can mend your Monk and give him valuable buffs like Shield of Faithwhich expands AC by 2. Furthermore, he can drench a portion of the harm by focusing on it on himself, instill your weapons and cast an incredibly valuable Bless. Shadowheart fit this job flawlessly.

When it comes to Mages, we have one of the most useful spells, which is Haste. This spell changes an ordinary Monk into a unstoppable killing machine, as it increases **your attack speed**, **your AC**, and **adds Bonus Actions**.

Equipment and bonuses from it

In Act 1, there are several items which you should consider getting. **Bloodguzzler Garb**is received after defeating **Bullet in Underdark**. It activates **Wrath** each time you're attacked. In turn, in Goblin Camp, you can find **Crusher's Ring** that increases your movement speed **by 3m** and **Amulet of Misty Step** that adds **Misty Step** spell to your repertoire.

In Act 3, as the game slowly proceeds to its final phase, you'll need following items:

- For defeating Raphael in House of Hope you'll receive Gloves of Soul Catching. This is probably the best Monk item in the game, as it makes damage dealt increase by 1d10 with every hit.

- Additionally, after defeating Prelate Lir'i'c you can receive Boots of Uninhibited Kushigo, which make your attacks receive a Wisdom modifier.

- Finally, Vest of Soul Rejuvenation will provide you with an advantage to defense because of **+2 bonus to AC**, and healing with a successful check against an incoming spell.

Consumables

Below you will find a list of consumables that will make your Barbarian even stronger.

- **Oil of Accuracy** - provides +2 to Attack Rolls.

- Elixir of Heroism - gives additional 10HP temporarily and applies "Blessed" status.

- Potion of Flying - additional mobility is something that is always needed.

- Potion of Hill Giant Strength - perfect if you don't have 20 Strength yet.

- Elixir of Vigilance - provides +5 to Initiative, make sure to drink it before tougher battles.

Bard

Guide

The Bards, who venerate workmanship and information, are one of the most flexible classesavailable in Baldur's Gate 3. Proficiency in the utilization of spells, unimaginably valuable class capacities in light of capacities, or productivity in fortifying partners makes them ideal associates while going through the Forgotten Realms. The accompanying page will assist you with understanding the fundamental standards of the Bard class, making your initial steps as this class simpler.

Best race for a Bard

In the full arrival of Baldur's Gate 3, the designers have taken out select racial rewards. From this point forward, while picking a race, you can add +2 and +1 rewards to any detail you'd like. In spite of this, a few racial capacities prove to be useful for specific classes.

- **Tiefling** - each subrace innately knows a different, useful spell. The best fit for a Bard is a Zariel Tiefling with their Thaumaturgy cantrip. The cantrip grants advantage on Intimidation and Performance checks - both Charisma-based skills.

- Elf - the High Elf subrace grants one additional cantrip. Wood Elf, meanwhile, increases your **movement** in combat to **10,5 meters** per turn.

Ability Points

While apportioning capacity focuses, first focus on Charisma, since the strength of your spells relies upon it. The adaptable idea of the Bard class will guarantee that it performs well in many assignments, so the resulting skills will rely upon your play style. Among the choices, nonetheless, you can consider:

- Dexterity, since it will pleasantly supplement the Bard's proficiency in guarded tosses connected with this capacity. It will likewise emphatically influence your abilities with light and medium protection.

- Constitution will furnish you for certain extra hit focuses, as well as assist in keeping up with centering while at the same time projecting explicit spells.

Best origin for Bard

Your Bard's origin should correspond with their high Charisma and Dexterity. Interesting options include:

- **Urchin**, offering proficiency in Sleight of Hand and Stealth. These, in turn, will come in handy if your party lacks a Rogue or if you are faced with a task that requires cunning and finesse.

- Criminal - this origin will give you proficiency in Stealth and Deception, which will complement your Bard's abilities.

- Entertainer - proficiency in Acrobatics and Performance nicely fits a Bard, since they rely on Charisma and Dexterity.

Bardic Inspiration

Bard's class ability. An action, during which your Bard motivates close by partners. Motivation gives them a 1d6 reward to their next attack roll, expertise check, and protection roll. At level 5, the motivation modifier changes to 1d8.

The quantity of purposes of Bardic Motivation is equivalent to the Bard's Charisma modifier. In the wake of utilizing all charges, the capacity will open up in the future after an extended rest. At level 5, you get the expertise Textual style of Motivation, which permits you to recover expertise charges after a brief reprieve.

Song of Rest

Class ability opened at level 2. The soothing melody permits the party to recover as though they had a brief reprieve. Particularly valuable in blend with, for instance, a Warlock, who recuperates some portion of the spell slots during a brief reprieve.

Jack of all Trades and Expertise

The Bard's adaptability is presumably shown best by his capacity you get at level 2. Handyman permits you to add half of your proficiency reward (adjusted down) to any expertise roll in which your personality isn't proficient.

Proficiency is likewise connected with Aptitude, which the Bard accesses at level 3. With it, you can pick 2 abilities in which your personality is as of now proficient. From this point forward, for each check connected with these abilities, your proficiency reward will be multiplied.

Best spells for Bard

The wide range of spells available to the Bard makes this class useful in many situations. Here is a list of several interesting spells worth considering:

Cantrips:

- Vicious Mockery - a series of unpleasant comments that inflict 1d4 psychic damage to the target and gives them a penalty to their next attack.

- Friends - enchant a person to gain advantage on Charisma skill checks against the target.

- Minor Illusion - creates a small illusion that distracts nearby creatures. Useful for diverting attention.

Spells:

- Heroism - the Bard or allied companion cannot be frightened, and they also gain 5 temporary hit points every turn.

- Tasha's Hideous Laughter - the target falls to the ground in hysterical laughter. They are exposed to attacks from opponents.

- Healing Word - a simple healing spell restoring 1d4 hit points through eye contact. Useful as a backup healing option for your party.

- Disguise Self - allows to temporarily change the character's appearance. Useful for outsmarting other creatures.

- Feather Fall - fall down slower. The target does not receive damage from falling.

- Blindness - a level 2 spell that blinds the opponent.

- Calm Emotions - all humanoid creatures within the spell's range become resistant to being frightened and charmed.

- Lesser Restoration - a level 2 spell that removes negative effects and poison from the target. Especially useful when the party lacks another healer (Cleric, Druid).

- Fear - a level 3 spell that creates an image so terrifying that the target drops whatever they are holding to the ground and becomes frightened. Exceptionally useful for crowd control during combat.

- Stinking Cloud - the spell creates a paralyzing, stinking cloud. Creatures within its range cannot perform actions.

Best subclass for Bard

After the full release of *Baldur's Gate 3*, the Bard will have a choice between **3 subclasses**, known as **Colleges**. Each of them has their own set of special abilities and will fit a different play style.

- **College of** Lore -a subclass zeroed in on procuring information and broad abilities. By choosing it at level 3, your Bard will promptly acquire proficiency in 3 abilities of your decision. The unique capacity of the College of Lore, Cutting Words, permits the legend to utilize a charge of Bardic Motivation to force a - 1d6 punishment on the rival (increments at resulting levels) to one of their next tosses.

- College of Valor - a specialization zeroed in on reinforcing the party during battle. Picking it gives the Bard admittance to the alleged Battle Motivation. From here on out, sidekicks who got Motivation will actually want to add a reward 1d6 (higher at ensuing levels) to the harm managed an attack and to their transitory defensive layer class. The subclass' proficiency in utilizing medium reinforcement, shield, and military weaponswill additionally make the Bard of the College of Boldness ready to excel on the cutting edge.

- College of Swords - a subclass for Bards wishing to show their fencing skills. Choosing this subclass gives you Battle Styles and medium armor proficiency - which will undoubtedly come in handy in combat. The Blade Flourish ability lets you use a Bardic Inspiration charge to use one of several special actions in combat.

Best build for Bard

As a summary, we present below an exemplary build for a level 3 Bard:

- **Race:** Zariel Tiefling

- **Subclass:** College of Valor

- **Background:** Criminal

- **Abilities:** Charisma and Dexterity around 16, Constitution around 14, Wisdom about 13/12, Intelligence about 10, Strength about 8.

Spells

Bards in Baldur's Gate 3 are a very helpful class that is fit for filling numerous different jobs in the party. Despite the fact that Bard's collection principally incorporates backing and group control spells, there are a few offensive and utility spells accessible to him/her that when utilized right, could change the result of a battle.

The best offensive spells for Bard

Cantrips:

- **Vicious** Mockery - only damage dealing cantrip in Bard's repetoire. This is a magic insult dealing 1d4 physical damage and applying Disadvantage on the target that is active for one turn.

Level 1 spells:

- Thunderwave - a powerful level 1 spell dealing 2d8 Thunder damage to the target and pushing it away.

- Dissonant Whispers - aside from dealing 3d6 physical damage to the target, the target has Frighten applied if they don't complete a Wisdom save.

Level 2 spells:

- Cloud of Daggers - an offensive spell creating a zone with a diameter of 2 meters lasting for 10 turns. All targets affected by the zone receive **4d4 Slashing damage**.

- **Phantasmal Force** - the target's mind has an illusion implanted that deals 1d6 physical damage to it each turn (spell lasts for up to 10 turns). When the affected target receives damage from a different source, the damage type changes to Phantasmal Force. Unfortunately, similarly to the previous spell, Phantasmal Force requires concentration from the caster.

- Shatter - a spell dealing 3d8 Thunder damage. Opponents made out of inorganic matter (e.g. stone) have Disadvantage applied on their Saving Throw.

- Heat Metal - 2d8 Fire damage, and the spell forces the target to drop his currently equipped metal weapon or receive a Disadvantage on Attack Rolls and Ability Checks. When it comes to armor items, the target will receive Disadvantage. If the target decides to keep the weapon, Bard can use a bonus action to deal additional 2d8 damage. A useful, albeit not often used spell, requiring a specific situation and opponent.

Level 3 spells:

- Glyph of Warding - a powerful spell triggering a certain magical effect. Aside from Sleep and Detonation, you can choose a variant that deals as much as 5d8 of chosen damage type to all targets in the range of the Glyph.

The best defensive and support spells for Bard

Cantrips:

- Blade   Ward -   the   chosen   target receives resistance to Slashing, Bludgeoning, Piercing, reducing damage received from these schools by half.

Level 1 spells:

- Heroism - the targeted character receives 5 temporary hit points, and cannot be Frightened. A useful skills, albeit, as most buffing spells, requires maintaining concentration.

- Bane - the enemies receive a penalty (-1d4) to Saving Throws and Attack Rolls. A spell useful when you don't have a Cleric with this spell currently in the party.

- Faerie Fire - targeted enemies are affected by magic light that makes them visible, while Attack Rolls on them have advantage. Especially useful when facing monsters that are hard to see or in dark environments.

- Tasha's Hideous Laughter - the affected target who doesn't pass a Wisdom Saving Throw, falls to the ground and rolls in laughter becoming completely Incapacitated. The Incapacitated target may try to shake off the effect after receiving damage. Only works against beings with 5 or higher Intelligence.

- Healing Word - a simple healing spell replenishing 1d4 hit points (you need to have the target in visual range). Useful as contingency healing if the main healer had fallen.

Level 2 spells:

- Calm Emotions - targets in the chosen area cannot be Charmed or Frightened. Useful in clashes against enemies that apply this effect often.

- Silence - the targets in the spell area are Silenced and are immune to Thunder attacks. For example, getting a magic wielder in the sphere makes them unable to cast spells.

- Level 3 spells:

- Fear - the affected targets that don't pass a Wisdom Saving Throw, become Fearful and break formation. When visual contact with the caster is broken, the targets may repeat the Throw to attempt to shake off the effect.

- Stinking Cloud - a stinking effect so strong that beings inside the spell range **cannot take action**.

Best utility spells for Bard

Cantrips:

- Mage Hand - a spectral hand allowing manipulating objects from a safe distance.

- Minor Illusion - a simple cantrip that distracts nearby targets, making them investigate the source. Useful when sneaking.

- Friends - when cast on a target, you gain advantage on Charisma checks against it. Unfortunately, after the spell ends, the targeted being knows that it has been Charmed and may accuse the caster.

- Light and Dancing Lights - simple spells that light the darkness. Useful in case not all members of your party have means to light the way.

Level 1 spells:

- Feather Fall - mitigates fall damage. The targeted beings don't receive fall damage. Use the spell actively as situation dictates.

- Disguise Self - Bard temporarily changes his appearance. An indispensable tool during Deception checks.

Level 2 spells:

- Enhance Ability - targeted ally receives an Advantage to Ability Checks with chosen Ability. Useful during major checks where you cannot afford to fail.

- Invisibility - the target becomes invisible for the duration of 1 minute (10 turns).

Level 3 spells:

- Speak with Dead - allows asking a dead character 5 questions. The corpse must have a mouth, and cannot be a reanimated undead.

Build

Bards are heroes inspired by art with numerous talents. Depending on the selected abilities, they can be used both as **a support class** and as warriors **on the front line**. On this page, we will present you tips that will help you create your dream Bard.

Character creation wizard

On this page, we focus on the support archetype of the class. A bard fighting in close combat may be characterized by a slightly different, optimal way of progression.

Many of the races available in Baldur's Gate 3 will work well with Bard, but for this guide, we recommend one of the following:

- **Tiefling** - all subraces offer natural knowledge of a particular spell, which will diversify the Bard's broad repertoire of abilities.

- Wood Elf - speed bonus and Stealth proficiency will help you maneuver on and off the battlefield.

- Human - proficiency in the use of various weapons and additional proficiency will complete the image of a multi-talented Bard.

When choosing the Background, pay attention to **Entertainer**. Proficiency in **Acrobatics**and **Performance** will be perfectly complemented by high Charisma and Dexterity statistics related to the Bard class.

Class progression

- At level one, you will gain access to the most important class ability - Bardic Inspiration. Allies will gain a bonus to their next Attack throw, Skill Check, or Saving Throw. The number of uses of Bardic Inspiration is equal to your Charisma modifierand renews after a long rest. When choosing spells at the beginning, especially pay attention to Vicious Mockery, Heroism, Healing Word, and Tasha's Hideous Laughter.

- The second level unlocks the Song of Rest, whose effect is similar to the short rest. Jack of All Trades will cause the Bard to receive half **his Proficiency bonus** on ability checks in which they are not proficient. Use this feature in case of check for which you lack the appropriate "specialists" in your team.

- At level three, choose the **Bard subclass**, the so-called **College**. In this guide, we will focus on the **College of Lore**. This specialization will allow you to choose **3 new Proficiencies** and unlock the **Cutting Words** action. It works like "negative Bardic inspiration", imposing **debuffs** on nearby opponents. The feature available to all subclasses, **Expertise doubles the Proficiency bonus** during the selected Ability check, making the Bard a true renaissance man. When choosing level 2 spells, we especially recommend: **Heat Metal, Calm Emotion, Enhance Ability**, and **Shatter**.

- The fourth level provides a **Feat**. We recommend choosing **Charisma improvement** to reach the maximum level of **20 points** as quickly as possible.

- At level five, your Bardic Inspiration bonus **will increase** (from 1d6 to 1d8), and you will also gain access to **Font of Inspiration**. This passive ability will restore your Bardic Inspiration charges after **a short rest** . When choosing level 3 spells, pay attention to **Glyph of Warding, Speak with Dead, Stinking Cloud**, and **Bestow Curse**.

- Level six will unlock **Countercharm** - a special ability that will give nearby allies **an advantage to Saving Throws against Charm and Frighten**. College of Lore bard will also gain access to **2 spells** from the **Magical   Secrets** category.   In   this   case,   we recommend **Fireball, Counterspell, Haste, Lightning Bolt**, or **Mass Healing Word**.

- At the seventh level, choose the level 4 spells. We especially recommend **Dimension Door** and **Polymorph**.

- At this level you once again pick a **Feat**. You can choose one **increasing   Charisma(Ability Improvements, Actor, Performer**) to reach **20 points**, providing the maximum modifier from this feature. An alternative could be the **War Caster**, who will help you **maintain concentration** while casting spells.

- The ninth level unlocks the level 5 spells. Consider choosing **Mass Cure Wounds** or **Hold Monster**.

- At this level, your Bardic Inspiration modifier will be **increased** once again (from 1d8 to 1d10), you will choose another **2 skills** with a bonus from **Expertise**, and you will also choose another **2 spells from the Magical Secrets category**.

- Level eleven is access to the last sixth level of spells. Of the two available options, we prefer the **Eyebite** spell.

- It is also the last chance to pick **Feat**. Pay attention to the previously mentioned **War Cater, Spell Sniper**, or **Lucky**.

Ilithild Powers

If you decide to use the power of Mind Raiders, invest in the abilities: **Shield of Thralls, Charm**, and **Stage Fright**. Powers granting buffa for allies and debuffs for enemies can turn the tide of many skirmishes.

Party members - their skills and spells

By taking on the role of a supporting Bard and using your abilities efficiently, you will be able **to unleash the full potential of your allies**. However, when composing your party, you must take care of **the first front line**, which will protect your hero from danger. A **Warrior**, **Paladin**, heavy-armed **Cleric**, or **Barbarian** will certainly be effective in close combat with the help of your buffs.

Song of Rest ability will be particularly helpful for all classes which key actions renews after a short rest, for example for a Warrior or Warlock.

If you decide to build a more **combat-oriented Bard** (e.g. by choosing the College of Swords subclass), ensure that you have adequate support from a **Cleric** or a **Wizard**specializing in enchantment and defensive spells.

Equipment and bonuses from it

In the early stages of the game, you will gain access to two items with particular statistics ideal for the Bard class. **Cap of Curing** will provide **healing** to your allies while casting Inspiration. **Blazer of Benevolence** will also buff companions adding some HP temporarily. The headgear can be found **next to Alfira in the Druid Grove**. You will receive the armor after rescuing **Volo from the Goblin Camp**.

In the later stages of the game, you should focus on items **that increase your stamina**and/ **or enhance your magical abilities**. It is worth mentioning the **Birthright** - a hat that adds **2 to Charisma**, and the armor **Potent Robe**, thanks to which you will receive a handful of bonuses scaling with the **Charisma modifier**.

Consumables

Here are some useful elixirs and potions that every Bard should keep in their inventory:

- **Elixir of Vigilance** - provides a +5 bonus to Initiative, thanks to which your allies will receive support during combat faster.

- **All kinds of healing potions** - will quickly allow you to regenerate lost HP.

- **Potion of Flying** - a mobility boost that will allow you to take a strategic position on the battlefield.

- **Elixir of Heroism** - gives +10 temporary HP and grants the Bless status. It will help you prepare for an encounter with the enemy.

Barbarian

Guide

While making the ideal Barbarian in BG3, you want to pick the right race and beginning. On this page, you will peruse which subclass to pick to completely use the main characteristics of this class, which are Fury and Unarmoured Protection. We propose what defensive layer the Barbarian ought to wear and what rewards you get for not wearing covering. We additionally list the best class actions. Toward the finish of the page you will track down the best Barbarian form.

Best origin for a Barbarian

While picking the Barbarian's background, search for proficiency in abilities connected with Strength or Dexterity. The ideal backgrounds for this class are:

- **Urchin**, granting proficiency in Sleight of Hand and Stealth.

- **Soldier**, granting proficiency in Athletics and Intimidation.

- **Outlander**, granting proficiency in Athletics and Survival.

Best race for a Barbarian

The main abilities of Barbarians are Strength, Constitution, and Dexterity, so the following races will work best:

- **Shield Dwarf** with a +2 in Strength and Constitution.

- **Strongheart Halfling**, with a +2 to Dexterity and +1 to Constitution.

- **Human** with +1 to every ability.

Barbarian's Ability Scores

- **The most important attribute of the Barbarian is Strength**, affecting attack rolls and inflicted damage.

- **The second most important ability for a Barbarian is Constitution**. It affects the maximum amount of hit points and provides better protection if you are not wearing armor. The Barbarian's Constitution should not be less than 14 points.

- **Dexterity affects armor class**. Regardless of whether you want your Barbarian to wear armor or not, this ability should not be less than 14 points.

Should the Barbarian wear armor?

A significant number of you most likely envision Barbarians as strong champions clad in cowhide scraps. In the event that you intend to play BG3 as a commonplace Barbarian, underneath we have made sense of one of the main highlights of this class - Unarmoured Defence.

Unarmoured Defence grants 10 base armor class points and adds your Constitution and Dexterity modifier to it when not wearing armor.

The Barbarian likewise accompanies a few highlights that makes them benefit from taking harm during battle. Rage is an extra class action that can last 10 turns. Rage closes early in the event that your personality has not attacked any animal or has not taken harm since the last turn. In the case of, during your turn, you utilize an action to accomplish some different option from attack, without taking any harm, Fury will end. Assuming that your personality will be wearing protective layer, the probability of getting any harm altogether diminishes. While making a Barbarian who's not to wear protection, you should in this manner put more focuses in Constitution and Dexterity.

If you give your Barbarian more Strength, you'll have higher armor class **wearing medium armor**, which grants about 15 Armor Class plus your Dexterity modifier. However, you should remember that playing such a Barbarian may cause your Rage to drop more easily in combat.

Best Barbarian class actions

- **Rage** -a reward action accessible from Level 1 onwards. While Seething, the Barbarian arrangements an additional 2 harm with skirmish weapons and while tossing things. They likewise get harm opposition and benefit in Strength checks and saving tosses. Rage closes rashly on the off chance that the Barbarian has not attacked anybody or has not taken any harm during their turn.

- **Danger Sense** - accessible from Level 2 onwards. An accomplishment that awards advantage on Dexterity saving tosses against traps, spells, and surfaces.

- **Reckless Attack** - a class action accessible from Level 2 onwards, giving benefit on attack rolls to both the Barbarian and all foes attacking the Barbarian.

Best Barbarian subclass

When your Barbarian reaches **Level 3**, you will be able to choose a subclass:

- **Berserker** - has a bonus class action, which **turns Rage into Frenzy**. In this state, the Barbarian gains access to two new actions and can attack with an improvised weapon as a bonus action. **One of the available bonus actions during a Frenzy is Enraged Throw**, which lets you pick up an object or a creature and throw it at a target, dealing bludgeoning damage and knocking it prone.

- Wildheart - lets you choose out of five different options based on animals:

- Bear grants resistance to all damage except for psychic damage and gives you access to self-healing.

- Eagle makes the character almost invincible, grants Diving Strike to attack an enemies on lower ground, and Dash as a bonus action.

- Deer lets you charge when Raging, dealing 1d4+2 damage and knocking targets prone. The charge does not trigger opportunity attacks. Rage increases your maximum movement.

- Tiger can deal damage to three enemies at once and inflict bleeding. Rage increases the range of the character's jumps.

- Wolf lets your allies move an additional 3 meters, while your Rage buffs them in combat.

Best Barbarian build

If you prefer a stereotypical Barbarian who doesn't wear armor, choose:

- **Race:** Strongheart Halfling

- **Subclass:** Berserker

- **Background:** Urchin

- **Ability Scores:** Strength 14, Dexterity 16, Constitution 15, Intelligence, Wisdom, and Charisma around 10.

- **Weapon:** Everburn Blade

- **Armor:** Barbarian Clothes

- If you prefer a more powerful armored Barbarian, choose:

- **Race:** Shield Dwarf

- **Subclass:** Wildheart

- **Background:** Soldier

- **Ability Scores:** Strength 17, Dexterity 14, Constitution 15, Intelligence, Wisdom, and Charisma around 10.

- **Weapon:** Blooded Greataxe

- **Armor:** Robust Chain Shirt

Build

Barbarian is a class centering and spend significant time in skirmish battle. Appropriately drove, he can have tremendous harm result, and a portion of his subclasses offer choices that permit him to endure discipline better compared to the excess colleagues. On this page of the aide, we tell the best way to appropriately construct a Barbarian.

Character creation wizard

The best race for a Barbarian is Half-Orc. This is because of his racial characteristics and proficiencies. One of them, Savage Attacks, changes a standard attack to crit whenever moved 19-20, while the second, Constant Perseverance, permits you to endure a killing blow - your legend will survive with 1 HP, and this might happen once per extended rest.

Elective race decisions are Wood Mythical person, who gets a reward to development speed, Gold Dwarf who has a reward to HP, or Githyanki who enjoys a benefit during capacity checks.

With regards to background, the most ideal decision for a Barbarian would be Soldier, following his Athletics and Terrorizing proficiency, or an Outlander that has rewards to Athletics and Survival.

Class progression

- At level 1, your legend gets the capacity to actuate Fury. This is a remarkable expertise on which Barbarian bases his harm managing capacities, as well as his survival on the battlefield. At the point when projected, it goes on for 10 turns, is enacted in the Reward Action, and increments harm managed scuffle weapons by 2. Rage likewise diminishes actual harm got and offers a Benefit on Strength Checks and Strength Saving Tosses.

- The subsequent level accompanies another capacity that is utilized often - Careless Attack is a sort of attack that gives a Benefit for your next attack in the following turn yet consequently, all attacks that are designated on the Barbarian likewise enjoy a Benefit. The second gotten spell on this level is Risk Sense, which when actuated gives a Benefit on Dexterity Saving Tosses against traps, spells, and surfaces.

- Level 3 outcomes in Extra Fury Charge and permits picking a subclass. From all suitable, we prescribe picking Berserker if you need to construct a harm managing character. With the Berserker picked, Fury changes to Free for all, and two special actionsare opened - first of them, Furious Strike, is just an attack, yet performed during a Reward Action. The second, Irritated Toss, permits tossing things and articles at foes and this way wreck them.

- On level 4, its time **to choose a Feat** - we recommend choosing **+2** to Strength. This is the most beneficial bonus on this stage of the character.

- With level 5, your Proficiency bonus is increased to 3, an Extra Attack is added and Fast Movement (increased movement speed) is unlocked.

- At level 6, you receive Additional Rage Charge, and Mindless Rage which makes you immune to Charmed, Frightened, or Calm Emotions.

- Level 7 means Feral Instinct unlocked - you gain a +3 to Initiative and can't be Surprised.

- At level 8, you receive another Feat - at this stage, we recommend choosing Great Weapon Fighter which changes -5 Attack Roll penalty to +10 to damage.

- At level 9, your proficiency bonus is increased to 4. Additionally, your critical hits deal extra damage.

- Level 10 means Intimidating Presence unlocked, which means you can try to instill Fear in an enemy during your action. Unfortunately, this is an action that you'll use sporadically.

- Level 11 means Relentless Rage unlocked - if you receive a blow that is supposed to kill you, instead of losing consciousness, you return with 1HP - this bonus can be activated once per short rest.

- Final level 12 allows choosing **another Feat** - you can decide on **Ability Improvements** or **Savage Attacker**, that increases your overall damage.

Ilithild Powers

Don't be afraid **to unlock and use these skills** - focus especially on **Cull the Weak, Repulsor** and **Black Hole**. Unleashing the full power of Ilithild Powers doesn't affect the character negatively, so leave every tadpole for yourself.

Party members - their skills and spells

As a Barbarian, you're defenseless to wizardry harm, so try to bring partners that will address these deficiencies. Furthermore, try to have a Rogue or Bard in the group, in view of their Skillful deception expertise and exceptional spells in the event of the Bard.

If you have any desire to expand your true capacity, add a Cleric or a Mage to the party with Hasteunlocked.

Equipment and bonuses from it

As a Barbarian, you have a one of a kind choice of leaving the introduction currently exceptional. In the event that you have Lae'zel in your party, take her covering. This is a decent impermanent defensive layer, even with your Reinforcement Class rewards. Additionally, toward the finish of the preface, assuming you kill Satan with whom the Ilithid is fighting, in the wake of looking through him you'll find an extraordinary two-handed sword that bargains 1d4 fire harm.

Besides, in Act 1, you'll track down Reason's Grip - gloves that gives an impermanent 15 HP reward assuming you end Fury physically - this is a significant thing with regards to protection.

Furthermore, in Act 1 you can get +1 reward to picked attribute on the off chance that you let Aunt Ethel pursue fighting her - utilize this choice so you'll have a +5 to Strength on level 4.

In Act 3, make a point to track down Rudder of Balduran. It offers outstanding rewards to safeguard, which will make your Barbarian a lot harder to kill.

Besides, consider picking Balduran's Giantslayer weapon for your Barbarian - this strong two-handed sword pairs the harm from your Solidarity modifierand gives a Benefit on Attack Rolls against Enormous, Immense, or Colossal animals.

Consumables

Below you will find a list of consumables that will make your Barbarian even stronger.

- Oil of Accuracy - provides +2 to Attack Rolls.

- Elixir of Heroism - gives additional 10HP temporarily and applies "Blessed" status.

- Potion of Flying - additional mobility is something that is always needed.

- Potion of Hill Giant Strength - perfect if you don't have 20 Strength yet.

- Elixir of Vigilance - provides +5 to Initiative, make sure to drink it before tougher **battles.**

Sorcerer

Guide

Sorcerers have a natural capacity to utilize sorcery starting from their natural ability acquired from their predecessors. Contingent upon who the hero's precursors were, the wizardry of the Sorcerers appears in different structures. In any case, major areas of strength for a mastering sorcery is without a doubt a superb friend during an excursion through the risky Sword Coast.

Best race for Sorcerer

In the full release of Baldur's Gate 3, the developers have removed exclusive racial bonuses. From now on, when choosing a race, you can add +2 and +1 bonuses to any stat you'd like. Despite this, some racial abilities come in handy for certain classes.

- **High Elf** - this subrace grants you access to **one additional cantrip**. Useful when composing a spell list.

- **Human** - proficiency in **light armor** could come in handy when creating a non-Draconic Heritage Sorcerer.

Ability Points

When distributing skill points in the character creator, **make sure to invest many points in Charisma.** Besides it, consider allocating the rest of available points in:

- **Constitution** provides a few extra Hit Points and helps maintain focus when casting spells requiring concentration.

- **Dexterity** - a higher status of this ability will give you a few additional armor points.

Best background for Sorcerer

When choosing your background, it's worth going for choices with numerous Charisma-based skills. This will complete your hero's build.

- **Criminal** proficient in **Deception** will help to lead your interlocutors astray. **Charlatan** also offers similar proficiency.

- **Noble** with proficiency in Persuasion will help you convince the heroes of your point of view.

Sorcery Points and Metamagic

The main mechanics of Sorcerers. **Sorcery Points**, available from **level 2**, you can use to **enhance the effects of your spells**. The most interesting **Metamagic effects include:**

- **Quickened Spell** with which you can cast a chosen spell as a bonus action.

- **Extended Spell**, which doubles the duration of a given spell effect.

- **Twinned Spell**, which causes the selected spell to apply its effect not to 1 but to 2 creatures simultaneously.

Progressing on the resulting Sorcerer's level will give you admittance to extra Divination Focuses and Metamagic impacts. Utilizing them skilfully will give you a benefit during experiences with perilous adversaries.

Adaptable spellcasting likewise permits you to trade accessible Spell Slots for Divination Focuses as well as the other way around. Divination Focuses recover after each Extended Rest.

Best spells for Sorcerer

The Sorcerer has access to a wide range of useful spells. Among the most interesting are:

Cantrips:

- **Fire Bolt** - a ranged attack dealing **1d10** damage.

- **Bone Chill** - a spell dealing **1d8** damage and preventing the target from healing in the next turn. Additionally, undead targets receive a penalty during an attack.

- **Mage Hand** - a useful cantrip that allows you to manipulate objects from a distance.

Spells:

- **Mage Armour** - an unarmored target receives an Armour Class equal to 13 and its Dexterity modifier. Especially useful when playing a Sorcerer other than the Draconic Bloodline subclass.

- **Magic Missile** - the spell creates **3 projectiles** that deal **1d4+1** damage to the target each. They never miss.

- **Thunderwave** - a wave of energy causing **2d8** damage and pushing everything away in its path.

- **Chromatic Orb** - a powerful spell inflicting **3d8** damage. The type of damage can be modified, and casting the spell using higher-level Slots further increases the damage.

- **Hold Person** - paralyzes selected target. Great in combination with the metamagic **Twinned Spell.**

- **Cloud of Daggers** - an offensive AOE level 2 spell, inflicting 4d4 damage.

- **Fireball** - a classic offensive level 3 spell, dealing powerful **8d6** damage.

Best subclass for Sorcerer

Sorcerers, in contrast to other spell clients, are conceived sorcery wielders utilizing their acquired potential. Thus, the subclasses of the Sorcerers will be founded on the background of a given legend.

Draconic Bloodline - the magical power inherent in this subclass comes from dragon blood, which was introduced into the family generations ago. **Draconic Resilience**provides the hero with an additional **Hit Point** for each level of the Sorcerer class. Additionally, the **scales** covering the body of the dragon Sorcerer increase his **Armour Class** by 3 when he is not wearing any armor. Depending on which **type of dragon** was the ancestor of your Sorcerer, you can use a range of diverse effects:

- **Red Dragon** - Your hero acquires **fire** resistance over time, and spells based on this element inflict more damage. You also learn a spell **Burning Hands**.

- **White Dragon** - The Sorcerer at the appropriate level acquires **cold** resistance, and attacks related to cold become more powerful. The hero learns the spell **Armour of Agathys**.

- **Black Dragon** - This Draconic Ancestry is associated with **Acid** resilience and damage bonuses. The Sorcerer learns the spell **Grease**.

When choosing your Draconic Ancestry, remember not to accidentally duplicate the spells with ones received with Draconic Bloodline

Wild Magic - this subclass is associated with the Sorcerer's inherited magical potential, which manifests from time to time in the form of **sudden and unexpected effects**. A characteristic feature of this specialization is the random **effect of wild magic**, which can be activated when the Sorcerer casts a spell of level 1 or higher. The effects of wild magic can be **positive** (for example, an additional action, restoring Hit Points) and **negative** (uncontrolled transformation of the Sorcerer or their environment, unexpected attack towards an ally), and their effect is determined by **blind luck.** The effect of the **Tide of Chaos** allows the hero to gain an advantage during the next roll but, at the same time, increases the chance of a random effect occurring when casting the next spell.

Storm Sorcerer - an elemental spellcaster wielding **air**. It is characterized by high mobility and numerous offensive spells with air and electricity element affinity. Their **Tempestuous Magic** ability lets them **fly** as a **bonus action** after casting at least a spell of at least **Level 1**. Flight lasts until the end of their turn and it **doesn't provoke opportunity attacks**.

It's also worth noting **Sorcerers must choose their subclass on level 1**. For this reason, think carefully about which one you want to play.

Best build for Sorcerer

In the end, we present to you an example build for the Sorcerer:

- **Race:** High Elf

- **Subclass**: Draconic Bloodline

- **Backround**: Noble

- **Abilities**: Charisma and Constitution around 16, Dexterity around 14, Wisdom and Intelligence around 11, Strength around 8.

Build

Sorcerers are a class including extraordinary people with natural ability and partiality for enchantment. Their remarkable gifts, when appropriately tackled, may end up being a genuine gamechanger on the battlefield. On this page of our Baldur's Gate 3 aide, we tell the best way to lead this class through improvement for your legend to turn into an almighty Sorcerer.

Character creation wizard

This form bases on Tempest Divination subclass. Creating different prime examples might vary marginally from what we arranged underneath.

To take advantage of your Sorcerer in the underlying phases of character improvement, we suggest High Mythical being, Human, or Dragonborn as the race of decision.

- The first variant means access to an additional Cantrip which will broaden your magic repertoire.

- Choosing a Human as the race for your Sorcerer means proficiency in light armorwhich when equipped should help you survive longer during the most dangerous of battles. Additionally, an extra Proficiency of your choice is definitely a useful bonus.

- Dragonborns, on the other hand, with their natural resistances and **the ability to spew fire/ice/poison have access to more tactical options** and ways to hurt the opponent or mitigate his attacks (especially at the beginning of the game).

When choosing a background, we recommend **Noble**, **Charlatan**, or a **Criminal**. All of the above options mean **Proficiency in Charisma-related skills** - which should be the defining stat of the Sorcerer.

Class progression

- Sorcerers make the choice **regarding the subclass** already at level 1 (as we mentioned earlier, on this page we focus on Storm Sorcerer). The subclass we're discussing here has a big starting advantage in the form of **Tempestuous Magic** skill which **after casting a spell of level 1 or higher**, allows the hero **to fly as a Bonus Action** available until the end of the turn. Flying is a very useful tool, increasing **your mobility**immensely. Use this advantage to cleverly position yourself on the battlefield and run from trouble (once in the air, the enemies won't be able to use Opportunity Attacks on you). When choosing initial spells, we recommend **Fire Bolt**, **Ray of Frost**, **Mage Hand**, **Magic Missile**, **Witch Bolt**, **Thunderwave**, and **Mage Armour**.

Spells based on electricity and sound will prove to be essential at later levels of the Storm Sorcerer.

- With the ascension to level 2, you'll receive access to a signature class feature - Sorcery Points. You can use these points, renewed every long rest, to alter the properties of the spells you cast. The available modifiers differ in terms of application and operation, and once chosen, they cannot be changed. We especially recommend these metamagic modifiers - Distant Spell and Twinned Spell. An interesting feature of a Sorcerer from level 2 onwards is the ability to exchange unspent Spell Slots for Sorcery Points and vice versa. Thanks to this feature, you can decide on the fly which "resource" you need the most at the given moment.

- At level 3, you'll have to choose 1 additional metamagic modifier. From the options available at this stage, we recommend Heightened Spell or Quickened Spell. Additionally, you'll receive access to level 2 spells. From the available options, we recommend Scorching Ray, Misty Step, or Cloud of Daggers.

- On level 4, you'll need to choose a Feat. We recommend Ability Improvements and improving Charisma ability. The better this statistic the larger the damage-dealing potential of your spells.

- With level 5, you'll get to know your initial level 3 spells. Among the available options, consider Lightning Bolt, Fireball, Counterspell, or Haste.

- After reaching level 6, Storm Sorcerer receives access to a choice of useful features. Heart of the Storm makes level 1 spells or higher dealing Lightning or Thunder damage summon a small, local thunderstorm. It damages enemies caught in its radius. The Storm Sorcerer himself with this feature has improved Resistance to the aforementioned damage types. Finally, your hero automatically learns **a variety of spells connected to his troubled heritage**.

- Among level 4 spells, consider Ice Storm, Dimension Door, and Confusion.

- Level 8 means choosing another Feat. Once again, we recommend Ability Improvements and improving Charisma (in order to reach max level of the ability as fast as possible). Alternatively, you can choose War Caster or Spell Sniper.

- When choosing level 5 spells, consider: Cloudkill, Insect Plague, or Cone of Cold.

- At level 10, you can choose another Metamagic modifier. It is best to choose the one that you've omitted during the choice at level 3.

- Having reached level 11, as a Storm Sorcerer you receive the final unique feature for this subclass - Storm's Fury, - that makes opponents that struck you in melee combat receive 11 Lightning Damage. Moreover, such an opponent will be additionally pushed away. When choosing your level 6 spells, consider Chain Lightning, or Disintegrate.

- Finally, level 12, means choosing another Feat. If you have previously chosen Ability Improvements and thus have full Charisma, choose one of the Feats that we listed at level 8.

Choosing Illithid Powers

If you decide to harness Illithid Powers, consider activating Charm, Repulsor, and Stage Fright. The universal nature of these powers, however, means that every single one may turn out to be useful in combat.

Party members - their skills and spells

Indeed, even the most remarkable Sorcerer will not do much without a group. Consequently, is worth to painstakingly design the party sythesis so abilities of individual colleagues complete one another. While playing as a Sorcerer, ensure you have a "tank" character that will drench all harm from skirmish battle and if necessary, divert the consideration of approaching foes. This job is best played by a Paladin, Fighter, intensely heavily clad Cleric, or Barbarian.

Don't forget about support. A Cleric, Druid or Bard with prepared healing spells will help your team get through the most dangerous encounters.

Equipment and bonuses from it

When choosing equipment for a Sorcerer, focus on items that increase magical powerand the defensive potential of this fragile hero. In the early stages of the game, in the cellar below Blighted Village, you'll find Bracers of Defence, that add +2 to AC if you aren't wearing armor or a shield. Another noteworthy item is the Psychic Spark which is an amulet that adds an additional charge for your Magic Missile.

Same as with Bard, in later stages of the game, consider equipping Birthright hat that adds +2 to Charisma. If your Sorcerer is a Human, you can consider equipping him with a set of Light Armor.

Consumables

Here is a list of useful consumables that the Sorcerer should keep at hand:

- **All** kinds of healing potions - they will quickly allow you to regenerate lost health points.

- All kinds of resistance potions - they will help you when fighting opponents who specialize in specific types of attacks.

- Potion of Speed - gives haste, provides an additional action, and temporarily increases your AC.

Party

How to recruit Us in BG3?

Us is the primary buddy you'll have a chance of enlisting, which happens not long after beginning the introduction of BG3. On this page of our aide, we show where to find the Brain Flayer locally available the Nautiloid, as well as rundown and clarify the essentials for enlisting him, and answer the inquiry whether he has any battle capacities. Besides, we answer the inquiry whether Us can stay as a sidekick in the wake of progressing to Act 1.

How to unlock the Mind Flayer as a companion?

- The opportunity to recruit Us appears during the Prologue. This is the Escape for Nautiloid quest, which involves escaping the titular vessel.

- In the initial part of the exploration, you'll encounter Myrmath - a victim of experiments. Interacting with Myrnath will activate a conversation with a talking brain asking to be released.

- Do not choose the option to destroy the brain and don't ignore the interaction with Myrnath, as this will make you unable to recruit Us. Instead, there are some skill checksyou can pass:

- Investigation check - involves examining the talking brain.

- Medicine check - only possible if you've successfully completed Investigation check. It involves the precise extraction of the brain.

- Strength check - involves cracking the skull to extract the brain.

- Dexterity check - involves delicate removal of the brain from the skull.

- The Myrnath puzzle is described in detail on a dedicated page Myrnath and the talking brain - Nautiloid.

- After successful retrieving of the brain, agree to recruit the Mind Flayer. Do not choose the option to part ways permanently.

- Us is not only a conversationalist - he can take part in combat making your job easier. He has claws that he can use.

Us leaving the party

- Us is tragically just a brief buddy, and don't anticipate keeping him in the wake of progressing to Act 1 of the mission.

- Subsequent to completing the Preface and making the Nautiloid crash, the hero will awaken near the ocean without the Mind Flayer in the group. The supposition that will be that he passed on in the calamity.

Us - best stats

Us is a Mind Flayer, and doesn't have a set class. By default, he has 21 health points and and 12 armor. His maximum carrying capacity is 20kg.

Her base statistics are as follows:

- Strength - 6

- Agility - 14

- Constitution- 13

- Intelligence - 12

- Wisdom - 11

- Charisma - 10

How to recruit Laezel in BG3?

A githyanki lady named Lae'zel is one of the primary characters that you can add to your party as a sidekick in Baldur's Gate 3. On this page of our aide, we show where to find her as she is a potential friend showing up in two distinct areas during Preamble and Act 1. You will likewise find out about the prerequisites you might need to satisfy to enlist the female hero, as well as the fundamental insights, gear, and class of Laezel.

How to recruit Laezel during the Prologue?

- The primary gathering with Laezel is a story occasion occurring during the Preface For example over the span of Break the Nautiloid journey.

- You'll meet the githyanki fighter either alone or joined by an impermanent sidekick Us. You'll experience her during the excursion through the side region of the boat - a cut-scene with the showdown will be initiated naturally.

- You'll start a discussion, during which you can either debilitate all discourse choices or skirt the prelude by picking the final remaining one.

- You can not add Laezel to the party during the Introduction for example you want to take her with you during your way to the extension. She will remain your friend up to the furthest limit of the Introduction, which last goal sees you crash the Nautiloid.

Laezel might kick the bucket during the Preface because of awful choices. In such a circumstance, she will not show up and you will not have the option to save her during Act 1.

Where to find and how to save Laezel in Act 1?

- Act 1 beginnings without Lae'zel in the group, however this doesn't mean you've lost the opportunity to go with her. She can be found and requested to rejoin the group once more.

- Arrive at the area north of Side of the road Bluffs (displayed in the screen capture above). You'll experience Lae'zel being detained in an enclosure by a gathering of tieflings.

- There is plausible that you won't arrive at Lae'zel in time. This can occur on the off chance that you lay out a Camp prior to handling the mission, and in such a circumstance, you will not have the option to keep her from passing on. We suggest setting the Free Lae'zel mission as vital once you come to Act 1.

- During the confrontation with tieflings, you can act in two fundamental ways:

- Attack tieflings - you can either begin with an unexpected attack or the battle might be started by picking a relating discourse choice.

- Pass an expertise check - you can either utilize Trickery (frightening away the tieflings) or Influence (destroying the enclosure). Assuming you've picked Influence, also decide to align with Laezel and not ganging up with the tieflings to kill her.

- On the off chance that subsequent to managing tieflings, Laezel is still in the enclosure, annihilate its base part to free the githyanki. That's what to do, play out any gone attack (for example an arrow fired from a bow - screen capture above) and target it at the enclosure after physically turning on turn-based battle.

- Presently you can either request that Lae'zel join the party, or send her to the Camp. Try not to pick the choice to forever head out in different directions.

How to gain favour with the companion?

You can gain favour with Laezel thanks to:

- treat different characters (NPCs or colleagues) in a horrible way;

- meet other githyanki on the planet.

There is a possibility of romancing Laezel and the romance is available to both genders. We described the romance in a separate chapter of the guide.

Lae'zel - best stats

Laezel is a female githyanki. Her character class is Fighter, and her default equipment is plate armor, leather boots, longsword, and a short bow.

His base statistics are as follows:

- Strength - 17

- Dexterity - 13

- Constitution- 14

- Intelligence - 11

- Wisdom - 12

- Charisma - 8

How to recruit Astarion in BG3?

In Baldur's Gate 3, one of the conceivable friend decisions is High Mythical being Astarion. On this page of our BG3 guide, we show where to track down the vampire in Act 1 of the mission, as well as what are the essentials to enlist this rogue. On the base piece of the page, you can find essential details of Astarion.

How to recruit Astarion in Act 1?

- You can experience and enroll Astarion not long after the start of Act 1 for example subsequent to showing up on the ocean front following the accident of Nautiloid.

- Explore the region west from Congested Vestiges. A cut-scene ought to be started where the Mythical person endeavors to outfox the hero. You can either set off in quest for the supposed beast or wait.

- Astarion might thump you to the ground in the event that you followed the mythical being's structure and bombed the detached discernment test. This is related with the chance of taking one of the expertise tests (for example dexterity, strength, hand-to-hand battle, to free oneself quicker.

- During the gathering with Astarion, a mind connection will happen. Through this, the mythical person will understand that he is experiencing the same thing as the legend and his mentality will change to more agreeable.

- In the last piece of the discussion, you can either request that Astarion join the party immediately, or send him to Camp. Try not to pick the discourse choice to for all time head out in different directions.

How to gain approval of the elf?

You can curry favor with Astarion on account of:

- settling on choices as per his perspective for example assist trolls with attacking the Druid Woods.

- being wry in discussions with NPCs;

- permitting him to benefit from the hero and foes.

- Romancing Astarion is conceivable, and is accessible to the two sexes. We depicted the sentiment in a different part of the aide.

Astarion - best stats

Astarion is a male High Mythical being. Moreover, he is a vampire, with abilities like vampiric bitethat permits him to benefit from his casualties. Astarion doesn't need to stow away from the sun, however he can't interact with water - erring on this on a devoted page (Why waters hurt Astarion?).

The mythical being is a Rogue, which makes him a decent possibility for secrecy actions and ambushes.

His base statistics are as follows:

- Strength - 8

- Dexterity - 17

- Constitution- 14

- Intelligence - 13

- Wisdom - 13

- Charisma - 10

How to recruit Shadowheart in BG3?

In Baldur's Gate 3, the list of potential colleagues is very broad, and one of ouroptions is a female half-mythical being cleric Shadowheart. On this page of our aide, we show every single imaginable way and examples of enlisting Shadowheart in Baldur's Gate 3 - you can do it during the Preamble or Act 1 of the mission. Further down the page, we clarify how for gain endorsement and fabricate positive relations with this character and supply essential data in regards to this legend.

Where is Shadowheart in the Prologue?

- You can meet Shadowheart interestingly during the Introduction on Nautiloid for example during Getaway the Nautiloid story mission.

- On the upper level of the boat, individuals are being held hostage and Shadowheart is being kept in one of the units. You can free her then, at that point, and this includes a riddle that we have portrayed on Detainees in cases - Nautiloid page of the aide.

- Once liberated, Shadowheart will join the group for the length of the Introduction, finishing in the wake of arriving at the scaffold and disrupting the flying vessel.

Where to look for Shadowheart in Act 1?

- In the event that you assist the cleric in the preamble, you with willing track down her oblivious near the ocean soon after the beginning of Act 1. She is near where the primary character will awaken.

- You can awaken her and afterward Grave Heart can rejoin as a buddy. Either request that she join the group immediately or send her to the Camp.

- In the event that you didn't figure out how to free Shadowheart installed the Nautiloid, luckily you actually get an opportunity of selecting her. Directly from the ocean side, travel north-east to Congested Remains.

- The cleric is found at the entry to a prison and presently you can request that she join the group or send her to Camp. She will remark on your bombed endeavor to save her on the Nautiloid, however it won't influence the enrollment cycle.

- In the event of missing the above interaction, Shadowheart might show up in the Druid Grovein the later piece of Act 1. Search for her in the preparation region. In this area enlisting additionally does without issues.

How to gain approval with Shadowheart?

To acquire endorsement with Shadowheart, you can:

- pursue choices steady with her perspective for example showing goodness towards different characters;

- try not to coordinate her with Lae'zel - the two ladies have clashing perspectives and serious struggles might emerge from this.

There is plausible to sentiment Shadowheart, and this is accessible to the two sexual orientations. We portrayed the sentiment in a different part of the aide.

Shadowheart - best stats

Shadowheart is a delegate of half-mythical beings. Her character class is Cleric, which makes her ideal for supporting job in the party. Her default gear incorporates a mace and shield.

Her base insights are as per the following:

- Strength - 12

- Agility - 14

- Constitution- 14

- Intelligence - 10

- Wisdom - 16

- Charisma - 10

How to recruit Gale in BG3?

The wizard Storm is one of the more significant characters to join the group in Baldurs Gate 3. On this guide page, you will track down point by point data on where to track down Storm in A,ct 1 of the mission, the proper behavior during the main discussion with the wizard, and the essential details of this buddy.

Where to find Gale in Act 1?

- You can track down Hurricane not long after the start of Act 1 of the mission, for example subsequent to finishing the Break the Nautiloid journey and awakening on the ocean front.

- Travel north-west from the ocean side and Congested Ruins.Explore the Antiquated Rune Circle situated close to the huge Nautiloid wreck.

- While moving toward the Rune Circle, Hurricane will emerge from the entryway, and you will naturally start a discussion with him. Picked discourse choices (for instance, about the parasite in the character's body) won't influence the possibilities enrolling the man.

- Toward the finish of the discussion, pick the choice to welcome Hurricane to the group or send him back to camp. Try not to deny his proposition to travel voyages.

Gale - best stats

Gale is human male. He addresses the wizard class and can be extremely valuable for projecting different sorts of spells. His qear incorporates a Staff and a Mage Robes.

His base statistics are as follows:

- Strength - 9

- Dexterity - 14

- Constitution- 15

- Intelligence - 16

- Wisdom - 11

- Charisma - 13

How to recruit Wyll in BG3?

During your visit to the Druid Grove in Baldurs Gate 3, you can recruit the companion Wyll, who is a Warlock. In our guide, we included information and tips on how to recruit Wyll and the basic stats of the Warlock.

Where to meet Wyll in Act 1?

- You should progress to Act 1 of the game, then visit the Druid Grove as a component of the principal journey, Eliminating the Parasite.

- At the entry to the Druid Grove, helping rout a gathering of goblins is mandatory. Solely after winning the battle will the occupants of the grove let the group in.

- Never in the principal act would it be a good idea for you pick the choice to join the trolls from their camp to attack the grove. Any other way, Wyll will never again need to go along with you.

- In the wake of entering the Druid Grove, track down the Warlock in the preparation region - he is displayed in the photos above. Start a discussion with Wyll and remark on his preparation with any exchange choice.

- During the discussion you can look into his mind. You'll learn he additionally needs to dispose of the parasite, and that you could search for Halsin together.

- Toward the finish of the gathering, welcome Wyll to join the active group or send him back to the camp. Try not to decline his proposition for voyaging together.

Wyll and Karlach - confrontation

- Wyll and Karlach get going loathing one another. Wyll should chase her. On the off chance that you enlist the two of them, they might wind up going up against one another.

- It can happen subsequent to getting back to camp for an extended rest. You can uphold Wyll in two ways - convince him to see reason (pick the primary exchange choices) or kill Karlach. We don't suggest the subsequent choice, as you'll lose her as a party part.

Wyll - basic information

Wyll is a human Warlock. His spells are rather useful to the party. His starting equipment includes, among others, medium armor and a rapier.

His base statistics are as follows:

- Strength - 9

- Dexterity - 13

- Constitution - 15

- Intelligence - 14

- Wisdom - 11

- Charisma - 16

How to recruit Karlach in BG3?

One of the likely allies to select in the main act of Baldur's Gate 3 is a tiefling called Karlach. In our aide, you will track down clarifications of where to track down the concealing Karlach, how to help the lady, and how to inspire her to join the party. You will likewise find out about Karlach's most significant details.

Where is Karlach hiding in act 1?

- You can track down Karlach in the main act of the mission. The injured lady conceals by the stream in the Risen Street locale - the above pictures show this spot. Arrive from the west, by first getting the Blighted Village and hopping over the harmed piece of the extension.

- Paladins under the initiative of Anders are hunting Karlach, and this is connected with the Chase Satan mission - we portrayed it on a different page. You can begin this journey by meeting with the paladins or when you track down the lady.

- Subsequent to beginning the discussion, don't turn forceful in light of the tiefling's flames. Continue to talk and make reference to the parasite.

- Consent to help Karlach - you'll have to deal with the paladins. Try not to pick the choice to help the paladins, since you should kill the lady.

- You can select Karlach right away. If you have any desire to manage the paladins guilefully, send Karlach back to camp and dispose of them without her. In any case, take Karlach directly to the expense house toward the north, where the paladins are. Try not to reject her.

How to gain approval of the tiefling?

To get endorsement with Karlach, you can:

- settle on choices predictable with her convictions;

- support her in retribution on individuals who made her a slave.

Karlach and Wyll - confrontation

- • Karlah and Wyll get going abhorring one another. Wyll should chase her. Assuming you select the two of them, they might wind up facing one another.

- It can happen in the wake of getting back to camp for an extended rest. You can uphold Karlach in two ways - convince Wyll to see reason (pick the principal exchange choices) or simply kill him. We don't suggest it, as you'll lose him as a party part.

Karlach - best stats

Karlach is a female tiefling. She is a barbarian and her default equipment includes a large axe and a crossbow.

Her base statistics are as follows:

- Strength - 17

- Dexterity - 13

- Constitution - 14

- Intelligence - 11

- Wisdom - 12

- Charisma - 8

How to recruit Halsin in BG3?

Enrolling the druid Halsin can make it more straightforward for you to finish missions and win battles in Baldur's Gate 3. On this guide page, you will find point by point data on where Halsin is detained, how to free the druid and how to inspire him to join the party. We additionally portrayed the main insights of this wood mythical being.

How to meet Halsin in act 1?

- You can figure out that druid Halsin vanished during your visit to the Druid Grove in act 1, yet this is a discretionary step. The man is detained in a troll camp. We depicted the penetration of this area in more detail on the How to get to the troll camp?page in the FAQ segment. There are a few accessible ways of entering that area.

- It's vital not to align with trolls and attack the Druid Grove. This could destroy the possibilities of Halsin joining your party.

- While investigating the troll camp, get to the Broken Sanctum, and afterward to the Worg Pens.

- You will watch a cut-scene in which trolls are tossing stones at a bear in an enclosure. The underlying reaction is superfluous, on the grounds that the bear will continuously get out in the wake of breaking the gate - this starts the battle. Help the bear in killing trolls and worgs from the close by confine. Likewise expect that the foes will get fortifications (they will show up through the entryway you used to arrive at this area). Try not to allow the bear to bite the dust.

- After the battles are finished, you figure out that druid Halsin you are searching for is the bear.

- You can converse with Halsin and ask him for help. You can now add him to the party or send him back to camp. Try not to reject Halsin.

- There is likewise an elective variation in which you crushed the heads of the troll camp without saving Halsin, significance without arriving at the enclosure wherein he was detained while in the bear structure. This won't destroy your opportunities to get this character. You can find Halsin in the Druid Grove after some time has elapsed. This will permit you to enlist him.

How to gain the approval of the druid?

To get endorsement with Halsin, you can:

- settle on choices reliable with his convictions;

- try not to have characters in that frame of mind with whom he might contend.

Halsin - best stats

Halsin is a male wood mythical being. He is a druid equipped for changing into different sorts of creatures. His fundamental gear is a calfskin reinforcement and a club.

His base insights are as per the following:

- Strength - 16

- Dexterity - 16

- Constitution - 16

- Intelligence - 12

- Wisdom - 18

- Charisma - 16

How to recruit Minthara in BG3?

One of the lowlifes in Baldur's Gate 3 is a drow named Minthara, whom you might experience in the Broke Sanctum in the Troll Camp. In our aide, you will track down tips on the best way to stay away from a conflict with Minthara and how to assist the paladin with selecting Minthara as a buddy.

Where is Minthara in act 1?

- Minthara is one of the heads of the Troll Camp, which is a bigger area accessible in act 1. You should pick one of the choices that permits you to invade the camp without stirring up some dust with the trolls. We have portrayed every one of the strategies to get to this area on the page How to get to the troll camp?.

- You can track down the paladin inside the Broke Sanctum - the entry to it is inside the campgrounds. Then, at that point, make a beeline for the northeastern piece of the area.

- Be cautious while conversing with Minthara. You can without much of a stretch estrange her or she can become one of the supervisors. This will occur, for instance, assuming that you uncover your aims about finding and needing to save the detained druid Halsin.

- You need to take the side of the trolls, that is to say, demonstrate the right area of the Druid Grove and advise her that you need to partake in the joint attack on this area. Try not to bamboozle Minthara by giving her the misleading area of the Druid Grove, as it will just postpone your connection getting deteriorated.

- The opportunity to enlist Minthara shows up after a joint attack on the Druid Grove - don't let her bite the dust. Welcome Minthara to join your party or send her back to the camp. Try not to dismiss the choice to add her to the party.

Alert - Minthara's presence in the party might meet with a negative reaction from a mates or lead to their demise on the off chance that they were in the Druid Grove at the hour of the troll attack.

How to gain the approval of the paladin?

You can amass positive relationship focuses with Minthara by:

- in settling on choices reliable with her convictions;

- taking part in the attack on Druid Grove and proceeding with collaboration with them;

- not having mates with whom Minthara might have a contention.

You can sentiment Minthara as any of the sexual orientations. We portrayed the sentiment in a different part of the aide.

Minthara's main stats

Minthara is a female drow. She addresses the Paladin class (she was a Cleric in the early access of BG3). As a matter of course, she has 57 wellbeing focuses and a defensive layer class of 15, and her conveying limit is 50kg. Her gear incorporates protection, boots, a shield, and a one of a kind scuffle weapon called Xyanyde. Minthara can likewise utilize spells.

Her base measurements are as per the following:

- Strength - 15

- Dexterity - 12

- Constitution - 15

- Intelligence - 12

- Wisdom - 19

- Charisma - 16

How to recruit Minsc?

Minsc is one of the potential partners in BG3. The Ranger and his fuzzy companion, Boo, return in Act 3 of the game. On this page, we have portrayed the method involved with adding this agreeable legend to your party. We review at which phase of the game you will meet Minsc and what actions you should perform ahead of time.

Who is Minsc?

Minsc, or rather Minsc and Boo, are known from the principal Baldur's Gate from 1998. Minsc could be enlisted to your party in section 2 and you could assist him with tracking down his companion, Dynaheir. Minsc and Dynaheir come from a far off land called Rashemen, otherwise called the place that is known for Berserkers.

Minsc returns as a buddy toward the start of Baldur's Gate 2: The Shadows of Amnfrom 2000. In the principal act, your character meets Minsc and Jaheira in the prisons of Irenicus, the fundamental adversary of the game. Dynaheir was killed by Jon Irenicus' partners in crime, and Minsc promised retribution on the mage.

His most impressive weapon, as Minsc himself claims, is the hamster Boo. As indicated by Minsc, Boo is actually an immense, grandiose hamster with huge intelligence, having the capacity to talk, albeit just Minsc can grasp him.

How to recruit Minsc as a companion in BG3?

You should begin getting ready to enroll Minsc in Act 2. At this stage, you should enlist Jaheira's friend. This is a critical character in Minsc's later essential for the storyline. You can peruse more about the half-mythical being on the How to enroll Jaheira in BG3 page.

After arriving at Act 3, proceed with the story until you activate The High Harper journey. This will ultimately lead you to the Vault, where you will actually want to meet Minsc interestingly. Notwithstanding, incidentally, the man's mind stays heavily influenced by the Outright, and it is furthermore controlled by the bogus Jaheira. After a short battle, accumulate data from around the Vault and make a beeline for the sewers.

In the Lower City, travel west and address the water valve puzzle (your errand will be to change the valves and set the suitable temperature appropriately).

In the wake of going through the line, a battle looks for you. Significant: THE Foe MINSC Should Endure THE Battle! In the wake of wiping out the excess adversaries, when the Ranger has next to no wellbeing left, utilize the Stagger action accessible from the latent abilities board. You can peruse more about dazzling foes on the How to utilize Thump Oblivious? page.

Killing Minsc at this stage will bring about him not going along with you, and also, troubled Jaheira will leave your party.

After an effective battle, an easy route scene will play, during which you should ask the Sovereign for insurance and intervention for Minsc. From the outset, the Illithid won't have any desire to consent to this thought, however pick conclusive discourse choices until he at long last concurs.

Purged from the impact of Without a doubt the, the Ranger will return to his detects, however after a second he will take off looking for his fuzzy companion. Pursue him and after a second you will experience Boo the hamster. Thankful Minsc will offer you his assistance. Acknowledge it and the incredible Ranger and space hamster couple will join your party.

How to recruit Jaheira in BG3?

In BG3 you will meet many characters that you will actually want to add to your party. One of the discretionary partners is Jaheira, a strong Druid/Fighter accessible from the second act of the game. In our aide, we clear up where for meet Jaheira and how to build a relationship with her.

Who is Jaheira?

Jaheira is a buddy from the principal Baldur's Gate from 1998. You can meet Jaheira alongside her better half Khalid toward the start of the main section in Cordial Amn Hotel. They guaranteed Gorion they would deal with your character after he passed on in the snare.

In Baldur's Gate 2: The Shadows of Amn, we meet Jaheira again at the absolute starting point of the game in Irenicus' prisons. In the wake of liberating her and Minsc from the enclosure, they will join the party. At the point when we find Khalid's body in one of the following rooms of the prisons, Jaheira swears retribution on Irenicus.

Jaheira is a half-mythical person Druid/Fighter, having a place with the Faerunian association called Harpers, liable for keeping up with balance by keeping both malevolent and great factions from acquiring an excess of force.

Jaheira's double class makes her a very valuable buddy in battle. She battles well with two weapons and has a few strong spells. She can restore the dead, make crowds of bugs, and effectively handle even the most impressive foe.

How to recruit Jaheira in BG3?

Between the occasions of Baldur's Gate 2 and Baldur's Gate 3, that is close to 125 years, Jaheira has progressed in the positions of the Harpers association, and her name is well known in the grounds of The Sword Coast.

We experience Jaheira in the second act of the game, before she sent her representatives to investigate the Religion of the Outright. You will actually want to join Jaheira to your party when you converse with her in Last Light Hotel.

Party management

On this guide page for the game Baldurs Gate 3, you will track down the main data about driving a party. You can learn, in addition to other things, how to join and send away potential party individuals, how to order friends, impact the union's mindset toward the primary character, and how partners are advanced.

Recruiting companions and maximum party limit

- You will begin the BG3 lobby alone, making your own character or picking one of the instant personas. We don't suggest going through the whole game with one character since thanks to group winning greater battles is simpler. Plus, you will have different attacks, spells and abilities available to you (for example a different structure for projecting spells or taking).

- The leftover party individuals you should find and enroll in the game world. Their rundown is on the aide page All Partners. You can track down there prerequisites for going along with them.

- In the wake of meeting the necessities (for example (arrival of a partner) you can welcome the character to the active party - pick the suitable discourse choices (model in the image). In the event of an absence of free space, you can on the other hand send it back to the camp where he will hang tight for additional interactions (more about this on the Party Camp page). Try not to completely dismiss different characters, since you will lose possibly significant sidekicks and related discussions as well as missions.

- In BG3, the active party (those going all over the planet of the game) can comprise of up to 4 individuals. This is 1 principal hero with 3 picked associates.

- At the point when you pick allies for an active party, focus on having an expanded group. Preferably, they ought to be characters from totally various classes, like hero, rogue, cleric and mage. On account of this, they can complete one another in battles and expertise tests. Every one of them will offer special actions, attacks, or spells.

Positive or negative companions attitude

- You ought to go with individuals who share a comparable perspective. This will permit you to acquire their help for journey decisions. The game illuminates about the endorsement or objection regarding a given friend (model in the image) for example during a discussion or finishing a mission.

- Positive connections can prompt opening sentiments and buddy missions. There might be clashes between party individuals. Try not to have them on a similar party. Conflicts can aggravate connections and even lead, for instance, to the parting separated a singular character.

- Buddies could wish to remark on late occasions or discuss them - interjection marks over their heads show this. This is a decent chance to further develop relations, yet be cautious while picking the response. Likewise, they can meddle in discussions with different NPCs if, for instance, they know the subject or the speaker.

How to unlock companion quests?

- Each sidekick has their own mission. They show up in the journal subsequent to adding a character to the party. You can regard them as discretionary errands, since they are not expected to finish the principal storyline. We portrayed all buddy mission in our answer.

- The game may not let you go further in the sidekick mission immediately. Search for chances to talk with a given friend in the party camp to get to know one another better and further develop relations. Going further with the mission may likewise require taking a particular sidekick on the excursion.

How to develop party members?

- All party individuals advance to higher levels, in addition to the fundamental character. You have full command over their turn of events and you can pick new subclasses or spells for them, in addition to other things. This will permit them to change their beginning forms.

- Colleagues, those you left at camp, can likewise get XP. This wipes out the need to shuffle the party just to acquire insight. You can get data about the advancement of inactive individuals from the party in the wake of getting back to the camp.

Companions inventory

- In BG3, in lined up with creating mates, you can likewise deal with the stock and current gear of your party individuals. Each enlisted character has beginning hardware, yet you ought to consistently overhaul it - give better weapons and shield components as well as single-use things (for example (mixtures).

- Each character has a different stock, and this is extremely useful concerning gathering a lot of gear. Divide the plunder between your partners (particularly heavier weapons and protective layer) to try not to over-burden you legends. We examined this point in more detail on the page Is there a weight limit?.

How to control a party during a battle?

- During battles, you have full command over the whole active party - you should provide them orders. While laying out orders, focus on the special attacks or capacities of a given character, for example, the capacity to bargain fire harm. Likewise look out for their weaknesses, for example unfortunate shield.

- Setting up the group before the battle is fundamental. You can separate the party, for instance, a rogue can sneak in from the back, and a long-range attacker can be put on a high rack.

- Try not to set your partners near one another, as they could all get harmed after a foe's region attack or a snare explosion.

- Attempt to try not to wreck or killing somebody from the party. Resuscitating or reestablishing such a character to a typical state can be truly challenging, and can likewise bring about squandering a given turn.

- Search for extra counsel on the most proficient method to take on conflicts in the game on the pages Battle and Secrecy.

Selection of characters for skills tests

- For the majority expertise tests, you can pick a particular colleague, and the fundamental character doesn't need to step through the exam. Change to an alternate character before discussion or interaction with an item.

- Pick characters most firmly connected with a given test, or with proficiency from the test or the best evolved characteristic (for instance. (Strenght). Sadly, the consequences of each test are irregular and in any event, when completely ready, it merits saving the game ahead of time to rehash a bombed endeavor without any problem.

Team composition tips

In this section of the Baldurs Gate 3 aide, you will figure out how to appropriately form a group to acquire however much benefit as could be expected during the ongoing interaction and have the option to deal with any rival experienced on your way.

While making your group in Baldurs Gate 3, it merits focusing on a few significant issues to be ready for any conceivable circumstance. You will surely require a capacity to cause harm in direct contact and from a good ways, approach strong spells that cause harm to one and many focuses without a moment's delay, as well as use helpful spells that recuperate, reinforce and put curses on rivals. Not insignificant will likewise be the non-battle abilities of the characters, which can work with discussion checks or make it conceivable to get specific things.

General tips

- Before you begin making a group in Baldurs Gate 3, worth realizing a few helpful hints will significantly work with this cycle.

- Various wellsprings of harm: while making your fundamental character and selecting allies to your group, ensure they can incur harm of different kinds: penetrating, slicing, otherworldly. A few rivals who are more shielded will be substantially more impervious to actual harm, yet they might be helpless to enchantment harm;

- Scuffle battle: in some cases it merits having serious areas of strength for an in weighty defensive layer (Fighter) in the group, who will actually want to tie a few foes without a moment's delay so the remainder of the group can start to dispose of individual targets individually;

- Gone battle: Rangers are very compelling in run battle. At times they can polish off an objective before it figures out how to draw near. Tragically, in Baldurs Gate 3Early Access you won't track down a recruitable Ranger, so you really want to make such a legend yourself. To do this, it merits ensuring that a few colleagues in length range weapons as helper weapons (Rogues, Fighters);

- Area of impact harm: some character classes, like Wizards, can bargain area of impact harm, yet remember that in Baldurs Gate 3, all offensive spells can likewise harm your partners. On account of Wizard, the Conjuration School subclass can help, however with different characters, you want to focus on this;

- Healing and buffs: each group will profit from having a Cleric who not exclusively can successfully keep the whole group alive, however can likewise eliminate adverse consequences from them, dole out certain rewards (for protective and attack rolls), and even restore a brought down colleague from a significant distance;

- Sneaking: having no less than one sneaking character in your group will be exceptionally helpful when you need to astonish the adversary, take something or simply slip securely right under the nose of a preoccupied rival;

- Abilities: it merits attempting to guarantee that in your group there is no less than one character with abilities that work with exchanges with experienced animals: Influence (Charisma), Misdirection (Charisma), Understanding (Astuteness). Remember about Discernment (Shrewdness), as well as Examination (Intelligence);

- Situations with: battle, you can put negative situations with your adversaries, which will, for instance, lessen their development speed, thump them to the ground or put them to bed, in this manner barring them from the battle. Character classes with valuable spells and control curses are Wizard, Cleric, and Warlock.

Exemplary team compositions

Baldurs Gate 3 is still in early access for the second and to that end we are offering group organizations in view of autonomous characters that you can join your group as you progress through Act 1. The setup of the group will rely upon the decision of the fundamental character.

Ranger is main character

- The primary proposed line-up includes a principal legend that is a Ranger - as a reminder, you won't find a Ranger sidekick in the Early Access of Baldur's Gate 3.

- Ranger (Tracker specialization): trackers are gifted in went weapons, so they can cause tremendous harm from long reach particularly while utilizing long quits. At the point when you provide your character with a second arrangement of weapons, for instance, two solitary weapons (ideally short swords), the character can likewise play out an attack that completes the objective close to him.

- Astarion (Criminal specialization): it appears to be that a Rogue with Hoodlum specialization is the most grounded of the accessible classes up until this point. Besides the fact that he perform strong can sneak attacks and ran attacks, utilize the capacity to run, which pairs the speed of development of this legend, and now and again, he can likewise perform two extra actions during one turn. This implies that you can play out a sneak attack, and afterward polish the foe off with a twofold attack (an extra action when the character uses two independent weapons). Astarion likewise has a whole scope of helpful abilities: Covertness, Quick Hands, Discernment, Influence and Terrorizing;

- Gale (Conjuration specialization): the primary wellspring of enchantment harm for your group. Entertainers approach the biggest number of spells, and likewise, they can advance new spells from scrolls, so their potential outcomes are practically limitless. On account of the Conjuration subclass, unified animals naturally prevail in cautious rolls and take no harm from his spells. Likewise, Gale has a proficiency in Understanding, Examination, and History;

- Shadowheart: sadly, you can't pick your own specialization for this character since he as of now has one. By and by, Shadowheart offers a ton of healing, supporting, and control spells, as well as has highlights Understanding and sneaking - he will be a welcome expansion to any group.

Cleric is main character

On account of the second proposed group organization, we have a Minister with Light Space as the primary person. Tragically, in the Early Access of Baldur's Gate 3, the personality of Shadowheart isn't grown as expected.

- **Cleric (Light Domain specialization)**: by fostering your pastor in a to some degree eccentric way, you can get a supporting person fit for managing a ton of harm from a good ways. The primary capacities of such a pastor ought to be Intelligence (liable for projecting spells) and Smoothness (liable for the person's protection and the capacity to go after from a good ways), and the principal weapon ought to be a long bow. The space of light furnishes the priest with the very helpful Faerie Fire spell, which can check rivals and hence bring about better going after rolls. Besides, Priest approaches mending, building up, and control spells - he is an important ally to each group.

- **Astarion (Thief specialization)**: it appears to be that a Maverick with Cheat specialization is the most grounded of the accessible classes up to this point. Besides the fact that he perform strong can sneak assaults and ran assaults, utilize the capacity to run, which pairs the speed of development of this legend, and at times, he can likewise perform two extra activities during one turn. This implies that you can play out a sneak assault, and afterward polish the foe off with a twofold assault (an extra activity when the person employs two courageous weapons). Astarion likewise has an entire scope of valuable abilities: Secrecy, Quick Hands, Insight, Influence and Terrorizing;

- **Lae'zel (Battle Master specialization)**: since the fundamental person of the player will be a priest with recuperating capacities, worth having a colleague battles in scuffle range. By picking the Fight Expert subclass, Lae'zel will turn into an entirely significant individual from the group, who will constantly be at the core of the fight. Lae'zel flaunts a few helpful abilities: Sports, Tumbling, Endurance, as well as Terrorizing;

- **Wyll:** the only Warlock you'll meet along the way, and he already has a chosen speciality (The Fiend), which in the *Baldurs Gate 3* Early Access is probably the best choice. Warlocks can deal massive damage to a single target, but they are also capable of dealing area of effect damage and hurling powerful curses at opponents. Wyll is proficient in the following skills: Persuasion, Intimidation, History and Arcana.

Camp

A critical area in BG3 is the party camp. On this page of the aide, we make sense of, in addition to other things, how to get back to the camp and how to rest there, what other significant capabilities the group's campsite serves, and which NPCs can show up in the camp (Owlbear, Scratch, Caught Skeleton, Volo and others) and what extraordinary scenes can be capable there.

How to get to the party camp?

- There are 2 methods for getting to the party camp:

- Choosing the huge fire button (base right corner of the screen) and afterward the choice to head out to the camp (Go to Camp).

- Utilizing Quick Travel - The campsite ought to be at the actual first spot on the list of areas with a quick travel choice accessible.

A long rest at the camp

- In the camp, you can fundamentally enact an extended rest - connect with the sleeping pad. This requires the utilization of 40 camp supplies. You can utilize a prepared camp supplies or select food items. You can find or purchase these things in the game world. Accumulate whatever number of them as could be expected under the circumstances and send them back from the stock to the camp (they won't trouble the legends).

- An extended rest brings the game into the following day. He can reestablish legends' Hp's, as well as eliminate negative situations with to them, or restore the restriction of ability and spell utilizes.

- The game likewise includes a Brief Reprieve. His fundamental benefit is that you don't need to set up a party camp. As a matter of course, the game permits 2 brief breaks, yet with a poet in the party you can build this cutoff to 3. At the point when he is depleted, you should go for an extended rest, and afterward cutoff will be reestablished.

The most important activities in the camp

- In the camp you can meet with buddies and foster your relationship. This will let you to realize them better, gain their compassion and do whatever it may take to progress in sentiments with them, as well as get remarkable friend journeys.

- An interjection mark over a colleague's head might demonstrate another significant discussion, for instance, about late occasions. It seems in the camp, yet in addition during joint travel all over the planet.

- The rundown of potential party individuals is on the page All Buddies.

- The camp is likewise a spot to change the ongoing enrollment of the dynamic party. You select up to 3 different characters going with your fundamental person.

- You can constantly begin a discussion with any picked sidekick and request that he stay at the camp (he will leave the party) or join the you. This subsequent choice will possibly end in a positive reaction in the event that your dynamic group at present doesn't comprise of 4 individuals.

- The last principal utilization of the camp is to utilize the Voyager's Chest. You can place all undesirable things in it unafraid that they will be lost.

- A chest is an extraordinary method for managing as far as possible. Your legends can be effectively over-burden. We suggest putting away protection, weapons, supplies, and any remaining pointless heavier articles inside it. We have portrayed the subject of thing weight in additional subtleties on the page Is there a limit?.

Unique NPCs in the camp

- Individuals and animals who are not individuals from the group may likewise show up in the camp. This normally occurs subsequent to meeting such a person in the game world and welcoming them to our camp.

- The Hooded Skeleton is an undead character that you can experience in the tomb of the Congested Remains in act 1. You need to arrive at the mystery chamber in the sepulcher (stowed away button), rout beasts and analyze the stone casket - it's essential for the mission Neglected Remnants portrayed in our aide.

- From here on out, Wilts will show up at the party's camp. He offers administrations of character restoration (for 200 gold) and changing the legend's class (for 100 gold).

- Scratch Canine is a creature that you can track down close to the carcass toward the upper east of the Scourged Town in Act 1. You need to tame the canine by conversing with him or breezing through one of the ability assessments. This will permit to pet the canine and let him sniff around to get to the camp.

- In the group's camp you can pet the canine once more and gather the little things he has found.

- The Owlbear Fledgling is an exceptional youthful creature, which you meet without precedent for Act 1 at the Owlbear's Home, west of the Druid Woods.

- The showdown with the bear should be taken care of so that the Owlbear won't bite the dust (for example (deadening him). After the battles will end, you should permit the youthful creature to benefit from its killed mother and leave the cave.

- After the occasions at the home, you should visit the Troll Camp to watch the cut-scene with trolls pursuing a bearowl. It's important to lay out an agreement with the creature (discussion with creatures, the capacity to deal with creatures) and "welcome it" to the group's camp. Eventually, you should manage the trolls (for instance). force of the ilithid, breezing through the expertise assessment.

- The showdown from the home was depicted in more detail on the page Owlbear in the section about managers.

- Volo is a man detained in a troll camp from act 1. After you meet him in the principal part of the camp, he will be tossed into jail.

- You have dare to the Demolished Asylum and analyze the eastern rooms. You should break into the enclosure or converse with the troll who claims Volo. Pay her for the detainee or take the ability test. The freed Volo will move to the party camp.

Important unique scenes in the camp

- While getting back to the camp, you can observe new, extra scenes which are connected with different occasions or characters. We have assembled the main ones beneath.

- While going on a rest, you might go over a person from the primary person's fantasies. You might have decided her appearance toward the finish of the person creation process. Her personality is obscure toward the start, however you will rapidly figure out that a parasite "living" in our mind is liable for the scenes in the fantasy.

- They can likewise incorporate scenes of gatherings with Satan Raphael and they will concern the craving to dispose of the parasite.

- Different scenes might happen either after the butchering of troll pioneers or subsequent to aligning with the trolls. In the two cases, the game will permit you to go through the night with somebody (this relies upon the relationship level with various characters).

Unique scenes may also involve selected **party members**:

- Laezel might choose to end the enduring of the primary person and any remaining characters contaminated with the parasite (counting herself). You can go after her, concur (and that implies the hero's demise), or prevent her from the choice (ilithid power or influence/medication/trickery test).

- Astarion might uncover that he's a vampire and wish to taste the legend's blood. You can permit him to do this (improvement of relations with the mythical being) or stop him.

- Wyll chases after Karlach and the showdown scene might happen in the wake of enlisting both of these characters. You can stop the contention and make them coordinate, or betray one of the gatherings and kill Karlas or Wyll.

How to leave the camp?

- You leave the camp likewise as you show up at it. The principal choice is the Leave Camp button in the base right corner of the screen. You will get back to a similar spot from which you set out for the camp.

- The subsequent choice is to summon the guide and picking a quick travel point. The group magically transports to this spot.

Bosses and difficult fights

How to defeat Phase Spider Matriarch in BG3?

The Phase Spider Matriarch is one of the managers experienced in BG3. On this page we've depicted how to battle the monster spider and what you'll get for beating her. We clear up how for plan for the battle and what spells to use to cripple the adversary rapidly.

How to reach the Whispering Depths?

You'll arrive at the Whispering Depths from the Cursed Town. In the wake of getting the region free from foes, move toward the well on the town's focal square and pass a Discernment check. You'll then, at that point, have the option to go down the rope.

The Whispering Depths are associated by tacky spider webs, on which the party should move between the floors. Sadly, at whatever point the person steps on a spider web, they should pass a saving toss or become Enwebbed - this status fundamentally impedes investigation and battle. Enwebbed characters can't move, use activities and ready all close by animals of their presence. Consequently, you ought to ensure no less than one of your characters is wearing the Spiderstep Boots.

How to get the Spiderstep Boots?

After entering the Whispering Depths, turn left and continue to push ahead until you arrive at an enormous chamber, where one of Lolth's devotees once stayed. Plunder the skeleton to one side of the exit, against the wall, to get the Spiderstep Boots.

Spiderstep Boots give the wearer insusceptibility to being Enwebbed, allowing them unreservedly to cross the region without cautioning close by beasts.

Destroy Phase Spiders' eggs

174

Prior to drawing in the chief, annihilate all the Phase Spiders' eggs. On the off chance that you don't, the Matriarch will open the fight by magically transporting close to them and promptly incubating them all. The little spiders don't have a lot of wellbeing, yet are a genuine disturbance and hit hard, particularly in the event that they all multitude a similar person.

The eggs can be obliterated by a toxophilite, or a person having bunches of throwable things. Make sure to furnish them with the Spiderstep Boots as well, as need might arise to continue on the spider webs.

Take positions on the strong ground inverse the Phase Spider Matriarch. The main pack of eggs is at the base left of the cave. Assault the eggs until you break them all. Prior to continuing on, ensure you haven't missed any.

There are more eggs on the stage to one side of the Matriarch. You can arrive through the spider webs. These eggs can be annihilated with skirmish or ran weapons. Ensure you've crushed them all.

The last pack of eggs is right close to the Matriarch, so you should be exceptionally cautious. Conceal in the shadows, trusting that the Matriarch will pivot and begin going the alternate way. When she does, shoot the egg or toss something at it, then promptly stow away once more. Rehash until all eggs are annihilated.

Preparing for the battle against the Phase Spider Matriarch

In the wake of obliterating all eggs, you should plan for a difficult experience. Ensure all your colleagues approach Fire spells.

Non-spellcasters can utilize consumable Looks to project spells, giving them a role as an activity. You'll require no less than two such spells to win this battle, so check your hardware cautiously.

Support spells, for example, Favor, will likewise prove to be useful, allowing your party rewards to their assault rolls and saving tosses. This is likewise a great chance to project Mage Armor and increment your soft spellcasters' Armor Class.

Fighting the Phase Spider Matriarch

Subsequent to annihilating all eggs and projecting every vital spell, you can connect with the chief. Make certain to adhere to the fundamental region and avoid different stages. The Phase Spider Matriarch will begin the fight by magically transporting onto one of the spider webs.

Contingent upon which of your personality goes first, ensure they're all on strong ground and afterward cast a Fire spell, or utilize a Fire look on the spider web under the chief, not on the manager herself.

The web is combustible and will consume rapidly, dropping the manager to the lower part of the cave, thumping her Inclined and managing bunches of fall harm.

Presently trust that the Matriarch will stand up and get on the other spider web. Once more torch it and drop her. Make sure to go for the gold, not the adversary.

At the point when the Matriarch returns at the top, you can polish her off in two unique ways. The foe has little wellbeing left, so you can simply kill her straight-up.

Once more then again, assuming that one of your spellcasters knows Thunderwave, you can push her off. The third fall will be deadly, finishing the fight. Note that while pointing with Thunderwave, you can figure out where the adversary will be pushed to - ensure the white line focuses to the lower part of the cave.

The Phase Spider Matriarch is too enormous to possibly be impacted by the normal Push activity. You want spells, for example, Thunderwave to move heavier rivals.

Rewards for defeating the Phase Spider Matriarch

Plunder the supervisor to track down an intriguing green thing, the Poisoner's Robe. The robe has 10 Armor, +3 to Skill, and an extremely intriguing property that causes an extra 1d4 harm from Toxic substance each time its wearer enchants that arrangements Toxic substance harm.

Lump The Enlightened - how to beat?

On this page of our manual for BG3 we've made sense of how for rout Irregularity the Enlightened. You'll track down tips on the most proficient method to immediately beat Chock, Fank and their chief. Toward the finish of the page, we've recorded the prizes you'll get for killing him.

Lump the Enlightened

Protuberance the Enlightened is an incredibly persuasive, wise beast, recruited by Trolls to go about their grimy responsibilities. He battles close by his followers, Chock and Fank, both way stupider than him.

You can employ Irregularity the Enlightened for the perfect proportion of gold and call him into fight if necessary, or outtalk him to recruit him free of charge. You can likewise assault and kill the Monstrosities to get an important thing.

Preparing for the battle against Lump the Enlightened

Prior to connecting with Protuberance's party, check out the annihilated room and observe a few expected dangers. There are a few items close by the Monsters can use during fight.

Take a gander at the snare balancing over one of the Monsters. You can implode a point of support to drop a rock on its head, however be cautious - the Monster close by can do likewise. Assuming any party individual from yours stands close to the rock, they'll wind up squashed, harmed and possible dead.

There are many items dispersed all through the room, like barrels and seats. The Monstrosities will attempt to contact them and toss them at you. Fortunately they don't bargain a lot of harm (going from 2 to 4) and the Beasts have inferior precision.

Prior to drawing in Knot and his partners, you ought to situate your party on key position ahead of time to expand your possibilities.

Climb the stone moves toward the left of the demolished cottage to arrive at the rooftop. On the off chance that you can't climb the low-hanging rooftop, simply hop there.

When you're at the top, put your party individuals on the uncovered shaft. This will give them some strong ground and a view of the Monsters underneath them.

How to defeat Lump the Enlightened?

With your party situated on the rooftop, they'll have Key position advantage on the foes, radically expanding their precision. Protuberance's gatekeepers will not have the option to contact them, so they'll be restricted to tossing things. That is not the situation with Knot however, as he can in any case effectively hurt you.

He's equipped for spellcasting, making him extremely hazardous. This makes him your essential objective - dispense with him quickly.

When he drops to half wellbeing, he'll make three perfect representations of himself, which essentially diminish your exactness against him, as the pictures can endure shots for him. Continue to go after until he falls.

When he's down, center around one of this gatekeepers. Chock typically stands to one side, involving close by objects as ad libbed weapons. A couple decent hits ought to be sufficient to bring him down.

Fank, the last enduring rival, shouldn't present an over the top danger after that - you'll doubtlessly complete him rapidly, completing the fight without losing any party individuals.

Rewards for defeating Lump the Enlightened

Overcoming the Orgres will, obviously, be compensated likewise. In the gut of Knot the Enlightened, you'll track down a diary, some gold, and an uncommon green thing, the Distorted Headband of Mind. It's a very strong curio, which builds the wearer's Insight to 17.

Auntie Ethel/Green Witch - how to beat?

This part of the Baldurs Gate 3 aide portrays how to effectively and immediately rout a lot more grounded rival at Old Home - Aunt Ethel (the Green Witch), and what reward you can get subsequent to following through with this job.

Aunt Ethel is an apparently honest old woman. Yet, don't be tricked by her affable appearance and calming voice, as they are simple appearances. The Green Witch, as this is her actual name, gives her very best for gain what she thinks often about most, and won't hesitate to forfeit the existences of guiltless creatures all the while. The showdown with this enemy happens in the Old Dwelling place - an underground cavern that can be gotten to through a hovel called Teahouse, which you will track down in the wetlands.

Potential threats

Before you enter Aunt Ethel's lodge, it merits understanding what perils you could look before your battle the Green Witch.

It's absolutely worth focusing on the well close to the witch's cottage. Assuming your personality hydrates from this well at the earliest reference point the individual will feel invigorated, and this impact will expand their greatest wellbeing by up to 10 focuses. Sadly, after your most memorable discussion with Aunt Ethel, incidentally, the water was harmed and your characters will experience the ill effects of stomach afflictions.

In the vestibule of the Congested Passage you will discover a few weird wooden covers. Try not to wear them for any reason, on the grounds that your legend will be moved by the witch and will begin going after individuals from their own group. I'm certain you can manage without that dull curio.

When you enter the Congested Passage, you will experience adversaries wearing the previously mentioned covers. It merits going after them off guard gain an additional assault turn and polish off no less than one rival before the match begins for good. Really focus on characters who use sorcery, as they can recuperate their partners and cast curses on your sidekicks.

Preparations

To get past the Congested Passage securely, the Plume Fall spell that your Wizard ought to have will be incredibly helpful. In the event that this isn't true or you don't have a Wizard in your group you can continuously utilize the suitable parchment. Feather Fall makes the characters resistant to harm from falling, and it will be a very valuable capacity as they meander through the Congested Passage.

How do I get to the Overgrown Tunnel?

When you enter Auntie Ethel's cabin, you can lead the discussion some way you wish. After beginning the battle, the adversary will rapidly utilize the intangibility mixture and afterward stroll through the chimney to different areas of the area.

Note that the chimney is brimming with consuming coals, which should be put out first so your group can securely continue on. To put out the chimney, you want to tap on the consuming coals.

In the remainder of this area, you will track down a terrified Mythical person and consequently continue to converse with him. During the discourse, you discover that the entryway close to the Mythical being is a smart deception intended to get excluded visitors far from Aunt Ethel's Old Homestead. In the wake of completing the discourse, simply stroll through the entryway and the characters get through the deception and think of themselves as on the opposite side.

How to safely pass through the Overgrown Tunnel?

In the wake of entering the Congested Passage, your group should stroll through a genuine labyrinth of winding ways canvassed in green and harmful exhaust. At the point when a person is remaining on a tainted region the individual in question will begin getting harm - so it merits staying away from. Beneath, we clarify how for walk securely and with no mischief through the Congested Passage straight into the Green Witch's Antiquated Homestead.

From the primary stage, follow the thin way to one side - you should turn the camera likewise to see it. Here it merits parting the group and moving every legend independently, as they can obstruct one another and attempt to sidestep their partners and consequently enter the region covered by the harmful cloud.

Right now, you ought to utilize the Plume Fall spell to keep colleagues from fall harm while leaping off high edges. Recollect that the spell just endures ten seconds so you need to play out the whole effort productively. Empower the leap activity and hold back nothing featured in the picture above, then, at that point, move somewhat forward to make an arrival spot for the other colleagues.

Subsequent to landing, slip marginally lower and hop again so the person lands on the left half of the noxious cloud, around the spot displayed in the picture above. At the point when you land, push somewhat ahead to account until the end of the group.

Move toward the edge of the stone, and bounce by and by - hold back nothing set apart in the picture above. Subsequent to landing, move somewhat forward or sideways with the goal that the remainder of the group can land unhindered.

Presently you should simply take one final jump toward wind up in the Antiquated Habitation and head off to war against Aunt Ethel. Hold back nothing set apart on the screen above, and subsequent to landing set aside some space until the end of the group.

Bug - how to start a fight?

Numerous players experience difficulty setting off the cutscenes with Aunt Ethel, which ought to regularly begin the battle. This is because of the way that the Green Witch was affected by the intangibility elixir while heading to the habitation, and obviously, this state is as yet continuous and can't be intruded. In the event that nothing happens to a large number of you enter Old Dwelling place, you can attempt to incite a battle in two ways.

To begin with, check whether utilizing the bowl (and subsequently liberating Mayrina, who was being held hostage by Auntie Ethel) set apart in the above picture will begin the battle. In the event that that doesn't occur, you can in any case attempt to get into Myrina's enclosure and check whether it works.

In the event that the above techniques have not worked and you have neglected to call Auntie Ethel, pick a person with region spells and afterward highlight the spot set apart in the picture over (a wooden extension associating two stone pieces). The spell ought to uncover the place of the witch, who is still affected by the imperceptibility mixture - this impact must be lifted. Project a region spell and hold on until the rival has effectively executed a protective dice roll.

When Aunt Ethel gets harm, her position is uncovered, nonetheless, she won't play out any forceful activities - she won't assault however she can in any case move sideways and make guarded tosses. Take a position higher than your rival to make it more straightforward for you to go after her with your standard weapon or Cantrips (utilize your spell openings) until the witch passes on.

Confrontation with the Green Witch

When Ethel emerges from stowing away, she promptly calls a few of her deceptions - these you can obliterate by going after from a good ways, utilizing went weapons, spells or tossing things. At the point when just the genuine witch stays on the guide, you can battle her in a conventional way, while likewise dealing with the group's wellbeing level.

During the battle, it merits utilizing some sort of assault or spell that will put a debuff on the foe, causing reward harm each turn - along these lines, you will continuously sort out which rendition of the witch is genuine.

At the point when Ethel loses sufficient wellbeing focuses, she'll begin asking for her life and proposition up an incredible power in the event that you let her leave Mayrina. Passing one of the checks could score you the power presented by the Witch (like getting "+1" to a picked characteristic, strength, finesse, and so forth), and it'll likewise permit you to save the young lady. Nonetheless, you will not get the prize you'd track down in a crushed witch's body - she'll essentially vanish, promising vengeance.

You can likewise drive her into the chasm and dispose of her right away, yet provided that you couldn't care less about the award. You'll get a similar measure of involvement focuses, yet you will not get an uncommon thing. While doing this, you need to pick the person that has the most noteworthy conceivable solidarity to build the likelihood of coming out on top. The Wizards likewise have a valuable Thunderwave spell that will likewise be viable.

Rewards

Overcoming Aunt Ethel's Green Witch will, obviously, be properly compensated. In the paunch of the crushed rival, you will find an uncommon green item called Corellon's Effortlessness. It is a generally excellent weapon for Wizards, as it gives a person who uses it and doesn't have armor with d4 reward to cautious dice rolls.

Owlbear - how to beat?

Owlbear is one of the more grounded early-game rivals you'll experience while investigating the huge universe of Baldur's Gate 3. The animal abides in its Home close to the Druid Forest. Owlbears are forceful and defensive of their young. It ought to be noticed the Owlbear is a totally discretionary foe, however beating it gives extra rewards and experience.

How to reach the Owlbear Nest?

You can undoubtedly get to the Owlbear Home from the Druid Forest. Assuming you're far away, twist to approach the Druid Forest or the Cursed Town.

We've denoted the Owlbear Home's area above. You can undoubtedly arrive by leaving the Druid Woods and following a way through the backwoods. Then you will arrive at a cascade and a hurrying stream.

To get to the Owlbear Home, you should cross the stream, and afterward follow the way down to the cavern. You'll see huge tracks on the ground.

Preparing to fight the Owlbear

Not long before the beginning of the battle with the Owlbear, consider projecting helper spells like Favor, which will give legends a reward to assault and protective rolls. This is likewise a great chance to project Mage Armor and increment your soft spellcasters' Armor Class.

To kill the Owlbear Whelp, you will require some sort of control spell to prohibit it from the battle. We suggest Rest in the event that you have a spellcaster on the party. In the event that none of your party individuals know this spell, you can utilize a look all things being equal. You'll have to upcast Rest at Level 2, as the Level 1 form won't be sufficient to influence the Whelp.

On the off chance that you choose to save the Owlbear Fledgling, you can welcome him to your camp sometime in the not too distant future. You'll dive deeper into it on the Camp page.

You can likewise concentrate down the bigger Owlbear. The battle closes the second it passes on.

During the battle, the Owlbear will attempt to abbreviate the distance isolating it from the party individuals however much as could be expected to go after with its sharp hooks. This will give your legends a negative Compromised impact, which diminishes the viability of their ran assaults. Before you assault, you should create some distance from the objective to expand your hit opportunity.

A red bolt will show up close to the Owlbear on the off chance that it's ready to get an open door assault off as you leave. It can in any case miss, obviously, however don't take a chance with it in the event that you're falling short on wellbeing.

How to defeat the Owlbear?

The Owlbear is a difficult enemy, particularly at lower levels. You can converse with it first assuming you'd like, however you'll be in an ideal situation starting the battle yourself to acquire a benefit.

It is ideal to begin the battle with an unexpected shot when the foe pivots and starts watching the remainder of the cavern - this will shock it and skirt its turn, allowing you to go after once more. While sneaking, be mindful so as not to enter the area of vision of the Owlbear, which is set apart in red.

During the battle with the Owlbear it merits keeping it in one spot or possibly out of scope of any of the colleagues by immobilizing or diminishing its development speed, for instance, by nailing it down (through bow assaults) or by utilizing one of the spells like Beam of Ice. Spells allowing Benefit on assaults are additionally valuable, for example, Pastor's Directing Bolt, which keeps up with its impact until the following time you hit the adversary.

It will likewise be essential to track down a raised position, particularly when your personality utilizes ran weapons (short or long bow) or uses spells that gain a level benefit reward like the Warlock's Eldritch Impact.

You ought to dispense with the Owlbear quickly, so center around managing however much harm as could reasonably be expected, ensuring your assaults have moderately high hit possibilities. A portion of the spells, like Enchantment Rocket, can't miss - use them.

Reward for defeating the Owlbear

Overcoming The Owlbear will, obviously, be compensated appropriately. In the stomach of the crushed animal, you will see as a thing expected to make the Vision of Irrefutably the an uncommon blue lance.

In the home, you will find an Owlbear egg, which merits a genuine fortune, and in the wake of looking through the close by skeleton, furthermore, an uncommon thing - The Oak Father's Hug.

This is some generally excellent light armor, with 13 AC, +3 Skill and the Request for Nature attribute, which bargains 1d6 brilliant to all undead going after its wearer. Sadly, this armor likewise makes the wearer take extra 1d6 harm from creatures, so you ought to change the armor at whatever point you're going to confront any.

Toll Collector Boss - BG3

Gerringothe Thorm Toll Collector is one of the discretionary bosses in BG3 in Act 2. Our tips will assist you with overcoming this troublesome adversary and acquire the Scrooge prize. We additionally clarify how for search the whole Tollhouse and get to the Tollhouse Expert's Office.

Toll Collector Gerringothe Thorm w BG3

In Act 2 BG3, you will go over the Tollhouse while navigating Shadow Revile Terrains. This building will be close to the graveyard, not a long way from the street prompting the Moonrise Pinnacles.

On the second floor of the obliterated Tollhouse, you will meet Gerringothe Thorm, a goliath brilliant beast who will request installment for crossing the waterway. The collector won't give you a particular sum, and each time you hand her mint piece, she will request more.

The battle against Gerringothe Thorm is basically difficult to win. The beast has especially strong assaults equipped for killing your personality right away. Be that as it may, there is a method for outfoxing it and immediately dispose of the danger.

How to get the Penny Pincher trophy?

Most discretionary boss battles in BG3 can be handily tried not to by cheat or persuading your rival to consent to a détente. You can dissuade Gerringothe Thorm and stay away from a battle while procuring the Tightwad prize. Pick somebody with high Magnetism to converse with the brilliant beast.

This is the very thing that you really want to do while conversing with Gerringothe Thorm Toll Collector:

- Ask her what she needs.

- Ask her what you will receive consequently.

- Give her a coin.

- Ask her how much gold she needs.

- Tell her you won't give her any more gold.

- Pick one of the Moxy checks and roll at least 18 on the dice.

- Pass another skillcheck by moving at least 21.

At the point when the discussion closes, the Toll Collector will fall to pieces. On her carcass, you will discover some gold, the Bit of Fortune weapon, a letter, and the Tollhouse Expert's Office Key.

Tollhouse Master's Office

You will track down the workplace in the western piece of the structure, close to where you talked with the Toll Collector. Open the entryway with the critical tracked down close to her carcass. There will be some gold and an Ironvine Safeguard in the enormous chest close to the closet.

After an effective Discernment check, you will find spoiled sheets on the floor. Obliterate the sheets with a ran assault and hop down. Search the room and take every significant thing, similar to parchments and bolts. Pass another Discernment check to find a button on the wall that will initiate the entryway driving outside.

Drider Boss Karniss - BG3

Drider Karniss is one of the bosses in Act 2 of BG3. He has solid assaults, a few allies to safeguard him, and a valuable spell that will make the battle more troublesome. Continue to peruse if you have any desire to know how to dispose of the Asylum status and rout Karniss.

How to defeat the drider boss named Karniss?

While finishing the Follow the Escort mission in Act 2 of BG3, you will battle a strong boss, Karniss, to get the Moonlantern. You will get a few partners from Jaheira to support this fight.

On the other hand, you can pick contrastingly and partner with the cultists - then Karniss will direct you through the Shadow Reviled Grounds, and you won't need to battle him.

At the point when you stand in the assigned spot, let your partners know when to go after the passing escort to acquire a benefit over the rivals. Karniss is a 6 level drider and goes in the organization of 5 buddies. His followers shouldn't represent a huge issue. Your partners can manage them, while your group can zero in on the principal adversary.

How to remove Sanctuary status?

Karniss will project a Safe-haven spell on himself, which will keep you from going after him. Just area-of-impact assaults work on a person with Safe-haven status. There are additionally a few straightforward ways of disposing of this status.

At the point when Karniss projects Safe-haven on himself, eliminate this status with spells, for example,:

- True Sight

- Detect Invisibility

- Bolts of Doom

In the event that you have no Safe-haven invalidating spells, hold on until Karniss assaults you, which will make the status vanish. Recollect that the adversary will project the defensive spell on himself in the future at the following an open door. In the event that you have no spells to eliminate this status, use area-of-impact spells like Billows of Knifes or Fireball.

On the carcass of the crushed driver, you will track down the Moonlanter and the Awful Sting weapon.

Raphael boss fight

Assuming you chose to break your statement and slipped into the Place of Trust in BG3, you'll need to confront the outcomes. In the wake of crossing the return gateway, Raphael, perhaps of the hardest boss in the game, will be hanging tight for you. On this page you can track down tips on the most proficient method to plan for the experience and a breakdown of the fight against the boss and his helpers.

How to set Hope free?

At the point when you meet Raphael in Act 3 of BG3, you can make a settlement with him. Whether or not you decide to do so and got the sledge consequently or totally tried not to get well disposed, you can slip into his home. To get more familiar with how to complete the custom in Villain's Charge, visit the How to go into Place of Trust? page of our aide.

Trust will welcome you when you go into Place of Trust. This is a potential partner that can assist you with battling Raphael, so we suggest liberating her from detainment before you leave through the gateway.

To free Expectation, you'll require the Arcane Mallet, and in the event that you haven't got it from Raphael, you can take it. On the off chance that you caused a settlement with Raphael and right now to have the Sledge, you'll have to take your agreement.

Go to the File and converse with the documenter. You can perceive that you are Verillius Receptor or get into his brain. With the ability check fruitful, you'll get a solicitation to the Boudoir. Enter the Boudoir and snap on the enchanted drape at the entryway. You can now go into the room.

You'll meet Haarlep. It is possible that you battle him and his assistants or keep away from the fight by finishing expertise checks during the discussion. One way or the other, you'll get the way in to the safe and presently you really want to press the button underneath Raphael's painting. Take everything from the safe and read the acquired notes. You currently know the secret phrase to the enchanted obstruction that safeguard the mallet or the agreement. Get back to the Document and gather what you really want.

Remember to take Gloves of Slope Monster Strength and Ornament of More noteworthy Wellbeing. To gather them, you'll have to incapacitate the snares on the points of support.

Continue to the jail hatch toward the finish of the passage and kill any unfriendly objective en route. In the jail, you'll need to overcome 2 Observers and a couple of Pixies. At the area, prepare the Arcane Sledge and obliterate 2 precious stones detaining Trust.

The lady will briefly join your dynamic party and you will actually want to control her during the fight against Raphael.

How to convince Yurgir to betray Raphael?

Vurgir is first enocuntered in Act 2 during your excursion through Glove of Shar. Regardless of whether then, at that point, you've persuaded him to end it all, Yurgir will show up next to Raphael. At that point, you can persuade him to deceive Satan.

To effectively persuade Yurgir, you really want to finish a Mystique check. This check is undeniably challenging, as need might arise no less than 30 Allure focuses. In the event that your Moxy is low and you don't have any suitable rewards to apply to the dice toss, save the game and attempt the check until you roll 20. Throwing 20 on the dice implies basic achievement, permitting you to finish the check.

How to defeat Raphael?

Before you start the battle, save your game, and ensure that your legends have their hit focuses completely renewed. On the off chance that you saved Trust and figured out how to persuade Yurgir to help during the battle, the following fight ought to be very simple.

Korilla, Trust's sister will join the fight on Raphael's side. You can attempt to convince her to double-cross Raphael, or thump her oblivious during the fight to try not to kill her.

Here are a few hints on the best way to rapidly overcome Raphael:

- You ought to have no less than one Savage and Contender in your dynamic party. This is on the grounds that Raphael and his assistants are impervious to pretty much every component. Scuffle assaults bargain the most harm.

- Try not to prepare a Paladin or a Minister for the battle, as everything brilliant harm is diverted by Raphael, and as the assaults return, they might kill the given legend in a split second.

- Great tip for this battle is to obliterate all support points from which Raphael channels energy at the earliest reference point of the fight. Each point of support has 99 hit focuses, however it will just take 2 gruff weapon assaults to annihilate every one.

- Begin with killing Raphael's associates.

- When Raphael brings another partner and it shows up close to one of your legends, move away from them and assault with went harm. Subsequent to denying a helper of wellbeing focuses, they will detonate, with another beast showing up in its place.

- Utilize Trust's spells to mend the whole party. Beside mending spells, Trust has helpful abilities like Favor.

- Block Raphael's assaults with Illithid Powers like Psionic Kickback or other uninvolved capacities.

- Raphael is helpless against Necrotic, Clairvoyant and Power harm.

Walkthrough
Prologue

Escape the Nautiloid

This page of the Baldur's Gate 3 aide has a walkthrough for Break the Nautiloid mission. This walkthrough will assist you with finishing the preamble.

Quest objectives

- Find a way out of the Nautiloid;

- reach the bridge;

- connect the relay nerves.

Walkthrough

This mission begins consequently toward the start of the game. You are on the Nautiloid boat, and you are one of the overcomers of the Psyche Flayers' assault on Baldur's Gate.

When you start (M1;1), take the main open section to the following room. From that point, you can get out to the external piece of the boat. Before you do that, you can take a gander at Myrnath, found undeniably higher than you. You can contact him by means of a lift, set off by utilizing the system presented beneath.

Associate with the man. In the event that you effectively complete a skillcheck for strength, smoothness, or medication (you want to move an adequate number of focuses), you will eliminate the mind. Assuming you succeed, you will discover that this is an Insight Devourer - Us. Assuming you concur, it will go with you.

Then, at that point, go to the beyond the boat. Get around the opening in the deck to get further. You'll run into Lae'zel. After a concise discussion, you will unite to expand your possibilities arriving at the transponder and getting away.

Just from that point forward, you'll confront your most memorable battle experience. Your adversaries will be 3 Pixies. They move rapidly and can bargain harm from a good ways. They're likewise impervious to fire, so in the event that you are playing as a Wizard, bargain them harm from cold.

After the battle, go to the steps. You'll be outside once more. The way driving further is to one side of the steps. You'll track down another passageway, impeded by a layer. The best way to break it is to go after it.

This way will lead you to a room with cases and a board with three cerebrums. To battle, don't contact the mind in that frame of mind of the control center. It will free detainees who are unfriendly towards you.

Shadowheart is in one of the units here. Sadly, nothing remains at this point but to attempt to get her delivered. Be that as it may, it won't deliver any outcomes.

In the event that you stroll into the passage to one side of the entry, you will arrive at a way driving directly to the transponder. Utilize the recuperation gadget to reestablish your group's wellbeing to full.

In the transfer room, you'll find Leader Zhalk battling a Brain Flayer (they're centered around one another, so you can leave them be) and more devils. The game doesn't drive you to battle them (in any case, you can acquire extra experience focuses). You can just go to the transponder and initiate it.

Act 1

Explore the ruins

Quest objectives

- Enter the ruins;

- explore the ruins;

- talk to the hooded figure.

Walkthrough

You actuate the journey toward the start of the game. Strolling close by the ocean side you've crashed on, you'll run into Shadowheart. She will be remaining by a locked entryway. Converse with her and you will discover that she is attempting to get in. During this discussion, you can likewise select the female Minister to the party. There are a couple of ways of entering the sanctuary.

Variant 1 - Breaking in

The simplest method for getting inside is to open the entryway close to which you and Shadowheart stand. Actually take a look at the close by barrels - you will track down criminal's devices. Use them to get inside. This will quickly allow you to arrive at the Wet Sepulcher, the journey's vital area.

Variant 2 - Entering through the chapel

The subsequent choice is to go up the slope. You'll experience a gathering of thieves. You can manage them in two ways:

- Calmly - follow the base way directly to the two thieves. This will set off a discussion. To keep away from slaughter, you should pass one of the skillchecks - influence, terrorizing, or misdirection. Before you pick, check which one has the best chances of succeeding. Remember to save the game as well;

- Viciously - surprise the bowman on the slope. That way you will acquire a benefit in the battle.

Whenever you've managed the foes, save the game once more and set out toward the entryway. Draw nearer to them to set off some discourse - a presentation or misdirection check will get you inside. In the event that you come up short, you can constantly open the entryway with criminal's apparatuses.

This will allow you to arrive at the Bedchamber. You will experience one watchman. You shouldn't disapprove of overcoming him. Then, make a beeline for the locked entryway. Obliterate them to continue on.

Behind them is another foe watching the region. You need to kill him in one turn. If not, he will call for fortifications from the adjoining room.

You really want to get to entryway in the right corner of the room. After the fight, you can utilize one out of the two methods for opening them:

- battle - you should go into the room that has a gathering of rivals. On the off chance that they haven't been cautioned, you can amaze them. Really focus on bowmen, as they can cause serious harm to the party. A button for opening the entryway is at its finish (you want to pass discernment skillcheck);

- annihilating the entryway.

The entry to the grave is behind the gate.

Variant 3 - Trapdoor

There is a way toward the east of the church. At its end, there is a hidden entryway. You need to open it with criminal's devices. Your party will enter the Damp Tomb.

Variant 4 - Hole

There's a colossal stone draping over the thieves in the sanctuary. Put a match to the rope holding the stone - it will fall and make an opening in the ground. Go through it to a destroyed room. At the point when you receive in return, you will be in the very room that can be gotten to utilizing different strategies.

When you get into the grave, you need to get a key to the locked entryway. It is situated in a stone casket in the Moist Tomb (Darkvision will be helpful here). There are 8 gas traps in the room - you really want to pass a discernment skillcheck to see them. To try not to enact them, you need to cover the snares with something. On the off chance that you can't distinguish one of them, you will not have the option to incapacitate that snare - it will actually want to enact.

There is a button on one of the segments (likewise identified by passing an insight skillcheck). Subsequent to taking the key and actuating the snare, you can squeeze it to impair the snare once more.

At the point when you get the key, go to the opposite side of the passageway (through which you entered the grave assuming that you utilized variant 2 or 4) and open the entryway. Go directly to the left corner of the room. After effectively passing the discernment skillcheck, a button will appear.Pressing it will make the close by cadavers to go after you. During battle, ensure your mages are beyond the quiet spell. Assuming that they get hit with this spell, they will not have the option to project spells.

At the point when the battle is finished, you can enter the burial chamber. Communicate with the stone coffin and a hooded figure will show up. Converse with that individual to finish the journey.

Free Lae'zel

Quest objectives

Path 1:

- Resolve the conflict;

- help Githyanki by the name of Lea'zel;

- recruit Lea'zel to the team.

Path 2:

- Resolve the conflict;

- kill Lea'zel.

Walkthrough

Note: this undertaking won't be accessible assuming that Lea'zel is killed during the preface.

This mission begins consequently toward the start of the game. Close to the church you'll experience two tieflings keeping Lae'zel caught. Approach them and begin a discussion. It might end in following ways:

- you can concur with the Tieflings and assist them with killing Lea'zel.;

- pass a duplicity or influence skillcheck to free her easily;

- lose the check to set off a battle against the tieflings, after which you can free Lae'zel.

You can likewise annihilate the lower part of the enclosure and assist Lae'zel with killing the tieflings.

At last, you can choose if you need to enlist Lae'zel to your group. Regardless of whether you intend to select her, you can send her back to camp.

Child's trial

Quest objectives

- Save Arabella;

- find Arabella's parents.

Walkthrough

This mission is actuated while remaining in the Druids Forest. While heading towards the heavenly lake, you'll go over a gathering. You'll learn Khaga has detained a young lady, Arabella, in the Emerald Forest.

Go to the assigned spot and save the game right away. Assuming you choose to converse with Khaga, you'll figure out why she's holding Arabella. As of now, you will actually want to impact the course of occasions:

- pass the nature or influence skillchecks - this will save the young lady. The expected qualities are extremely high, so you will likely have to stack the game a few times to accomplish the ideal impact;

- try not to meddle - the young lady bites the dust;

- assault Khaga - you should battle Khaga. In any case, arabella will bite the dust.

Despite how the circumstance finished in Emerald Forest, return to the region where individuals accumulated before. That is where you will track down the young lady's folks. In the event that Arabella made due, you will get a reward.

Get help from Healer Nettie

Quest objectives

- Find the healer - Nettie;

- go with Nettie;

- find an antidote to the poison.

Walkthrough

Assuming you figure out how to free Lae'zel from her enclosure calmly, you'll have the option to attempt another Influence check. On the off chance that you pass it, you'll find out about Nettie, a druid's understudy who can assist you with eliminating the parasite.

Assuming the tieflings watching Lae'zel pass on, you'll have the option to begin this mission during your most memorable visit to the Druid Forest. While conversing with Zevlor, let him know you want clinical assistance and he'll point you towards Nettie.

She can be found at the Druid Woods, explicitly at the Emerald Forest region. Go to her and inform her concerning your concern. She will actually want to help and advise you to follow her to the assigned spot.

At the point when you follow her, you'll get to a room where another discussion will happen. This time, Nettie will offer you a "fix." On the off chance that you pass an examination skillcheck, you'll understand it's a toxin and deny in time. Then, in the event that you can pass the influence skillcheck, she will let you go.

Be that as it may, assuming you choose to take the particular, the person will be given the situation with "distress". To take it off, you'll require a remedy. Assuming you effectively pass the skillcheck, she will give it to you herself. If not, you'll need to battle and take the antitoxin forcibly (you need to look through the body). Then, at that point, you have nothing else to do except for to leave the room.

Save the Goblin Sazza

Quest objectives

- Free Sazza;

- escort Sazza out of the Grove

- get to the Goblin camp.

Walkthrough

This mission will enact while in the Druid Woods. At the rear of the area you'll track down two tieflings close to the enclosure Sazza's secured. You can do the accompanying during a discussion:

- try not to meddle and allow Sazza to be killed.;

- stop the execution and save the troll (in the event that you pass the influence or terrorizing skillcheck, you'll have the option to do it easily).

In the event that you've chosen to favor Sazza and you managed the Tieflings, you can converse with the troll. She will enlighten you regarding the priestess in the camp. After you discharge her, she will consent to take you to her.

You can open the enclosure with stealing devices or by basically annihilating the entryway. Whenever that is finished, lead Sazza out of the forest. To do this, the most secure thing to do is to go up the stone rack found right at the edge of the cliff. Get around there, and in the wake of passing the discernment skillcheck, you will find an entryway prompting the cavern.

Inside, you'll experience a gathering of trolls which you'll need to battle. Focus on the toxophilite on the slope. Because of Sazza's low endurance, it is smarter to get her far from the conflict.

You'll likewise track down oblivious Findal there. In the event that you utilize a mending spell on him, you will actually want to converse with him.

Note: you can likewise enter the cavern from the opposite side (be that as it may, you should pass an inclination skillcheck). Use it to get to the jail. Like that, it'll be simpler to battle. You will actually want to surprise your adversaries.

Finally, you must follow Sazza to the Goblin Camp.

Deal With Auntie Ethel

Quest objectives

- Get Auntie Ethel's help.

Walkthrough

Heading towards the Riverside Teahouse, you will experience two siblings - Johl and Demir - blaming Auntie Ethel for grabbing their sister. On the off chance that you pass the examination skillcheck, it'll turn out the lady is lying. During this exchange, you can take the side of siblings and help them in their pursuit. After the discussion, the lady will vanishes.

To view as her, you need to dive deep into the bog. Assuming you pass the mysterious information or influence skillcheck, it'll turn out that the entire situation is only a deception. Assuming that you neglect to pass it, you can likewise bring down the deception by conversing with the sheep. Bombing will bring about the local actually looking amazingly bright, as in the image underneath.

Auntie Ethel lives in a Teahouse close to the quick travel point. When you go inside the house and choose to converse with the old woman, the cutscene will begin.

During it, the witch will offer you to eliminate the parasite in return for one eye.Agreeing won't help you. All you'll learn is that the parasites inside your heads have been adjusted by wizardry. You'll likewise get a super durable debuff, diminishing your discernment and keeping you from truly landing basic hits.

Teahouse in BG3

Question Auntie Ethel

The Save Mayrina side mission will start in the wake of meeting two siblings, Johl and Demir, contending with Auntie Ethel. Look at the above video, which will direct you bit by bit through all phases of the journey.

You will meet three characters in the timberland, south of the troll camp. During the discussion with Ethel, pick the exchange choices blaming her for hijacking the lady. After the discussion is finished, the witch will vanish, and the siblings will head towards the bog. Follow them to find the witch's safe-house.

At the point when you arrive at the bogs, you should pass an insight check. On the off chance that you don't pass, you will require converse with the sheep. During the discussion, play out the Creature Taking care of expertise check, and afterward select the BAA exchange choice. At the point when the deception vanishes, the landscape will change and every one of the captivated Redcaps will return to their actual structure.

The Redcaps won't understand that the deception has been broken, so they won't go after you. In any case, it's smarter to overcome them now, since the witch hasn't arrived. Set your partners accurately on the front line and rout 4 little rivals.

Head towards the hut. Inside, you will find Mayrina. **During the conversation, tell the woman what happened to her brothers.** Mayrina will disappear - this will trigger the first fight with Auntie Ethel.

First fight with Auntie Ethel

In the event that you have proactively crushed every one of the Redcaps from the swamps prior, the main battle with the witch shouldn't give you any difficulty.

Utilize just fundamental assaults and don't allow yourselves to be killed. The witch will figure out how to run away to her refuge.

Save Mayrina

Subsequent to finding reality with regards to Auntie Ethel, follow her to her hideaway in the Teahouse in the marshlands. Connect with the hearth to douse it and continue to the mystery room. At the base, you will track down the Congested Passage.

Move toward the large entryways by the mythical being and associate with them. At the point when you pass the ability check, you will find that the entryway is another deception. Try not to put on the veils lying on the table. Turn the camera so the cursor is behind the entryway and send your friends there. The entire party ought to have the option to pass through the entryway easily.

In the following room, you will track down a few foes. Rout them all and bounce over the cascade to the further piece of the refuge.

To start with, attempt to appropriately situate your party and trap your rivals to acquire a benefit.

Be careful with poison mists and traps dispersed on the ground. To clear your path through, you can initially consume the gas, and afterward quench the fire (poison mists will return, so you really want to pick up the pace). Another choice is basically to run over an impediment. Continue to move further into the passage until you arrive at the room with the witch and Mayrina.

Defeat the hag

The second battle with Auntie Ethel won't be so natural. The witch knows many spells and projects a deception on herself which makes more witches. This battle likewise has a period limit. Mayrina is detained in a consuming enclosure, so watch the wellbeing points of the wooden enclosure to keep it from tumbling down.

Prior to beginning the fight, it's ideal to set up your party appropriately. The battle with the witch will possibly start when you approach the enclosure, so conceal every one of your friends in the shadow and send the ran characters and mages to the rear of the enclosure, ideally so they can remain on a higher ground.

Take out the phony witches first. Utilize strong spells like Wizardry Rocket for this. At the point when just the genuine witch remains, center your assaults around her. Nonetheless, on the off chance that you don't dispose of her quickly enough, Auntie Ethel will project a deception in the future and make more phony witches.

At the point when the witch has around 20 wellbeing focuses left, she will battling and ask you for a ceasefire. You can play this out in more than one way:

- proceed with the fight

- request that she discharge Mayrina

- haggle with the witch and get a prize from her

- pass the expertise check to free Mayrina and get a prize from the witch

Search the lair for a way to help Mayrina

In the event that you have saved Mayrina and driven away or killed the witch, you will in any case have to help her track down the remedy for her significant other.

Assuming you killed the witch, search her body. You will track down a wand there called Harsh Separation. Assuming the witch has gotten away, really look at the last room in her safe-house. The wand will lie on the table. Utilize the entryway and head outside.

Converse with Mayrina. You will have the accompanying choices to browse:

- break the wand and in this manner not restore Mayrina's better half

- restore Maryina's better half, however save the wand for yourself

- restore Mayrina's better half and return the wand

Assuming that you picked the last choice, Mayrina and her significant other will go to Baldur's Gate where you could meet them once more.

Hunt the Devil

Quest objectives

- Find the devil;

- kill Karlach (optional);

- kill Anders (optional).

Walkthrough

On The Risen Street, close to the cavern where you battled the gnolls, there's a little cabin. A gathering of Paladins has settled there. Converse with their chief, Anders, and you'll realize they're hunting the devil. Offer your assistance to begin the mission.

Their objective - Karlach - holds up by the stream close to the Paladin's quarters. Drawing near triggers a discussion. The tiefling will let you know the inverse - she has gotten away from heck, and the gathering you met needs to catch her and bring her back. You can settle this undertaking in two ways.

Kill Anders and the rest of the Paladins.

It's a more beneficial choice - you'll get more XP and better hardware. The battle will be decently troublesome. Really focus on Anders. He can bargain extreme harm and immediately thump down more vulnerable partners.

After the fight, gather the plunder from the crushed and return to Karlach. It just so happens, she is truth be told the devil, yet the Paladins are additionally couriers of misery. After this discussion, the journey is finished.

Kill Karlach

When you arrive at the stream and converse with Karlach, you can simply battle. This encounter will be less requesting than the one against Paladins and shouldn't cause you any issues.

In the wake of killing Karlach, leap to where the Tiefling's body lies. You need to detach her head to have evidence for the Paladins. You can likewise inspect her body, which requires breezing through an Arcana assessment.

At last, return to the head of the Paladins and hand him over the head. He will offer you an uncommon blade as a declaration of his appreciation. After this discussion, the journey will be finished.

Rescue the Trapped Man

Quest objectives

- Release the trapped man;

- bring Benrin to safety;

- find Miri;

- find the dowry;

- tell Benryn where Miri is.;

- talk to Benryn.

Walkthrough

You'll find the mythical being at Waukeen's Rest, on the principal floor of the structure you're breaking into. He's nailed somewhere near a recoil in a higher up room. When you arrive, you need to rush on the grounds that the fire is spreading quick. To eliminate impediments, you should effectively breeze through an Examination or Strength assessment.

When you get Benrin out of the structure, you can converse with him. He will request that you track down his significant other Miri. Her body is higher up in the structure nearby. Utilize your Talk with Dead capacity (you'll find out about how to get it from a different page of the aide) and you'll find out about the settlement concealed in the horse shelter.

The structure is profound inside the complex. You will see a sheaf in it - collaborate with it and an overlaid chest will show up. Take its items and return to Benrin. Let him know where his significant other's body is, and he'll run there. Follow him and converse with him again to finish the journey.

Rescue the gnome

Quest objectives

* Get close to the goblins;

* stop the windmill.

Walkthrough

You initiate this journey while visiting an unwanted town. There, you track down a windmill (M5;6) and a gathering of trolls who menace Barcus. When you draw near to them, the discussion begins. In the event that you can pass the influence skillcheck or utilize Illithid's power, you can drive the gathering ceaselessly. If not, you'll need to battle.

At the point when you manage the adversaries, enter the windmill. You'll find a brake switch there. Pull it, and the machine will stop.

Presently you can move toward the tied elf. In the event that you choose to free him, you'll need to talk with him and figure out how he arrived. When the discussion is finished, the journey will be finished.

Search the Cellar

Quest objectives

- Find the Ancient Tome

- Unlock the Ancient Tome (optional);

- Destroy the Ancient Tome (optional);

Walkthrough

There is a hovel in the unwanted town, right close to the quick travel point. Inside, you can find a lid prompting the basement. Enter it - you'll see a cavern loaded with chests. There is an undead in every one of them. Assuming you cooperate with them, you will be gone after.

On the contrary side of the room, you will find a mirror with which you can have a discussion. Sooner or later, it will get some information about the lich. To make it let you pass, you should affirm that you are its worker, and afterward pick the accompanying responses:

- " A foul lich. May he die a thousand more deaths.";

- "To clean a wound?";

- "I'd look for whatever spell will rid me of this worm in my head.";

In the event that you offer an off-base response, you will be gone after.

There is a studio behind the mirror. On the table found directly from the entry, you will find a book portraying tests.

Take a gander at the book behind the bars.Destroy the entryway, open it with a lockpick or utilize the key you can find in the room neighboring the studio (you can obliterate the wall to get to the following room). Before you enter, incapacitate the long snare before the bars. The following snare discharge system is right under the book, however you can securely take it in two ways:

- Incapacitate the snare under the book (insight expertise check required),

- Supplant the book with another thing - you can toss one of the things from the stock on the table.

It just so happens, you want a key to open the book. You can manage this in two ways.

Destroy the book.

The primary choice is to obliterate the book. This variant is extremely simple. It expects you to do magic that arrangements light harm on the book (Shadowheart can do that).

Find the key.

Assuming that you choose to open the book, you should go to the Whispering Depths. In the Cursed Town, you will track down a few sections:

- a very much situated close to the quick travel point;

- an opening in the stone situated in the storm cellar of the structure inverse the drug store.

In the caverns you will experience a gathering of phase spiders. These are a portion of the more troublesome rivals in the game. They can magically transport and can cause incredible harm. Furthermore, they are driven by a Phase Spider Matriarch, a strong rival. There you will view as the Dull Amethyst, which is expected to follow through with the responsibility. You can attempt to sneak past her or battle her.

In the wake of seeing as the key, you can actuate the book in the stock. You additionally need to conclude whether you need to save the book for you and get familiar with the Talk with Dead spell or give it to Hurricane or Astarion.

Ask the Goblin Priestess for Help

Quest objectives

- Follow Priestess Gut;

- drink the priestess's potion.

Walkthrough

When you get into the Troll Camp, you can undoubtedly make a beeline for the Broke Sanctum (M6;9). On the off chance that you utilize the force of the parasite, you'll go in there easily. Inside, you'll experience priestess Stomach. During the discussion, she offers to eliminate the parasite. Assuming you concur, she advises you to follow her to another room.

In any case, she doesn't consent to play out the custom when the person isn't the only one with her. So you need to isolate the hero from the others, lead the gathering out of the room, and begin the discussion.

In the event that you adhere to the priestess' guidelines, you will be caught and the worm will in any case be in your mind. You need to pass the skillcheck effectively to get free. It will incite a battle where you should confront a huge gathering of rivals. In the first place, kill the priestess, then, at that point, set the group at the highest point of the steps to acquire Strategic position advantage.

Find the Missing Shipment

Quest objectives

- Help trapped survivors;

- talk to survivors;

- meet Rugan's associates.

Walkthrough

When you arrive at The Risen Street, you'll experience a gathering of gnolls encompassing the train survivors. Draw nearer to start a battle. In the case of, during the fight, you draw near to Filind, you can drive him to comply and kill the survivors to take their effects. For this situation, nonetheless, you won't skirt the battle, since you will be gone after by the gathering later.

Be that as it may, assuming you search for the wellspring of the voice, you can likewise persuade the animal to remain with you against the gnolls. The last choice is undeniably more useful. Filind will assist you with overcoming the others, and afterward he'll rebel himself. All things considered, be that as it may, you will enjoy an upper hand over him since he will be separated from everyone else. After the battle, converse with the survivors - they'll request that you carry the chest to their base camp at Waukeen's Rest.

When you arrive, make a beeline for the structure at the rear of the complex (the entryway is concealed with containers). Inside, converse with the gatekeeper and give him the secret key, and you'll get the way in to the trapdoor prompting the cellar.

When you enter the underground, communicate with the wardrobe - another entry opens, prompting the appropriate concealing spot.

When you get in there, you will meet Zarys, and after a short visit, head towards her to converse with her once more and finish the journey.

Save the First Druid

Quest objectives

- Find Hasin in the goblin camp.

- Eliminate goblin leaders.

- Meet with Hasin in the Emerald Grove.

Walkthrough

After entering the troll camp, set out toward the entry to the Broke Sanctum. The entry to the prison where trolls keep Halsin is set apart in the above picture.

After entering the prison, an easy route scene will play in which you will see trolls torturing a monster bear secured in an enclosure - this is Halsin in his changed structure. During the discussion, side with the Druid and rout all adversaries. Halsin will uphold you in this battle.

Halsin will request that you rout three troll pioneers that you will track down in different rooms of the Broke Sanctum. The druid can go with you, yet you will not have the option to sneak around then, at that point, so the decision is yours.

When you manage the troll chiefs, converse with Halsin, and afterward meet him in the Emerald Forest. Go meet with Rath to gather the award and complete the journey.

Underdark in BG3

How to get to Underdark?

There are 4 ways prompting Underdark. The way you pick no affects the further story in Underdark.

One of the sections is situated inside the Troll Camp. At the point when you arrive at the Broke Sanctum, track down the way to the Debased Sanctuary in the western piece of the palace.

Go to the eastern piece of the sanctuary and find the room whose inside is enlightened by a light emission penetrating through the roof. You don't need to address the moon puzzle to open the way to Underdark. Find the switch on the wall by passing a Discernment expertise check and open it utilizing the Thievs' Devices.

In the wake of entering the Underdark, you will get to the Selunite Station.

You will track down the following entry in Whispering Depths in the Cursed Town. You'll track down the entry to the Depths in the well in the center of the town or one of the houses.

Not a long way from where you will battle the Phase Spider Matriarch is a gorge from which green light is transmitted. Bats will fly out of the gap. You should hop inside to get to Underdark. Simply make sure to project the Featherfall spell in all colleagues first. In the wake of landing, you will get toward the eastern piece of Underground.

The following entry to the Underdark is in the Zhentarim's safe-house an on the area of Waukeen's Rest. You will track down the entry to the safe-house in the little structures close to the outbuilding with bulls. After you get inside the hideaway, we exhort not to participate in a battle with the Zhentarims. There is a lot of oil and combustible barrels all over building. Hence, battling them can rapidly bring about the demise of the whole group.

Find the resting wolf named Istor. Close to him, you'll find an entryway with a deception spell forced on it. Pass through the secret entryways. Utilize the lift and go down to Underdark. You will wind up in the north-eastern underground, not a long way from the Myconid State.

The last entry is in Auntie Ethel's Teahouse in the Sunlit Wetlands. On the page Save Mayrina we have depicted the mission with the witch in subtleties.

At the point when you show up at her home, quench the fire to get to her refuge. Then, at that point, cooperate with the entryway. You will figure out that the entryway is only a deception. Pass through the entryway and arrive at the cascade. Leap to the opposite side. Not a long way from the cascade are the following entryways covered with a deception. Behind them you will find a green entry prompting the southern piece of Underdark.

On the off chance that you can't overcome the entryway, take a stab at putting on the covers found at the first wooden entryways.

What to pay attention to in Underdark?

The Underdark is divided into several regions, including 4 Waypoints. When entering the Underdark, your team should be at least level 4. You will encounter many tough enemies and minibosses there.

- Myconid Colony - here, you unlock side quests: Find the Mushroom Picker, Help Omeluum investigate the Parasite, and Defeat the Duergar Intruders. There are 2 merchants in the colony.

- Selunite Outpost - the entrance to the outpost is guarded by two statues. There is a minotaur at the gate.

- Arcane Tower - the entrance to this location is guarded by 2 magical turrets. To thoroughly explore all floors of the tower, you must first fix the broken elevator. You will find here the ingredients needed to complete the side quest: Help Omeluum investigate the Parasite and a lot of loot.

- Beach - here, you will find a ship that will take you to the Grymforge and the Find the Missing Boots quest. In the forge, there is a passage to the Moonrise Towers, which is the beginning of the second act of the game.

- Sussur Tree - here you will find the Sussur Bark, an item associated with the side quest: Forge a Master Weapon.

- The Festering Cove - it's a secret location in Underdark.

The underground is also full of various traps. Equip yourselves with tools to disarm traps, and remember to move carefully. When your character approaches the trap, they will automatically perform a Perception check.

Some traps can be shot down with a regular arrow or a fire ball. You can set fire to the poisonous gas cloud and wait for the danger to be gone.

How to advance to Act 2?

If you have any desire to avoid side journeys and immediately finish Act 1, go to the ocean side, rout the Duergars, and utilize the boat to get to Grymforge. From that point you will actually want to utilize the lift, which will take you to the Moonrise Pinnacles.

Find the Mushroom Picker

In the province, you will find a broker named Derryth, who will inquire as to whether you have seen her better half. In the event that you answer adversely and pose a couple of extra inquiries, you will open the journey Track down the Mushroom Picker.

Go to the put set apart on the guide. After moving toward the cavern with green mushrooms, a discussion with Baelen will start. You can help him in more than one way:

- In the event that you have the Dim Step look with you, toss it to him playing out a Strength check.

- Project a fly spell on the diminutive person.

At the point when Baelen can escape from the snare, he will thank you and offer you an imperceptibility look as a trade off. Get back to Derryth and gather the award, the Gloves of Uninhibited Kushigo.

Help Omeluum investigate the Parasite

In the Myconid State, there is a broker named Blurg. During the discussion with him, enlighten him concerning your concern with the fledgling. The dealer will call the Brain Flyer - Omeluum.

While conversing with Omeluum, let him know that you need to dispose of the fledgling. Open the mission: Assist Omeluum with researching the Parasite. You should bring him 2 fixings that you will track down in the Obscure Pinnacle, in the southwestern piece of Underdark.

At the point when you return to him with the obtained fixings, Omeluum will make an elixir for you. Subsequent to drinking, you will actually want to pass a few capacity checks to open new Illithid powers. Eliminating of the fledgling will fall flat, and the errand will be finished.

Subsequent to drinking the elixir, you can purchase (or get through terrorizing) a strikingly valuable thing from Omeluum called the Ring of Brain Safeguarding, which safeguards against Appeal. This ring will be exceptionally helpful in the battle against Nere in Grymforge.

Arcane Tower - how to destroy turrets and run the elevator?

The Arcane Tower is situated in the southwestern piece of Underdark. To get inside and analyze every one of its floors, you should first deactivate the turrets and actuate the lift.

The turrets will shoot anybody who attempts to move toward the entryway. They can be deactivated in two ways:

- Toss the Sussure Blossoms close to the turrets, which you can find close to the Sussur Tree toward the north of the Tower;

- or on the other hand utilize any electric spell and incur sufficient harm for them.

At the point when the turrets are presently not a danger, you can go to the Tower and begin the lift.

Project the Fly or Featherfall spell on one of the characters and move toward the turret close to the sculpture. Hop on the goliath mushrooms at the rear of the Tower. Get the Sussure Blossoms and utilize the lockpick to open the indirect access to the Tower.

Move toward the generator and put a bloom into it. The lift in the Tower will be opened. Go up the steps to the lift and go up 2 stories. Open the principal entryway of the Tower and let the remainder of the group inside.

Arcane Tower - what can you find there?

On the least floor of the Tower, you will track down a chest with the Revealed Secrets jewelry, a few books, mixture fixings, and recuperating elixirs.

On the first floor of the Tower, you will find Timmask Spores and the Tongue of Franticness and elements for the Assist Omeluum Investigate the Parasite with questing.

On the second floor, you will track down a Plated Chest on one of the overhangs. At the point when you remove every one of the things from the chest, you will get a few significant things, including the Mystra's Beauty boots, which give Featherfall.

On the third floor, you will find a chest with the Mage's Companion ring and many books and parchments. You will likewise track down a baffling button by the window. To tackle the riddle with the button, you want to uncover the substance of a grave north of the Arcane Tower first. You will find a Canine Choker there. At the point when you put on the neckline and press the button, a piece of meat will jump into a more healthy place.

On this floor, you will likewise track down an Engraved Githyanki Plate on one of the shelves. In the event that Lae'zel is in your party, in the wake of looking at the thing, you will open another discussion with her.

On the highest level you will experience robots. You can overcome them in fight or get a thing from them assuming you pick the right discourse choices. You will require 3 books for this discussion:

- Ragged Book - lies on a rack on the first floor.

- Dusty Book - an open book that lies on the work area on the second floor.

- The Ways to Haziness - it's on the work area on the third floor.

Peruse this large number of books, and during the discussion with Bernard, consistently pick the first conceivable response. On the table by the robots, you will track down a Directing Light ring. Put on the ring to find a button in the lift that prompts the storm cellar.

Go down to the storm cellar and search all the shelves. Remember to take the Staff of Arcane Gift. In the chest, you will track down a few parchments, bolts, and the Sparkswall ring.

Find the Missing Boots

You will open the Find the Missing Boots journey around the ocean in Underdark. As you approach the boats, a Duergar will confront you. Take any capacity check, then, at that point, get some information about the boots. Propose help in tracking down the elf.

You will find the dwarf in the Mykonid state, she will lie on a huge mushroom. Converse with her and deal help in return for boots. At the point when you get back with the boots to Duerger, he will allow you to utilize the boat, which will take you to Grymforge.

Cure the Poisoned Gnome

In the Mykonid settlement, you will find the elf named Thulla. Give her the remedy to save her from biting the dust. In the event that you don't have a cure with you, take a stab at visiting the closest dealer. Cure is an extremely normal thing in the game.

From Thull you will get another journey - Save the Grymforge Elves. The appreciative dwarf will provide you with the Boots of Speed, which the Duergar is searching for by the boats on the shore.

Defeat the Duergar Intruders

In the Mykonid province, on a huge mushroom stands Sovereign Spaw. You will get a mission from him - Rout the Duergar Interlopers. He will request that you dispense with the Duergars from Underdark ocean side.

Go to the ocean side and assault the dwarves. At the point when the fight begins, more adversaries will show up. The most grounded adversaries will be on the seventh level.

One of the diminutive people will drop the Exterminator's Hatchet, which bargains a ton of harm from toxic substance and fire.

Get back to the mushroom province and talk with the Sovereign Spaw. As a prize, you will get an Emissary's Talisman, and he will open a mystery space for you situated in the province close to the broker Derryth. There will be a few parchments and a Sad remnant of Menzoberranzan protective cap. There are a ton of mixture fixings close to Drowa's body, and you will likewise track down the book Flumph Mating Customs. Peruse the book and take the capacity check to get to know the mystery of the fashion.

Selunite Outpost

In the event that you got to Underdark through the station, hold on until the sculptures at the gate kill the minotaur. If you have any desire to get inside the station, you can project the Fly spell on yourself and attempt to bounce in through the open window.

At the point when you're inside, shoot the stone on the sculpture which radiates light. The sculptures at the gate will be deactivated. Then, open the gate with a lockpick and let the remainder of the group in.

In the chest by the campfire, you will track down the ideal stuff for the Paladin, the Protective cap of Destroying. In the excess chests there will be some gold, Hoodlums' Endlessly apparatuses for incapacitating snares.

Spectator

Spectator is a boss in BG3, which can be experienced in more than one way. It's ideal, in any case, to stand up to him in Underdark, close to the Selunite Station. This is the way to stir something up with the boss.

Not a long way from the station lies a few froze drows. Assault one of them to stir the Spectator.

To acquire a benefit over areas of strength for the, we suggest situating the group insightfully and beginning the battle remaining on the gallery of the station.

Spectator has many strong assaults and can play out a few activities in his turn. Assuming that your group is essentially level 4, you ought to rapidly manage him utilizing supernatural bolts. The crushed rival will drop the Spectator's Eyes jewelry, which has the spells Beam of Dread and Injuring Beam.

Phalar Aluve sword

Between the Selunite Station and the Mykonid province, you will track down a sword in the stone. To eliminate it, you should pass a strength or insight check and penance a couple of drops of your blood. The long blade Phalar Aluve is an artfulness weapon managing 5-14 harm 4 cutting harm.

Minotaurs

In Underdark, you can meet a couple of Minotaurs. A battle with these monsters ought not be excessively troublesome in the event that your group is basically level 4.

Assuming you utilize the section to the underground from the Whispering Depths side, you can promptly experience 2 Minotaurs. During the battle, ensure all characters in your group are not standing excessively near one another. Minotaurs can take a long leap and assault a few rivals immediately.

Bulette

A tremor? No, it's simply one more boss in BG3 - Bulette. You might experience this unusual beast between the Whispering Tree and the ocean side in Underdark.

Bulette can abruptly leap out of the ground and immediately thump down a few colleagues. The beast has a durable armor and can undoubtedly evade most assaults.

To overcome the boss rapidly, position all colleagues in the four corners of the front line so that each character assaults him from an alternate side. Utilize the most grounded spells, for example, Sorcery Rocket and Toxic substance Beam.

The crushed foe will abandon the Bloodguzzler Clothing, the ideal dress for a brute.

Festering Cove

If you have any desire to find every one of the insider facts of Underdark, you should visit Rotting Inlet. You won't track down numerous significant things there, however you can turn into a divine being for a happy pack of fishfolks!

A secret way prompts the inlet, not a long way from the spot prompting Auntie Ethel's cottage. First, shoot every one of the snares, then get around the mushrooms to the opposite side and slip the stone.

A discussion with the occupants of the bay can be led in more ways than one. You can battle with them and their 'god' or haggle with their chief and get the Sickle of BOOOAL from him.

There is likewise a third, considerably more pleasant choice - after a fruitful capacity check, you could be guaranteed as the new lord of fishfolks! Sounds great? This should be finished:

- For this discussion, pick a person with the best insight and mystique.

- Toward the start of the discussion, you need to pass a programmed Nature check.

- Pick the first exchange choice where you charge their bogus god.

- Take the picked capacity check for influence, strength or insight.

- At the point when the deception vanishes, pick the first discourse choice and get some information about the power.

- Pick the first exchange choice once more and say you will kill him and take the power for yourself.

At the point when you rout the redcap, the fishfolks will guarantee your personality as their new god. Also, that is all there is to it. Sadly, you won't get any extraordinary compensation for this, and you likewise won't track down such a large number of important things in the cove, with the exception of a couple of shells and starfish. Also, fish, obviously.

The main thing that could in any case show you the bay is a message in a container. Do you recollect the little Tiefling that could be saved from the nags on the ocean front in Druid Woods? Presently you understand what the kid was doing there. Doni sent a letter to his dad, expressing that he desires to see him in Baldur's Gate.

Grymforge

In this BG3 guide, you will figure out how to overcome Grymforge and complete demonstration 1. We clear up how for free Evident Soul Nere and how to eliminate the rubble. We portray the mission to save the dwarves in the manufacture, the way to the Firm Produce and where to track down Mithral mineral. Toward the finish of the page, you will track down tips on the most proficient method to overcome Grym and how to help the Reviled Priest.

Grymforge

You will get to Grymforge utilizing the boat secured on the ocean front in Underdark. To utilize the boat, you will first need to finish Find the Missing Boots journey. On the other hand, you can battle the Duergars and assume control over their boat.

In the manufacture, you will find a lift prompting the exit from the Underdark to the Shadow Reviled Terrains, the area that starts act 2. To rapidly complete demonstration 1, subsequent to entering the manufacture, travel east to the lift where a couple of Duergars are standing.

Grymforge is partitioned into a few districts, including 2 Waypoints.

- Grymforge - here you will begin investigating the manufacture. In this area you will open the journey Free Obvious Soul Nere and complete the mission Save the Grymforge Elves.

- Old Fashion - here you will find the entry to the Firm Manufacture and the things expected to produce inflexible armor and weapons.

- Utterly unyielding Fashion - here you will confront major areas of strength for a, Grym, and you will actually want to produce inflexible armor and weapons. Here, you will likewise find a baffling neckband connected with the mission Help the Reviled Priest.

After you leave the boat, Morghal will move toward you, requesting installment for entry. Pick the second discourse choice to go to the fashion without paying. You are currently ready to investigate this region freely.

Free True Soul Nere

Subsequent to showing up at the manufacture, you will be ship off Thrinn. Assuming you have the boots that were taken from her, you can return them now. During the discussion, you will figure out that Nere was detained by rubble in a noxious room. In the event that he isn't delivered soon, he will pass on. Consent to help in eliminating the stones.

If you have any desire to free Nere, you really want to pick up the pace. Investigating the manufacture for a really long time or venturing out to the camp over and over again will propel time fundamentally, and Nere will bite the dust from the harmful gases. So you ought to finish this journey first and ensure you have sufficient wellbeing, as this mission includes an avoidable battle subsequent to eliminating the rubble. At the point when the rubble is eliminated, you will actually want to pick who to overcome -

partner with Nere and rout the defiant dwarves or kill Nere and his brethren.

If you have any desire to free the little persons and pick the great side, you should kill Nere. At the steps, you will meet Brithvar. Converse with him and let the man know that you likewise need to dispose of Nere. The bantam will help you in the battle assuming you first dispose of the suspending circle watching the region. In any case, you should do this unobtrusively and without witnesses, if not you will be gone after or placed in jail. At the point when you get found out, you can likewise attempt to pay off the watchman.

Move toward the sphere. When the sphere begins following you, draw it to an isolated spot and assault. One exact shot or a solid spell ought to kill it in a flash. Let Brithvir know that the undertaking is finished. Presently you can deal with eliminating the rubble.

To obliterate it, you will require an option that could be more grounded than standard explosives. Connect with the dwarves and pass the ability check to listen in on their discussion. Let them know that Tulla sent you and proposition your assistance. Consequently , you will get the area of Philomeen's hideaway.

Open the little metal entryway in the eastern piece of the manufacture's most minimal floor.

Go to the furthest limit of the room and press the button on the wall on the right side. In the mystery chamber you will discover a few explosives.

Go now to the enormous entryways close to the assemblages of dead dwarves. Enter inside and take every one of the important things from the tables - you can sell the flatware at any vendor. On the left half of the chamber you will track down a button that opens a mysterious section. Follow the passage until you track down the huge entryways. Continue to travel through the rubble until you arrive at the steps where a gathering of foes will go after you.

Go up the steps and continue onward forward. Get around the gap and enter the hideaway through the entryway or circumvent the wall and track down an opening in it.

During a discussion with the little person, you will actually want to do an expertise check to convince her to give you the Runpowder vial. You can now get back to the rubble and free Nere.

Get back to the rubble and spot Philomeen's vial close to it. You can likewise put other hazardous materials. When you do this, the little persons will ease off to a protected distance. Do likewise and hit the vial with a fireball or another searing shot.

Move toward the blast site and hang tight for the cut-scene. Pick which side to take:

- Assuming you pick Brithvara and the little persons, you will battle with Nere and his cronies. As a prize, you will get Nere's gear and you will be all ready to remove his head to convey it to the Mykonid settlement in the Underdark.

- In the event that you pick Nere, you should overcome the defiant dwarves. What's more, as a prize, he will give you a fledgling. This situation won't help the elves.

Before you start the battle with Nere, furnish one party part with the Ring of Psyche Protecting, gave you got it subsequent to finishing the Assist Omeluum with researching the Parasite journey in the Underdark.

In the battle with Nere, you should overcome him and 6 Duergars. Assuming that you've recently concurred with Brithvar, you will get 6 partners for this fight. Center around overcoming the fundamental rival and the mages, who will frequently project mind control spells.

Subsequent to winning the battle, discharge the elves during the discussion with Brithvar. On Nere's body, you'll track down a Wrecked Moonlandern, a fledgling in a container, Deteriorating Night Walkers, a knife and a Blade of Shouts that bargains additional corrosive and mystic harm.

Save the Grymforge Gnomes

In the event that you saved Tulla, the elf you met in the Underdark, she gave you a journey to save the elves in the manufacture.

Converse with Beldron in the wake of killing Nere and shield the elves from Brithvar. You will get a little installment and discover that one of the elves, Wulbren, has been taken to the Moonrise Towers. You can offer them help and meet them later in act 3.

Deliver Nere's Head

In the event that you finished the Loss the Duergar Gatecrashers journey in the Underdark, in the wake of overcoming Nere, cut off his head and convey it to the Mykonid settlement. As a prize, you will get the Emissary's Special necklace.

Get Past the Rubble

You will experience a few Duergars and bulls close to the rubble. Project a discussion creature spell on yourself or drink an elixir and converse with the bulls. Persuade them to go after the Duergars. After the fight is won, talk again with the bulls and request that they eliminate the rubble.

How to deal with a trap with a burning gargoyle?

In the northern piece of the manufacture, on its upper floor, you will find a snare with a fire-breathing beast remaining behind a shut mesh. The most effective way to manage this trap is to send an individual there who has the Mage Hand spell.

You don't need to deactivate every one of the snares. In the wake of passing discernment check, you can find traps and will basically keep away from or get around them.

At the point when you get to the foreboding figure, summon a hand behind the bars and use it to pull the switch. This deactivates the beast and opens the gate.

By the foreboding figure you will find a Symbol of Shar which you can provide for Shadowheart and a chest for certain elixirs and The Protecty Sparkswall clothing.

How to get to the Adamantine Forge?

There is a stepping stool close to the snares and the fire-breathing beast. Go down and stand by the switches.

Pull the switches and hold on until a stage shows up, make one individual from your party bounce onto it. Once more, pull the two switches. Leap off the stage and go to the furthest limit of the hall.

Get around the pit and continue onward until you arrive at the steps and the following switches. On the way, look at the skeletons lying on the ground and take the Steel Molds - these things will prove to be useful in the Utterly unyielding Fashion.

Send the following individual from your party to the metal extension. Make this individual arrive at its end.

Get back to the first party part and pull the two switches. Hold on until the stage arrives at the second party part. Send them to the opposite side of the manufacture. You will track down there another Waypoint - the Old Manufacture. You can now magically transport the remainder of the party there.

Going further, you will experience 4 rivals. Rout them and go down the steps.

Hop down and pull the switch on one of the wheels to initiate the blacksmith's iron and slide.

How to defeat Grym?

Grym is a discretionary boss from the Firm Manufacture. You will arrive by going through the Underdark, making a beeline for Grymforge.

At the point when you go down to the Firm Manufacture, turn the Magma Valve. Grym will show up after the cut-scene.

At the point when you open the valve, the room will flood with magma. First, set all party individuals on round stages so they don't get fire harm.

Grym is an extremely impressive level 8 rival. Be that as it may, there are a couple of approaches to manage him without any problem.

First, to harm a Grym, he should be remaining in magma. In any case, Grym's armor solidifies, giving him assurance from each assault. Host one gathering part generally stand near the magma valve. Sometimes the magma will chill off - you should turn the valve once more.

Grym won't go after you for the first 2 turns. Then, at that point, utilize your most grounded assaults, while ensuring that your characters don't step aerobics the magma.

Grym has expanded protection from pretty much every sort of harm, his main shortcoming being beating.

Grym can play out a few activities during his turn. Nonetheless, there is a method for staying away from his assaults. Each time somebody hits Grym, they get Ideal objective status. You can utilize this for your potential benefit. Continuously assault last with the individual who is farthest away from the rival. Along these lines, when Grym begins his turn, he can not contact that individual.

One more technique to rapidly overcome Grym is to draw him to the focal point of the stage and drop an enormous blacksmith's iron on him.

For defeating Grym, you will receive the Grymskull Helm.

How to use the Adamantine Forge?

At the point when you get to the fashion and rout Grym, you will actually want to make armor or weapons.

To fashion new gear, you will require Mithral mineral and Steel Molds. You can undoubtedly track down molds in different pieces of Grymforge. There are many molds lying close to the entry to the Firm Produce.

You can track down Mithral metal in 2 spots. One of them is south of the Antiquated Manufacture Waypoint. Attempt to hit it with any weapon, or utilize a spell to smash the stone and get the mineral. The subsequent mineral is north of the Firm Fashion.

Put the Mithral metal into the iron block, and the shape into the projecting. Pull the switch to bring down the iron block and take the recently made piece of gear.

Contingent upon the form you utilized, you can make:

- Adamantine Split Armor

- Adamantine Scale Mail

- Adamantine Shield

- Adamantine Scimitar

- Adamantine Mace

- Adamantine Longsword

Think carefully about what you want to create. You will only have 2 Mithral ores at your disposal.

Help the Cursed Monk

In Grymforge, you might run over the Dim Justiciar's Diary. Subsequent to understanding it, you will open the Assist the Reviled Priest with questing.

You will track down the diary close to the skeleton, not a long way from the boat you used to get to the fashion. On the off chance that Shadowheart is in your party, looking at the body will open another exchange with the Priest.

To find the Priest, you should go to the Inflexible Manufacture. Leap toward the western piece of the area and go down the stones by the magma. Send one party part there, ideally somebody with a ton of Finesse and a reward to Skillful deception.

Continue to get around the stones until you arrive at the steps. Go up and open the chest. Keep an eye out for consuming surfaces and ejecting magma.

A Magma Natural will be watching the region close to the chest - it shouldn't go after you, we likewise don't exhort getting into a battle with it. This is an extremely impressive rival at a lot more significant level than your party.

To open the chest you need to move basically a 20 on the dice. At the point when you take the Conscious Special necklace, a cut-scene will play. Pas the Insight ability check and ask the soul for task subtleties. The priest will request that you give the special necklace to his little girl - you will meet her in act 3.

Mountain Pass

Stepping into the Mountain Pass

Subsequent to finishing the vast majority of the substance in Act 1 of BG3, the diary ought to direct you toward one of two ways: The Underdark or the Mountain Pass. To follow the last way, go to the northwestern edge of the first guide. You'll run over an obliterated extension, yet turning passed on prompts a more modest construction that will take you straightforwardly to the pass.

The game will caution you before you continue further. You'll in any case have the option to get back to the beginning guide subsequent to entering the pass. Ensure, nonetheless, to finish every one of the journeys that interest you ahead of time, as some of them will become inaccessible.

Strolling not too far off in the new region will lead you to a rune circle you can enact to open a quick travel point. The way divides in two headings right a short time later.

Assuming that you go right, you'll meet Woman Esther. She'll request that you take a Githyanki egg from the Creche further into the area. You can likewise exchange with her. Peruse this page to become familiar with the Creche Y'llek.

In the event that you're not keen on side journeys and might want to rush straightforwardly to Act 2, follow the left way after the rune circle. Be watchful, as there's a foe experience only a couple of strides ahead.

Battle against the Death Shepherds

You'll go over a gathering of hostiles: two Death Shepherds and some Ghasts. These animals are risky and have vexatious, abilities to deter. However, there's still an acceptable technique to this fight.

The Shepherds can be a serious danger even to a recently refreshed, arranged group. You ought to be essentially Level 5 preceding confronting them.

Prior to setting off the experience, you can acquire a little benefit by shooting them from stowing away.

Death Shepherds can restore their fallen partners. Not just Ghasts - they can resuscitate each other too. This can vigorously delay the fight and make it a lot harder. We in this manner suggest bringing down the Shepherds first. Without them, you won't have to stress over their revivals.

Bring them both to low HP and finish them both off one after the other. On the off chance that the enduring magician gets a turn before you kill it, it will utilize it to restore the other one.

In the wake of managing the Shepherds, the Ghasts shouldn't present a difficult situation.

The way the fight happens on is somewhat thin. Keep a battle development - your frontliners ought to hinder the way to the soft backliners.

Moving on and meeting Elminster

In the wake of managing the undead, continue onward down the left way. After a short walk, you'll arrive at a wooden scaffold and meet an old mage clad in red robes.

He'll present himself as Elminster Aumar. He'll likewise give some significant piece attached to Hurricane. On the off chance that the Wizard's in your party, he'll converse with his old coach which sets off a short plot-important discussion. On the off chance that Storm's not with you, Aumar will go to your camp and you'll have the option to see that scene once you're prepared.

In the wake of meeting Elminster, continue onward down the way until you arrive at the gate to Act 2.

Find the Githyanki Creche

On this guide page for Bladur's Gate 3 you will find a walkthrough for the Find the Githyanki Creche journey. You will figure out how to get to the Creche and how to attempt to eliminate the parasite.

Quest objectives

- Find the githyanki patrol.

- Find the githyanki creche.

Walkthrough

After arriving at the pass in the northwestern piece of the guide, you will experience a githyanki watch. Conversing with the watch chief triggers a battle, paying little mind to which exchange choices you pick.

After the battle, search the pioneer's cadaver (ideally with a high person Knowledge) and take the emblem. At the point when you pass the Arcana expertise check, you will gain proficiency with the area of the Githyanki creche.

Go to the mountain pass and move toward the turning wheel displayed in the above picture. At the point when you figure out how to pass the Strength expertise check, you will actually want to utilize the gondola to move the party close to the Broke Sanctum.

You can enter inside in more ways than one, in any case, we propose a mysterious passage in the precipice (you can open it with a lock pick) set apart in the image above - it is situated under the primary entry. You will arrive by going down the stones.

At this stage, it's great to have Lae'zel in your party - she will improve in every one of the discussions.

After entering, pick the passage displayed in the image above. At the point when you get to the crossroads with an image in the center, follow the way on the left and you will go directly to the hospital.

Talk with the githyanki specialist, then utilize the machine to attempt to dispose of the parasite. Assuming you permit Lae'zel to sit in the seat, you will acquire an extra endorsement level.

You don't need to attempt to save Lae'zel, in light of the fact that the endeavor to eliminate the parasite will end in disappointment at any rate. It's smarter to utilize this second to construct a relationship with the Warrior, so attempt to energize her.

Act 2

Reach the Moonrise Towers in BG3

This page of our manual for BG3 highlights an itemized walkthrough on the most proficient method to arrive at Moonrise Towers. We clarify where for track down the Moon Light to securely pass through the Shadow

Reviled Terrains. We portray how to save Isobel at the Last Light Motel and how to converse with Jaheira.

Shadow Cursed Lands - Underdark entrance

To arrive at Act 2 from the Underdark, go to Grymforge. Enter the lift the two drinking Duergar were once holding on. After the lift ride, you'll wind up in a destroyed sanctuary.

In the focal point of the sanctuary there's a chest - open it, you could utilize its items later on. Go higher up and proceed ahead until you meet a Fatigued Voyager. Converse with him - having Hurricane in your party opens extra discourse choices.

After some short discourse, you can take him straightforwardly to camp. Assuming you so want, you can request that he sit tight for you there all things being equal. No matter what your decision, you won't miss this discussion. Subsequent to conversing with the more bizarre, Hurricane will need to converse with you as well - do so and return to the overworld. Search the close by body and leave the sanctuary.

You'll wind up in the reviled lands. You want a steady light source to securely cross it. You can utilize standard lights or the Light cantrip. The Blood of Lathander mace will likewise prove to be useful, assuming you've figured out how to procure it in Act 1.

Without a light source, the revile will progressively hurt your party until you bite the dust.

Continue to go on until you arrive at a scaffold. You can converse with Shadowheart here, in the event that she's in your party.

Go across the scaffold to before long set off a cutscene, and afterward a fight. Assuming Hurricane's in your party, don't attempt to run before the fight - he will not support.

You'll confront six shadows - they're impervious to most harm beside Brilliant. They can likewise turn imperceptible in obscurity - spells, for example, Moving Lights and Sunlight will uncover them. In the event that you have a Priest in your party, the Soul Watchmen spell ought to make this battle paltry.

After the fight, follow the Harpers to a place of refuge. You can detect a dead raven en route - clicking it sets off a battle.

Assuming that you might want to end the fight rapidly, trigger it subsequent to projecting Soul Watchmen.

Continue onward forward until you arrive at a stone scaffold. You'll meet Jaheira - a druid, here to kill the evil at Moonrise Towers.

She gets going antagonistic and suspicious, however you can alter her perspective on you.

Assuming that you've saved Mol before by saving her companion and finishing her journey, she'll vouch for you.

One way or the other, you can either clear up everything for her or abstain from replying. No matter what your decision, you'll have full admittance to the Hotel. There are a few recognizable countenances here, like Alfira, Mol and Dammon. Talk with the Harper Officer by the scaffold and Dammon - both are selling some valuable stuff.

Whenever you're finished, enter the structure, converse with Jaheira, then, at that point, to Isobel.

Last Light Inn

After a cutscene you'll be tossed into a fight. There are numerous adversaries, who will more often than not center down Isobel. Keep her alive no matter what.

On the off chance that Isobel falls before you rout every one of the foes, the whole Hotel will turn unfriendly and everybody inside will kick the bucket. It will not be simple, yet whenever you're finished, converse with Jaheira to proceed with the journey.

After the fight, you can head towards the Moonrise Towers. After leaving the region, a Harper will request that you join a snare against a gathering of cultists, who can some way or another travel through the reviled lands solid. Concur, follow him to the trap site and plan for another fight.

How to get a Moon Lantern?

Before you can arrive at the cultists' nest, you should secure the apparatus they use to travel through the haze. In the event that you've saved Isobel, the Harpers will lead you to the snare site. On the off chance that the Hotel fell, notwithstanding, you'll have to think that it is all alone - make a beeline for the eastern piece of the guide, to a demolished side of the road house - the cutscene ought to set off naturally.

The fight against the guard is troublesome. The Drider frequently projects Asylum on himself, keeping you from going after him, while the Orc can project Fireball - focus on him.

After the fight, scan the Drider's carcass for the Moon Lantern, setting off a cutscene. You can deliver the pixie inside or keep her there - notwithstanding, you'll acquire insurance from the revile, allowing you to arrive at Moonrise Towers.

Moonrise Towers

Subsequent to clearing your path through the revile, you can now arrive at the faction's hideaway. You can generally move here however you see fit visit two of the brokers here (three, on the off chance that you haven't killed the halfling at the troll camp). They make them interest things in stock.

Go to the fundamental corridor to meet Ketheric Thorm. He'll pass judgment on a gathering of trolls for their disappointment. Their destiny ultimately depends on you - killing them will redirect doubt from yourself.

After the cutscene, go higher up and converse with Z'rell - don't attempt to go for an Insight check, it will set off a battle you can't win at the present time. Consent to find Balthazar at the Thorm mauseolum, go to his room and take the lantern. You can likewise peruse his notes and take one of the hearts on the table. Move toward the shelf and snap the books in the upper right corner. This enacts a platform, on which you should put the heart.

You'll open a mystery room. In the event that Storm's in your party, tapping the circle on the work area will set off some extraordinary exchange. Persuading Hurricane to utilize the dim enchantment here might actually madden Mystra later on, however will net you a tainted lantern that could prove to be useful later on.

Gauntlet of Shar in BG3

In act 2 of BG3 you will find the Excellent Mauzoleum, which will lead you to the Gauntlet of Shar. In this aide, we clear up how for find the Ketheric Thorm's Artifact and how to pass the trials in the Antiquated Shar Sanctuary to track down the 4 Umbral Jewels. We clarify how for manage Yurgir and Balthazar and how to track down the Nightsong and the Lance of Night.

How to obtain the Ketheric Thorm's Relic and solve the puzzles in the mauzoleum?

After showing up at the cultists' central command in the Moonrise Towers in act 2, go to the Thorm Mauzoleum - before you enter it you will meet Raphael, who will tell you not to deliver the animal inside for any reason. Finish the discussion with him and head inside.

Its an obvious fact that the Thorm's Catacomb is related with Shar, Shadowheart's goddess - to benefit from this string, you ought to host her in your gathering.

Peruse Thorm's journals found in the rooms, then continue forward. A little riddle looks for you - you really want to press the buttons properly aligned. Divide your characters and snap 'Moonrise Towers', 'Despondency' lastly 'General' - the gates to the further piece of the area will open. Utilize the lift.

Continue to go on until you arrive at a colossal corridor with a sculpture of Shar in the center.

Your errand here is to bring down four censers utilizing the switch. There are four switches in the four corners of the room. Actuate them and afterward quench every one of the consuming censers in the room.

This will uncover a way to the gem in the center - enact it and pass through the gate forward to the following room, where you can connect with the skeletons.

Pick the discourse choice in which you say that you were sent by Z'rell, and afterward plan to battle with the gatekeepers of the vestiges. Skeletons will be your partners - center assaults around the dark circles that call extra foes, and manage the rest a short time later.

When the fight is finished, move toward the system situated at the front of the room and collaborate with it. Shadowheart ought to have additional exchange choices here.

To continue further, you want to finish Shar's trials and gather the 4 Umbral Diamonds tracked down in the area.

How to deal with Yurgir and get 1st Umbral Gem?

Head right from the focal area - you will see a monster that looks like a dark jaguar.

You can follow it or attempt to go around - you will rapidly see that you can collaborate with the characters experienced here.

Yurgir is the adversary referenced by Raphael. Assuming you followed the puma, you will actually want to associate with it and look further into the historical backdrop of this spot. Assuming you've chosen to circumvent it, you'll see the trap early and have the option to begin the battle based on your conditions.

Conversing with him will uncover that he has an agreement with Raphael. After a fruitful Understanding roll, you will actually want to pick one of the two new choices - you can control him to kill his troopers, the jaguar, lastly himself, or you can scan the area for data.

The first choice is a lot quicker and permits you to get the Diamond immediately. The second requires going to one more piece of the sanctuary. To free the evil spirit from the agreement, then keep looking for the jewels until you see as every one of the three and afterward stand before the lift.

Whenever you have acquired 3 diamonds, go down two times from the spot of the last trial. Search for the pentagram on the ground and light a candle close to it. A rodent will show up - cooperate with it. You can consent to its arrangement, however at that point you should control the devil or battle him. The favored choice is to battle the rodent and its copies.

The most ideal way to win the battle is to have a Pastor with the Soul Watchmen spell in your party - rodents will naturally run towards you, venturing into the spell and biting the dust on the spot.

After the fight, a cut-scene will begin with the main enduring cleric of Shar.

Battling him is unavoidable, and overcoming him will at last break the evil presence's agreement. Get back to Yurgir - you will see a cut-scene in which Raphael shows up. After it's done, you will actually want to get a pearl.

The Soft Step Trial - 2nd Umbral Gem

The first trial is situated by the principal hall. Open the first entryway and snap on the Shar's landmark to make an offering. The objective in this trial is to slip inconspicuous past the gatekeepers to the furthest limit of the room.

Nonetheless, before you do that, you need to find the critical in the focal part, which opens the gate toward the end.

Subsequent to completing the trial, take the jewel and continue to the nearby found close by.

The Self Same Trial - 3rd Umbral Gem

The following trial requires crafty, as you will confront your appearance. They have similar things and capacities as you, yet they likewise have a couple of extra abilities that you don't have. You can't send your partners back to the camp, so you're compellead to battle as a four-individuals party. Begin sneaking, save the game and go into the room. After entering the first steps, make an Insight expertise check - in the event that nobody succeeds, load the game. Any other way, you will be surprised - this can rapidly prompt a wipe, contingent upon the strength of your party.

Assuming that you have passed the test, continue sideways staying away from the adversary's field of vision.

On the off chance that you have a Rebel in your party, target somebody who can be wiped out quickly with a Sneak Assault. Additionally make sure to polish off clones with their firsts. All in all, Storm should bargain the last catastrophe for Hurricane's clone - any other way, he will get a revile. Clones can vanish into the shadows - utilize the Light spell to uncover them - very much like with shadows and phantoms on a superficial level. After the battle is finished, get the exceptionally uncommon ring and jewel, and utilize the instant transportation gadget to get back to the start of the room. Then, head down the steps.

The Faith Leap Trial - 4th Umbral Gem

Pick the entryway straightforwardly inverse and plan for the trial, which, regardless of appearances, is paltry. You should stroll down an imperceptible way and essentially there are two choices for following through with this job.

The first choice is to retain the format of the way that is just before the Shar's landmark.

The subsequent choice is to utilize the Fly spell, on account of which you won't actually need to follow this way.

Moreover, assuming that you set up the camera in the correct manner, you will see the quietly framed plates. Simply make sure to hop on the last stage toward the finish of the way, rather than strolling, as your personality might follow some unacceptable way and pass on.

After arriving at the end, take the diamond and return to the hallway.

Spear of Night

Go to the library. To arrive, you need to go down the steps close to the immense sculpture. The library is close to The Confidence Jump Trial. Pass through the hindrance on the entryway and dispense with the circle in the middle, which projects an emanation of quiet. From that point forward, rout the leftover adversaries. Recollect that utilizing the Sunshine, Moving Lights, or Light spells makes your foes lose protection from most harm types.

After the battle is finished, incapacitate the snares and search all the shelves. Track down the book "Lessons of Misfortune: The Nightsinger". At the steps, you will track down a button - press it to open the gate to the following room. Put the book you tracked down on the rack and go to the last room. As Shadowheart, get the Lance of Night and search the room.

Balthazar

Magically transport yourselves to the Waypoint Gauntlet of Shar and go west. The way will lead you to the undead skeletons. You need to battle them. This fight works similarly - dark circles gather rivals, and they, at the end of the day, have protection from harm when they are uninformed. Rout them and converse with Balthazar. You can help out him to break into the complex or kill him here. Battling him will be a test, but with a decent party, you ought to have the option to deal with him - overcoming Balthazar at this stage might make future successions simpler for you.

Ketheric Thorm's Relic - Nightsong

When you procure every one of the 4 pearls, return to the Gauntlet of Shar Waypoint, and afterward head to the primary special stepped area. Place one of the jewels, step onto the stage and head down. At long last, communicate with the following special stepped area and spot the leftover three jewels. Pass through the gate, and afterward to the blue water.

Note! This is the place where occasions on the planet are pushing ahead. On the off chance that you haven't done the side missions on a superficial level, it merits returning and doing them now.

You are in the space of the goddess Shar - you should advance toward the finish of the area, bouncing on islands drifting in the air.

Toward the finish of the area you will track down Nightsong - an Aasimar who was detained by Balthazar and is the wellspring of Ketheric's everlasting status. In the event that you've worked with Balthazar, you will presently have a discussion with him and conceivably a battle. Be that as it may, assuming you have killed him, you will quickly complete the mission with Nightsong.

Assault Moonrise Towers in BG3

Subsequent to meeting the Nightsong and obtaining Ketheric Thorm's artifact in BG3, you'll have to attack Moonrise Towers. We depict the fight against Thorm and clarify how for secure partners for the finale of Act 2 - Isobel, Jaheira and the Harpers

Allying with Jaheira

In the wake of looking through the Gauntlet of Shar and finding the Nightsong, it's at long last chance to overcome Thorm and the Religion of the Outright. In the wake of leaving the sanctuary, converse with Shadowheart assuming that she's in your party. Get back to camp and take an extended rest. Then, quick travel to Moonrise Towers and converse with Jaheira.

It's the ideal opportunity for a fight. Assuming you've neglected to safeguard Isobel, you'll be all alone, making it significantly harder. Jaheira will join your party, being of extraordinary assistance.

Assuming you have the Harpers with you, the battle ought to be sensible. On the off chance that it's simply Jaheira, you'll have to go through every one of the stunts your sleeve to win. Use oils, parchments and projectiles. Wild Shape in every case completely reestablishes Jaheira's wellbeing, making her a great tank. Zero in on Z'rell, then, at that point, on the sharpshooters on the wooden bars above. On the off chance that you've helped the gnolls in a side mission, they'll battle next to you.

After the fight, converse with your partners and go higher up, setting off another fight. Kill the adversary spellcaster first. Assuming you've neglected to safeguard Isobel, there'll be one more adversary here as well. In the wake of beating them, go up to the roof.

Fighting Ketheric Thorm

You'll confront Thorm in a cutscene - you can attempt to persuade him you'll have pity, or assault out and out. This decision might matter later on. Rout Thorm's cronies. The pioneer will get away from once his wellbeing gets sufficiently low. After the cutscene, finish the battle.

Search the cadavers and enter the empty tower. This will take you to the Psyche Flayer Province.

As you clear your path through it, you'll ultimately arrive at a lift, prompting the last fight against Thorm.

Dive on the lift and stroll through the gate - this triggers a cutscene and a discussion with Thorm. On the off chance that you completely inspected his room, attempted to offer him kindness and saved Isobel, you can persuade him to give up. This skirts the whole first phase of the battle.

In any case, get ready for a challenege - Ketheric is undying for however long Aylin is contained. Your essential goal is to save her and take out Thorm's cronies.

The boss himself isn't excessively undermining at first. Kill the Psyche Flayer prior to aiding Aylin, as it can overwhelm her and carry her to its side. Subsequent to killing the Psyche Flayer, bring down the leftover flunkies and Thorm himself.

Overcoming him sets off a cutscene and begins the subsequent phase. You'll confront the Missionary of Myrkul, impervious to cold, poison and necrotic harm. Projecting Scramble on your essential harm seller ought to burst him down rapidly.

End of Act 2

Overcoming the Missionary triggers a cutscene. You'll address the Fantasy Guest and leave the region with another goal - go to Baldur's Gate, kill Gortash and Orin, then, at that point, take their Netherstones restricting the crown.

Subsequent to conversing with your partners, make a beeline for the passage at the west of the guide - go to Baldur's Gate to complete Demonstration 2.

Wake Up Art Cullagh

This page of our manual for Baldur's Gate 3 makes sense of how for awaken the secretive man finally Light Hotel and enroll Halsin as a party part. We make sense of what for do and where to go.

Wake Up Art Cullagh - side quest walkthrough, Baldur's Gate 3

You'll get the mission in the wake of addressing the man presented underneath. He's finally Light Hotel, close to Advisor Florrick you might have saved in the past demonstration. Analyze hm and converse with the lady overseeing him. You'll become familiar with he's spent quite a while in the Shadowfell, the domain of Shar, and was investigating the Place of Recuperating.

Get back to the camp - you can converse with Halsin. After a short discussion he'll go to Endure Light Motel.

Converse with the Druid again there and travel south to the Place of Mending.

Assuming Marcus figured out how to grab Isobel and Last Light fell, cast Speak With The Dead on Marcus' body. This will definitely accelerate the journey and skirt the Place of Recuperating.

On the manner in which south you might go over a few particular remains - be cautious, there's a trap here. The adversaries can limit your characters and magically transport, so trust you've passed that Insight check.

You'll ultimately arrive at one of the extensions prompting the intensely reviled region. In the event that you haven't gotten the Pixie's approval or the Drider's lantern, turn around to get them. You will not get far in any case.

Assuming you possess the ability to move freely inside the revile, continue. At the focal square you'll confront a few twisted Harpers. It ought not be excessively extreme. After the fight, follow to the mission marker.

You'll track down the entry to the Place of Mending at the directions X:- 189 and Y:- 19. Go into the House and glance around. Assuming you've saved Arabella from Kagha in Act 1, her questline go on here. Helping them sets off the journey "Save Arabella's Folks", which you can find out about here.

Subsequent to looking through the rooms, rest and make a beeline for the primary corridor where you'll find one of the Thorms, occupied with giving an ungodly talk on medication and Shar.

You can skirt the fight against Malus Thorm and his medical caretakers by prevailing at the discussion. To boost your possibilities, have a Minister converse with him. Having a Poet in your party will likewise allow you to utilize Bardic Motivation on troublesome skillchecks. In the event that you fizzle, prepare for a difficult fight - Malus can undoubtedly kill characters with a solitary hit, while his medical caretakers can cause Loss of motion. It's way simpler to Convince him to off himself and the medical caretakers.

Notwithstanding the way that you've managed him, search Malus' carcass and take the lute. Get back to Endure Light Motel and converse with Halsin.

Play the lute to awaken Craftsmanship Cullagh. You've finished the mission "Wake Up Craftsmanship Cullagh", opening its subsequent journey, "Lift the Shadow Revile". Completing it will allow you to enroll Halsin as a party part.

Lift The Shadow Curse in BG3

Following finishing the responsibility Wake Up Workmanship Cullagh's, you will get the mission Lift The Shadow Revile. You'll figure out how to lift the revile and enroll Halsin - you should finish this mission, or he won't join the party and will leave in act 3.

How to prepare for the portal defense?

Take an extended rest and go to the lake, where Halsin is pausing. Have a Minister in your party, like Shadowheart - they'll prove to be useful in the forthcoming battle.

How to defend the portal with Halsin?

Converse with Halsin and get ready for the fight to come - you should safeguard the entryway for four turns. The foes assault in waves, however there's just a single way to the entryway - through your party. Have your Minister projected Soul Watchmen and pick Brilliant harm - it will be important in this battle.

Place the Priest in the way towards the entrance and cast Soul Gatekeepers. As presented above, fighters and bowmen generate in the upper left corner - use AoE spells to manage them, for example, Fireball, Mass of Fire or Glyph of Warding.

After the fight, watch the cutscene. Gather the amazing measure of plunder dropped by the crushed adversaries. Get back to camp and converse with Halsin.

In the wake of conversing with Halsin, you can at last add him to the party. Presently you can begin looking for Thaniel's final part. Make a beeline for the area presented underneath - organizes X:61 Y:22.

How to defeat Oliver?

Go into the house and converse with the child.

Assuming Halsin's in the party, he'll let you know that is the child you're searching for. Let him know you know what his identity is, then, at that point, pursue him through the entryway.

You'll confront Oliver in the focal square. You want to obliterate the hindrance that protects it. This is finished by overcoming adversaries - center totally around them.

After the battle is finished, convince the child to join with Thanial. Get back to camp and converse with Halsin. Thaniel will make sense of there's something final he wants for lift the revile - the death of Ketheric Thorm.

Find Arabella's Parents in BG3

You'll get this journey from Arabella, in the event that you've saved her from Kagha in Act 1. You'll track down the young lady close to the Place of Mending, near the gate.

Find Arabella's Parents - side quest walkthrough, Baldur's Gate 3

You'll track down Arabella at facilitates X:- 152 Y:14. Converse with her to set off a cutscene. Let her visit at your camp and manage the two shadows.

Then, go into the Place of Recuperating and make a beeline for the conservative.

Converse with the undead nurture there.

You'll track down Arabella's folks - dead. You can trick the medical caretaker, opening her as a trader. Get back to camp and convey the awful news to the young lady.

Punish the Wicked in BG3

While investigating the land in act 2, you might go over a baffling mythical person who passes judgment on a departed lady. Tolerating his journey implies assisting him with passing judgment on the lady, who he blames for awful violations. On this page, we clarify where for track down the mythical person and how to settle the journey.

How to find the notebook?

Make a beeline for this region - the directions are X:115, Y:104.

Converse with the mythical person and consent to help him. He'll request that you go to the refinery and track down the charged's confidential note pad. The refinery is close to Moonrise Towers, so you can't finish this mission until you figure out how to travel through the revile.

Assuming you've proactively done that, quick travel to Moonrise Towers and head towards the mission marker.

When you're inside, you'll set off a discussion with the landlord - an individual from the Thorm family.

Assuming you might want to effectively prevail here, ensure the main person's great at Execution, Skillful deception and Constitution saving tosses.

You should dispose of the owner before you can get to the journal. You can simply go after him, however he's a troublesome enemy, similar to all Thorms viewed as here. Then again, you can converse with him all things considered. Thisobald takes a taste in the wake of passing checks. His third taste will be excessively and he'll explode, killing him easily. You'll have to prevail at five skillchecks - two social ones, and three saving tosses/Skillful deception.

The troubadour in this particular circumstance generally enjoys benefit on Execution checks - it merits recollecting that!

Subsequent to overcoming Thisobald, move toward the featured board, take the scratch pad and return to the mythical person. Converse with him and partake in his custom.

You can compel the denounced to regulate equity to herself, break her intellectually or excuse her. The first and third choices will turn the mythical person threatening, setting off a battle. The subsequent will fulfill him - he'll give you his gloves, which let you gather a raven, finishing the journey.

Act 3

Rivington

Act 3 is the most extensive and open of all demonstrations. Many undertakings interpenetrate with one another, and the storyline gives players numerous choices for taking care of issues. In the accompanying aide, you will track down data on finishing the Rivington locale in Act 3 and completing the side journeys from here.

Talking with Yenna

You start the act on a mountain path - move forward.

You will go over a redhead young lady with whom a cutscene will begin. You can overlook her or offer assistance - in the event that you consent to assist her, she with willing briefly join your camp.

Talking with refugees

Continue on until you arrive at the outcast contending with the powerful. The discourse will behave.

You can attempt to pursue the outcasts away or help them, the choice depends on you - recollect that assuming you attempt to help the displaced people, you might need to battle the strong's guardians. No matter what the arrangement, go into the house and track down the lid to the storm cellar.

Open it with the key from the first floor or with Skillful deception. Head inside - keep an eye out for traps - and make a beeline for the finish of the room. Search all that and read the notes on the table. One of them will naturally begin the Investigate The Dubious Toys journey you can learn about it later in the aide.

Leave the structure and head towards the displaced people - converse with the forlorn man from the image above - this will move the Shadowheart journey 'Little girl of Murkiness' forward.

Side quests

Right now, you can investigate the region and track down a couple of extra side undertakings.

- Settle the Open Hand Sanctuary Murders begins in a sanctuary on the fundamental street.

- Find Missing Letters can be begun in the mailing station working close to the scaffold - it merits having Hurricane in your group while following through with this responsibility.

- Investigate Cazador's Castle is given to you by the beast trackers on the slope - it merits having Astarion with you for this discussion.

- Assist the Devilish Bull with canning be tracked down close to the entry to the area, close to the enormous outbuilding.

- Find Spills the Jokester begins in the carnival.

- You start the Vindicate The Ironhands mission in a cavern, which you enter from the waterway side.

- Find the 'Harsh Administrator' Ffion is accessible in Sharess' Touch.

- We depicted every one of the above journeys on discrete pages in our walkthrough.

How to solve a murder case?

Head towards the city until you find out about the homicide of Duke Stelmane.

Purchase a paper from a child and enter the sanctuary where an exchange is occurring between a Halfling and a flying elephant named Valeria.

After it closes, begin a discussion with the Halfling - you will discover that Lorgan's dad was killed.

Continue to the room where his body is found, and afterward converse with the attendant. After this, cast Talk with the Dead on the dead dad of Morgan. You will learn more insights regarding the homicide.

Then, search for the trapdoor with a blood stain close to it and go through it.

Investigate the area. You can finish the side journey Help the Reviled Priest from Act I here. Search for a break between the stones in one of the rooms and afterward go through it.

Search the new piece of the area and battle with the doppelgangers. In the wake of overcoming the rivals, you'll track down an edge on a heap of rubble. To uncover it, make an Insight check.

Return to the Halfling , then, at that point, go across the extension. Enter Sharess' Stroke and address the lady by the entry, who will allocate you the assignment: Track down the 'Harsh Curator' Ffion.

Talking with Raphael

Then, go higher up and converse with Raphael - you will have the amazing chance to advance in the Free Orpheus, Help Kith'rak Voss, and The Githyanki Champion missions.

Assuming you consent to help out Voss, it will really intend that, eventually, the Head will turn into your foe, so it is savvy to confound him subsequent to leaving Raphael (assuming that you've consented to his course of action) and lie to Voss so the Ruler thinks nothing.

Disregard the above issue on the off chance that you don't have Lae'zel in your group or didn't visit Rosymorn Cloister during Act I.

Searching for a journal

Get back to the room with Raphael and go into the room nearby looking for the diary.

Then, hop onto the contiguous roof.

Stroll around it and go into the room through the overhang. Search it and you will find a rundown of homicide focuses as well as a body under the bed. Gathering the rundown of targets opens the Dazzle the Homicide Council story journey and pushes the Investigate the Killings story mission, which you began in the wake of purchasing a paper, forward.

Get back to Sharess' Stroke and converse with Valeria. Show her the cutting edge and the rundown of homicide targets - she will give you a pass to the city and furthermore suggest proceeding with the undertaking in the principal part of Baldur's Gate.

Talking with Gortash

Then cross the extension and show your pass. The robots from Steel Watch will stop you, and Gortash will make you a proposition. Go to the crowd with him at the watchtower, then start the discourse.

You can consent to his agreement, reject him, or attempt to go after him here - the battle is irrationally troublesome because of the robots here, which are extremely difficult rivals, so following one of the other two options is better.

From that point onward, leave the watchtower and head into the city. The first piece of Act 3 is finished.

Confront the Elder Brain

Confront the Elder Brain is a mission that finishes the game - it drives straightforwardly to the consummation, so assuming that you have a few side journeys left, don't begin it. If not, on the accompanying pages of the aide, you will figure out how to finish the Confront the Elder Brain mission and finish Baldur's Gate 3.

Initiating the task

Get back to Bhaal's Sanctuary and head the other way - a way you haven't investigated at this point.

You will arrive at a boat - get in it and a cutscene will be shown.

Then, go on along the way. There aren't many side ways here, so continue onward forward. In the long run you will arrive at the snare site - rout the adversaries. They shouldn't represent a significant danger to you, regardless of whether you are surprised.

Continue to move until you meet Gortash. Converse with him.

Confronting the Elder Brain

Follow him until a cutscene begins. The Netherbrain will show up before you in the entirety of its greatness, and your assignment will be to assume command over it. Passing the ability check will bring down HP in the forthcoming battle with the Netherbrain - aside from that, it makes no difference.

After the cutscene is finished, converse with the Sovereign who saved you.

How to save Orpheus?

He will propose to you to turn into an Illithid yourself to overcome the brain. On the other hand, you can give him the stones to cause him to do it without anyone's help. At long last, you can free Orpheus gave you have the Obscure Sledge - you could get it from Raphael on the off chance that you made a settlement with him or on the other hand on the off chance that you've taken it from the Place of Trust. In this walkthrough, we will save Orpheus.

Pick the last exchange choice - the Head will let you be, and you will actually want to free Orpheus. Assault two red stones, and afterward a cutscene will be set off.

During it, you should choose - it is possible that you will allow Orpheus to transform into Ilithid, on account of which he will control the Netherbrain, or you will do it without anyone else's help. After this, pass through the entry to Baldur's Gate to get done with the last responsibility - Annihilate the Elder Brain.

Consider Gortash's Bargain

You get this journey when you arrive at Wyrm's Stone. During the crowd, Gortash will propose a collusion to you. You can consent to the collusion with him, incite a battle, or recommend that you will unite with Orin. From this piece of the aide, you will figure out how to direct the remainder of the discussion.

Expecting that you have consented to combine efforts with Gortash, you can proceed with this mission solely after getting Orin's Netherstone.

After the battle with Orin, go to Gortash, who is in Wyrm's Stone. Converse with him and don't give him the stones - he will test you. Subsequent to persuading Gortash to participate, make a beeline for the Morphic Pool.

Destroy the Elder Brain

Obliterate the Elder Brain is the last assignment in the game. Finishing it drives straightforwardly to the finale and end credits. On the accompanying aide page, you will figure out how to finish the fundamental journey while staying an Ilithid.

How to gather a team?

Baldur's Gate is on fire, and you are its just expectation. Orpheus, who is a priest and can project a helpful fireball, is joining your party. Push ahead and converse with Voss - he will be extremely thankful to you for saving Orpheus and will loan you his solidarity in the battle against the foe.

Continue on until you enter the structure. A cutscene will set off in which the ongoing partners will pronounce their help.

- Volo will assist you with his insight - this is conceivable assuming that you've saved him from the irate crowd in the city.

- Valeria offers backing to the city watch - she will help on the off chance that you didn't kill her during the Homicide Court experience.

- Astarion may have the option to bring Animals of night into fight assuming that he has finished the custom in Cazador's Prison.

- The Peculiar Bull will assist you with its change capacities assuming you have carried him to the city.

Besides, you will track down a shipper here - stock up on elixirs and other essential things for the battles since there will be a lot of them in front of you.

How to get to the Netherbrain?

Push ahead - in front of you will be an immense square, where perhaps of the greatest fight in the game looks for you. Before you start it, attempt to climb the tower close to the gate on the right.

Begin the battle from that point. You can utilize the Call Your Partners choice to gather a strong region assault or essential partners. No matter what the choice, wipe out the rivals individually until you arrive at the gate.

Move to one side - another battle will begin briefly. This time, you will likewise need to deal with region assaults of the Nautiloid, which bargains around 30 to 50 fire harm toward the finish of the turn. Keep away from the undeniable regions and furthermore dispose of foes while remaining moving.

At last, you'll arrive at the highest point of the tower, where you'll have the option to move to the Netherbrain.

Take a brief reprieve or drink an elixir that makes a comparative difference. Set up your elixirs, in light of the fact that the last battle in the game looks for you.

How to defeat the Elder Brain?

You want to arrive at the Crown of Karsus and enchanted claimed by a person changed by Illithid. In the interim, your group should manage the four Dream Gatekeepers, who have a few control impacts like Appeal, Incapacitate, and Stagger. Furthermore, the Ruler with the red mythical beast will join the battle assuming that you have chosen to free Orpheus.

Toward the finish of the area, you will likewise find four Ilithids who cast an Enchanted Rocket each turn, managing around 50 harm.

On the off chance that you are playing on the most minimal trouble level and your group is portable, simply overlook the rivals and go to the Crown as fast as could really be expected. Use spells like Cloudy Step or Layered Entryway, and when you arrive, let the person changed into Ilithid cast command over the Crown of Karsus.

On the off chance that you play at higher trouble levels, the matter gets a smidgen more troublesome. Kill the Sovereign first assuming that you freed Orpheus, overlook the mythical beast, and have your quickest character go to the four Ilithids toward the back and dispose of them since you won't keep going long. Subsequent to disposing of about portion of them and the Head, you can abandon somebody to serve as an enticement for the leftover adversaries. In the event that any of your partners kicks the bucket here, it doesn't make any difference in light of the fact that after you rout the Netherbrain, they will be naturally restored, including Orpheus.

Go through the entry - you really want two characters who can bargain harm, ideally from a good ways.

The Netherbrain each turn will obliterate the stages where characters that have finished their turns are. Remain together and bounce from one to the next as you complete your activities. Once per turn, the Netherbrain will project a region assault that makes a one move and arrangements harm, yet on the off chance that you have a high Constitution trait, you can counter this impact. No matter what the strategy, you will ultimately kill Netherbrain.

End of the game

A cutscene will be shown, adding your achievements and permitting you to pursue a few choices connected with your buddies. For this situation - it's the way you will be recalled by individuals of Orpheus, the destiny of Lae'zel, or more all, the destiny of your personality transformed into an Ilithid. After so much, you will get another short cutscene with Shrivels, and at the end, after the credits, a scene with Raphael.

Find the Missing Letters

Find the Missing Letters is a side journey in Baldur's Gate 3, which you can finish rapidly, and as a prize, you will get some gold.

How to find the letters?

You get the journey from a diminutive person in the mailing station working before the sanctuary. You can haggle with him to get compensated ahead of time - yet it really doesn't make any difference.

In the wake of tolerating the journey, take Hurricane to your party and go to the Open Hand Sanctuary on the roof.

Bounce down to the lower level from the sanctuary tower and converse with Hurricane's Tressym.

Persuade it not to chase pigeons and afterward take the lost letters - you can understand them assuming you like. Notwithstanding, recollect that this may adversely influence the mission. Then, return to the midget and give him the letters and you will get a prize.

Find the Stern Librarian Ffion

'Find the Harsh Bookkeeper Ffion' is a side mission in Baldur's Gate 3 connected with the principal storyline. On this guide page, you will track down the answer for the assignment - how to arrive at the carcass and track down Ffion.

How to find Ffion?

Acknowledge the undertaking from the lady close to the entry at Sharess' Stroke. Then, go through Raphael's room and bounce onto the roof.

Stroll around the structure and hop onto the overhang. Open the entryway, search the room and associate with the carcass under the bed. Project the Talk with the Dead spell on it.

You've recently tracked down Ffion - you can get back to the lady in Sharess' Stroke and turn in the mission.

Investigate the Murders

Investigate the Murders is a story mission from Baldur's Gate 3 which straightforwardly prompts getting one of Orin's Netherstones. On this page of our aide, we give a walkthrough to this mission.

Initiating the task

The errand starts in Lower City region of Baldur's Gate. Make a beeline for the Elfsong Bar.

Head inside, converse with the owner to purchase a room, then go up the steps telling that you've been sent by Valeria. Converse with the halfling and offer her your assistance.

Get back first floor and converse with the midget. Caution him and consent to assist with his rodent issue.

Proceed until you arrive at an enormous room where you'll have to confront githyankas sent by Vlaakith.

Defeat them - **focus on appearing portals then on the enemies**. After the area is clear, approach the wall at the end of the room - there is a button behind the statue.

Search the new room.

Conversation with Orin

After appropriately looking through the room, you'll finish Visit the Ruler's Old Refuge journey. Turn left and leave by means of underground passages. You will go over a sidekick of yours, however it ends up, its Orin. She will illuminate you that she has seized one of your colleagues and you have brief period to save him - presently you can assist Orin with killing Gortash or attempt to get her without help from anyone else.

End the discussion and leave the sewers - you'll be back here, yet first you want to do one thing on a superficial level. Make a beeline for the point set apart on the guide as the Wine Celebration - converse with Cora Highberry and lead the discussion towards the wine. The wine ends up being harmed, and this will set off a fight - in the wake of overcoming all rivals, converse with Cora once more and you'll get a prize. Go to Facemaker's Shop (facilitates: X:- 189, Y:- 33).

Head inside, and a cut-scene will be started.

When it closes, a battle against the shapeshifters will be started - rout them and search the bodies. You will track down a pack with cut off hands and data about their safe-house.

Go to the safe-house - you will have to divert close by occupants - you can do it through Minor Deception spell. Open the locked entryway, yet save your advancement prior to entering.

Check out the room and complete an Influence check. Assuming that it falls flat, reload your save and rehash until you pass it. Communicate with the secret passage and say the password which you've tracked down in Dolor's notes.

As of now, consider doing a rest, as difficulties look for you.

Fighting Sarevok Anchev

Subsequent to resting, head inside and move ahead until you experience three Death Knights.

Show them the hands you took from Dolor and they will open the nearby. This is the second when you will meet quite possibly of the most requesting rival in the game - Sarevok Anchev. Search beneath for the quickest approach to managing him utilizing Otto's Powerful Dance spell.

Before you start a discussion with Sarevok, ensure you have first in class hardware and a decent party composiiton. Strong spells like Arcane Lock, Otto's Overpowering Dance, or Tissue to Stone will divert this battle from extremely challenging to inconsequential.

Before you start the battle, lead one of the party individuals to the entryway where Death Knights are found. Not long before the exchange that starts the battle, get this person to project Arcane Lock on the entryway - this ought to be sufficient to eliminate these three in number rivals from the battle. Next in the line is battling Sarevok - he is an extreme foe, yet conceivable to overcome. Assuming you have Dark Opening spell, use it on Sarevok and three spirits, then, at that point, utilize an area of impact spell to kill them. At long last, cast Otto's Compelling Dance spell on Sarevok and finish the battle.

Search the rooms, gather Talisman of Bhaal and save Valeria. Presently, Investigate the Murders and Intrigue the Homicide Council missions ought to be finished.

Get Orin's Netherstone

Getting Orin's Netherstone is just conceivable assuming that you figured out how to dazzle the Homicide Council. On this page of our aide, we tell the best way to get Orin's Netherstone by taking out Murder Council.

How to get the Netherstone?

Go to these directions in Undercity Remnants - X:- 139, Y:934, and cooperate with the locked entryway. Say that you've butchered the Homicide Council, and you'll be allowed in.

Go ahead and prepare to battle. In the event that you are here straightforwardly subsequent to battling with Sarevok, make sure to take an extended rest. In the event that the related Discernment check is fizzled, battle will be started with you being trapped by the adversaries.

Your objective in this fight is to take out the rival from the above screen capture - in the event that you don't figure out how to do this inside five turns, you will confront a party wipe. Recall that he has a capacity to invalidate first five occasions of getting harm.

You can stay away from the wipe by remaining farther than 55m from the foe.

Subsequent to overcoming the adversary go on down until you arrive at the entry to Sanctuary of Bhaal.

Open it with Ornament of Bhaal and enter.

Keep going down and cooperate with Orin at the special raised area.

To keep Orin from killing the casualty on the Special stepped area of Bhaal, you'll need to pass a beware of one of 3 potential interactive abilities.

The battle with Orin is more straightforward than the one with Sarevok, yet requesting. The six cultists that go with Orin will project support spells on the foe and what is more regrettable, they are resistant, as they have super durable Safe-haven cast on them. Notwithstanding, they can be pushed and moved - use spells like Thunderwave and Hurricane as well as things, for example, Bolt of Thundering Thunder that additionally push when struck. In the wake of dealing with six irritations, kill Orin - she shouldn't represent a danger.

Gather her Netherstone and pick the variant for the following piece of the journey - either go to Gortash to make a settlement with him or kill him and take his stone. The choice depends on you.

Help the Devilish Ox

Help the Devilish Ox is a side mission in Baldur's Gate 3 you ought to consider doing as the creature can help you later during the last fight.

Helping the Ox

This undertaking is gotten from an Ox that is in a pen on a bluff. Converse with it and consent to assist him with getting past the city gates.

Generally, you need to do no extra activities next to acquiring section to the primary piece of Baldur's Gate town. When you enter Lower City, the errand will be finished, and you'll get a ring and a note as remunerations, as well as the capacity to call the Ox to help you during the last fight - the Ox will take an alternate structure.

Solve the Open Hand Temple Murders

Settling the homicide secret in Open Hand Sanctuary is a side journey in Baldur's Gate 3 that is associated with the fundamental storyline. On this page of our aide, we show where to find the body and the rundown of homicide targets.

Conversation with Lorgan

To start the undertaking, converse with the halfling in Open Hand Sanctuary.

Continue to the room where his body is found, and afterward converse with the medical caretaker. After that utilization Talk with the Dead on Father Lorgan's body (more on this point On the most proficient method to converse with talk with dead? page of the aide). You will learn more insights concerning the homicide.

How to find the list of murder targets?

Search for a trapdoor with a blood splatter close to it and enter it.

Search for a gap between rocks in one of the rooms and go through it. Search the new piece of the area and battle the doppelgangers. Subsequent to overcoming the rivals, you'll track down a sharp edge on a heap of rubble. To uncover it, make an Insight check. You will likewise find a blossom key.

Return to the halfling, converse with her, and afterward continue to Sharess' Stroke through the room where Raphael is found.

Leap to the close by roof then, at that point, circle it and enter the structure through the overhang.

Search the room - you'll track down a rundown of targets and a body under the bed. Gathering the rundown of targets opens the Intrigue the Homicide Council story journey and pushes Investigate the Murders story mission forward.

Get back to Sharess' Stroke and converse with Valeria. Show her the cutting edge and the rundown of focuses to be killed - with this, the mission is closed.

Gather Your Allies

Here you will track down a rundown of all partners in BG3 and how to get them. Keep perusing if you have any desire to know how to begin the last fight ready and what mission or individual choices you want to make to enroll the assistance of every conceivable individual/groups.

How to gather allies?

During your experience in BG3, you'll meet a great deal of free NPCs and strong groups. The story decisions you make that influence the experienced people will affect the finale of the game. Individuals you left cheerful or that met their objective might turn into your allies that will remain close by in the last fight.

The Assemble Your Allies mission starts in Act 3, when you learn of the genuine risk to the universe of Faerun. By finishing side journeys or making a special effort during investigation to assist characters, you'll with getting their appreciation and backing once you want it. In the event that an individual vows to assist you in the battle, they with willing be added to the rundown of allies in your diary.

All allies and how to make them join in BG3

Here is a rundown of possible allies in BG3. If it's not too much trouble, note that you can not enlist every one of the characters recorded underneath in one playthrough, as which characters choose to help you relies upon the choices you make en route. For instance, on the off chance that under Astarion's tension you kill Yurgir in Act 2, he won't be accessible as a partner later.

- Battle-Ready Owlbear - during Act 1, kill the mother and spare the small Owlbear. Next, save it from goblins and invite to your camp. Take care of him at the camp for at least 3 nights.

- Dammon: save the Tieflings in Act 1 and don't let Isobel be kidnapped in Act 2. Dammon will join as an ally only if the Owlbear is in your camp.

- Arabella: rescue Arabella from the druids in Act 1 and find her parents in Act 2. Invite her to your camp and agree that Withers takes care of her.

- Volo: free Volo in the goblin camp in Act 1 and help him again in Act 3.

- Halsin : free Halsin in the goblin camp in Act 1 and recruit him to the party. Additionally, complete Lift the Shadow Curse quest in Act 2.

- Barcus Wroot and Wulbren: rescue Barcus in the Blighted Village and free the gnomes from Grymforge in Act 1. Help Wulbren in the Moonrise Towers in Act 2, and then in Act 3, broker a peace treaty between Wulbren and the Gondias with the help of Barcus.

- Nightsong: save her in Act 2. In Act 3, stand by her side against Lorroakan.

- Isobel: don't kill Nightsong and make sure Isobel survives in Act 2. In Act 3, do not ally with Lorroakan.

- Lorroakan: save Nightsong in act 2, then betray her by siding with Lorroakan.

- Rolan: help the Tieflings in act 1 and free them in the Moonrise Towers in Act 2. Find Roland in Shadow Cursed Land and send him to Last Light Inn. In Act 3, ally yourselves with Nightsong against Lorroakan.

- Yurgir: don't kill him in Act 2. In Act 3, complete the Helsik ritual and enter the House of Hope. Speak with Yurgir before the fight with Raphael and pass the DC30 test to temporarily add him to your team.

- Inspector Valeria and The **Watch**: solve the murder case in Act 3 and save her from Bhaal's followers.

- **Florric**: Save her from dying in Act 1 and 2, then free her from imprisonment in Act 3.

- Mizora: free Mizora from the Mind Flayer colony beneath the Moonrise Towers in Act 2 and let her stay in your camp in Act 3.

- Jaheira's Harpers: recruit Jaheira to your party in Act 2 and complete The High Harper quest in Act 3.

- Duke of Ravengard: complete Rescue Duke Ravengard quest and Wyll's side quest.

- Vampire Ascendant Astarion: Let Astarion complete the ritual and become a full vampire in Act 3 and kill the Gur hunters.

- Ulma and Gur: don't let Astarion complete the ritual in Act 3 and free the enslaved people.

- Strange Ox: complete the Strange Ox quest in Act 3.

- Viconia DeVir: don't kill Nightsong in Act 2 and make sure Shadowheart leaves Shar and becomes a Selunite. During Act 3, take Shadowheart to House of Grief and betray her by allying with Shar cultists.

- Orpheus: obtain the hammer from Raphael by allying with him or by breaking into his estate. Do not let the Emperor or anyone else eat the brain. Free Orpheus using a hammer.

- Bhaal's Slayer: Kill Orin in Act 3 and accept your destiny as Bhaal's Chosen. If you've chosen Dark Urge as your background, becoming Bhaal's Chosen will be easier.

Investigate the Suspicious Toys in BG3

While investigating Rivington in Act 3 of BG3, you will go over the Investigate the Suspicious Toys journey. In this aide, we make sense of how for find Arthur Gregorio's home and open the entryway at Felogyra's Fireworkshop.

Where to start the quest?

The mission "Investigate the Suspicious Toys" begins subsequent to exploring the chest with toys in the outbuilding east of the Rivington quick travel point. Converse with the watchman at the entryway and persuade him to give you access.

Be careful with the watchman watching the structure. Sit tight for him to get to the opposite side of the room and incapacitate the chest trap by passing a Smoothness really look at DC20. At the point when you inspect the items in the chest, a gatekeeper will move toward you. Persuade him that these are not your explosives.

Leave the animal dwellingplace and look at the Gift Record book lying on the table close to the watchman. From the notes you will discover that the toys were given by Arfur Gregorio.

Where to find Arfur Gregorio?

Arfur's home is close to the horse shelter where you found the toys chest. Talk with individuals contending before his home. You will figure out that the property was taken over by displaced people.

During the discussion, inspect Arthur's considerations. After effectively passing the Insight check, you will discover that the man is concealing something in his storm cellar. Propose to him that you will remove the exiles from his home.

At the point when you go into the house, go straight and actually take a look at the room inverse the entry entryway. Subsequent to passing the Insight check, you will find a portal to the storm cellar.

There will be a lot of traps in the storm cellar. Separate one person from the remainder of the party and completely search the room by hopping over or keeping away from traps. Open the chest by the work area and read the letter. You will figure out that Arfur is being coerced by somebody.

Get back to Arfur and let him know what you've found and request replies. After effectively passing the Appeal check, Arfur will educate you regarding Felogyr's Fireworkshop, situated in the Lower City. He will likewise give you a Confirmation Pass to the city.

How to get to the top floor in Felogyra's Fireworkshop?

At the point when you arrive at the Lower City, go to the Fireworkshop situated in the southeast piece of the guide. While conversing with the merchant, persuade him you were shipped off the shop by Gortash or utilize the mysterious password from Arfur. Avery will allow you to go to the upper floor.

Open the metal entryway close to the watchman and go up the steps. The following gatekeeper won't let you to the last floor. You need to sneak in there by drinking an imperceptibility mixture or assault the watchmen.

On the highest level, you will confront a gathering of rivals. In the event that you assault them, every one individuals from the shop will join the fight. There are a ton of explosives and barrels in the room. You can utilize them to rapidly take out adversaries.

Eventually, you can look through the whole structure and go down to the storm cellar. There will be a great deal of traps in the cellar, so be cautious with each step you take.

How to save Vanra

Subsequent to arriving at Lower City in Act 3 of Baldur's Gate 3, you can start and finish Save Vanra mission. Peruse on if you have any desire to figure out how to find what you're searching for in The Becoming flushed Mermaid and find the witch's refuge. Moreover, we assist with getting Vanra out from Auntie Ethel's paunch and how to overcome the witch at last.

Initating Save Vanra quest

The mission will be started during a discussion with Lora in Basilisk Gate Military enclosure in Lower City. Get some information about the subtleties of her little girl's vanishing. The path will lead you to The Becoming flushed Mermaid motel.

The Blushing Mermaid

Continue to the motel set apart on your guide. Converse with the man at the bar. Bosun Gannet will send you to Chief Grizly, who is on the upper floor of the motel.

Converse with Skipper Grizly and get some information about Lora. At the point when he offers you cash to make Lora dissapear, decline to gain proficiency with the genuine character of the lady.

Shock! Chief Grizly will end up being Auntie Ethel. The witch will concede that she snatched the child and assuming you attempt to kill her, the young lady will bite the dust with her.

At the point when the witch vanishes, a fight against 6 Redcaps will follow. Rout every one of the rivals and return to the bar proprietor. Close to the counter there is a way to the cellar, from which you can get to the witch's hideaway.

Getting Vanra out of Auntie Ethel's stomach

You can't kill the witch immediately assuming Vanra is to be saved. For the young lady to make due, you should first concentrate her from Auntie Ethel's stomach. There are two methods for doing this:

- You can connect with the witch in battle, diminish her wellbeing focuses to 1 and thump her oblivious. Then you can remove the young lady of the witch's midsection.

- On the other hand, you can utilize a unique mixture that will make the witch upchuck the young lady. The recipe for Witch's Curse (the elixir you want) can be gotten during Assist the Witch Survivors with questing.

Help the Hag Survivors

Converse with Zena before The Becoming flushed Mermaid bar. In the event that you get some information about Vanra, the lady will say that a gathering concealing in one of the houses at the docks is behind the seizing.

Go to the house displayed in the screen capture above and pick the lock on the entryway. On the work area, you will find an ousting notice. Subsequent to perusing the note, the Assist the Witch Survivor with questing will be started. In the house you'll likewise track down a letter from Kled, from which items you'll discover that individuals who resided in the house moved to Old Garlow's Place.

Old Garlow's Place is southeast of The Becoming flushed Mermaid. At the point when you go into the house, Adrielle and her allies will confront you. Persuade them that you at last need to kill the witch.

Assuming in Act 1, you've helped Mayrina (Save Mayrina mission), you'll meet her on the second floor of Garlow's Place. If you ressurected her significant other and gave the wand back to Mayrina, he will likewise be there.

Mayrina got changed into a sheep. At the point when you endeavor to converse with her, she will just mumble about a baffling doll.

Break the spell on Maryina by obliterating 2 dolls. One is at the steps, the second at the work area toward the finish of the room. A discussion with Jatlo will start, trailed by battle.

Peruse the letter found on Jatlo's body and converse with Mayrina, she will give you a prize - Staff of Interference.

Go ground floor and view as the safe. Take 2 books and Dried Fey Blossom. Peruse the journal to become familiar with the recipe for Witch's Blight. Create the required mixture and continue to Auntie Ethel's safe-house available from The Becoming flushed Mermaid.

How to find Auntie Ethel's hideout?

There are wooden steps prompting the basement close to the landlord. In the basement, you really want to finish a Discernment check to find a mystical entryway - this is the very deception that you've experienced in Teahouse in Act 1.

When you find the entryway, turn the camera so the cursor is on its opposite side and snap anyplace. Your party ought to have the option to move beyond the deception securely.

Progress forward to the following room and rout a gathering of foes. You can astonish them to acquire a benefit in the fight. You can likewise attempt to slip into the witch's refuge undetected and try not to battle them.

How to kill Auntie Ethel?

The battle with Auntie Ethel will be basically the same as the past confrontation. The witch will utilize deceptions and make clones. Notwithstanding, this time she will have extra assistance. Each time you kill Ethel, sorcery mushrooms will resurrect her.

Prior to battling the witch, furnish yourself with outfits or drink mixtures that offer toxic substance obstruction. Additionally ensure that you have See Intangibility parchment or spell.

Begin with saving Vanra. Thump the witch oblivious and eliminate the young lady from her body or toss Witch's Blight at her. At the point when the child is protected, you can polish off Auntie Ethel.

First and premier, manage the 3 mystical mushrooms. Each mushroom recovers its wellbeing focuses completely during its turn, so you want to annihilate it totally inside your turn. Thus, it merits concentrating of the whole group on a solitary mushroom. Whenever mushrooms are annihilated, begin going after the witch.

Mushrooms are impervious to toxic substance and skirmish assaults. The most ideal way to rapidly dispose of the mushrooms is by utilizing fire spells.

At the point when the enchanted mushrooms are obliterated, you can deal with Auntie Ethel. Her deceptions require simply a solitary hit to be scattered. On the off chance that your group is around levels 9-10, you shouldn't have a real problem in this battle. Center your assaults around the genuine witch and immediately end the battle.

On Ethel's body, you will track down the Corellon's Effortlessness weapon, Ring of Feywild Ignites and Discolored Appeal accessory. In the close by chest, there is a touch of gold and 2 bolts.

Presently you can return to Mayrina and tell her that the witch has been at long last crushed. You will get the Fey Semplance Talisman from her as a prize. Remember to visit Lora and Vanra as well. The young lady's mom will provide you with the Ornament of Windrider and the Duellist's Privilege weapon as a prize.

Puzzles

Myrnath and the Talking Brain - Nautiloid

On this page of our Baldurs Gate 3 aide we tell the best way to continue in the wake of experiencing the talking brain Us locally available the carrier Nautiloid. You will likewise figure out how to make the Keenness Devourer join your party.

Encountering Myrnath in the Prologue

- The talking brain can be experienced not long after starting the Introduction occurring locally available the carrier Nautiloid. At the point when in the subsequent roundabout chamber, analyze the southern region. You'll experience Myrnath, a casualty of investigations.

- In the wake of looking at Myrnath, a talking brain called Us will confront you. He will request that the legend discharge him.

Destroy or preserve the talking brain?

- Two choices here are obliterating or securely eliminating the Astuteness Devourer. Obliterating the brain is the least demanding choice here - just pick the ideal decision from the rundown.

- The subsequent choice - eliminating the brain - requires effective consummation of a few Expertise and Capacity Checks. These are - Examination (analyzing the brain), Medicine(careful expulsion of the brain), Strength (breaking the skull to eliminate the brain) andDexterity (cautious extraction of the Keenness Devourer) Different Checks might seem for example in light of class or Proficiency of the legend.

- Assuming that you have effectively taken out the brain, you can pass a discretionary Expertise checkto ruin it.

- On the other hand, you can leave the talking brain in salvageable shape.

Recruiting Us as a companion

- In the discussion that follows, you can permit the Mind Devourer to join the party, reject it, or assault it.

- Whenever selected, the talking brain helps in battle all through the preamble and arriving at the extension, as he is outfitted with hooks.

- The brain will bite the dust because of occasions of the finale of the Introduction, and that implies you start Act 1 alone. He will not show up in the future.

Closed chest - Nautiloid

On this page of our *Baldurs Gate 3* guide we show **how to open Elaborate Reliquary, a chest encountered during the course of the Prologue** taking place onboard the airship **Nautiloid**. You'll learn **where to find the key** as lockpicks are of no use here and what the chest contains.

Where is the chest?

- **Elaborate Reliquary** is one of the first locked containers found in the game.

To find it, you really want to arrive at the northern room of Nautiloid. This is similar room with the control center with 3 buttons and people held in cases.

Assuming you definitely dislike finding the compartment, hold ALT to feature intelligent articles nearby.

Where is the key to the reliquary?

- You can't open the chest with lockpicks - a key is required. Advance toward the eastern room, which investigation is completely discretionary.

- Find an intelligent body - one of them will have Gold Key on it. When you got it, return to the holder. Open the chest - the legend will naturally match the key.

Contents of the chest

The Elaborate Reliquary contains:

- gold'

- Onyx - a valuable stone that can be sold to a merchant later on.

Prisoners in pods - Nautiloid

On this page of our Baldurs Gate 3 aide we answer the inquiry whether during the Preface you can free Shadowheart and others held in the cases. This is significant data since it includes attempting to select a potential colleague.

Location of Shadowheart

- During the Preamble you'll get an opportunity of investigating the northern room. Inside the room, there are units with individuals caught by Psyche Flayers. In one of the units, you can track down Shadowheart, and freeing her has need as she can join your party once delivered.

- In the wake of looking at the case, you can converse with the minister, which will prompt an acknowledgment that to open the unit, straightforward connection will not do.

- Assuming you've moved an abhorrent person, you can leave Shadowheart in the unit and this won't bring about her death.

How to open the pod with the cleric?

- From the room with the units, go to the discretionary eastern room.

- You really want to find a thing - hold ALT to feature all intuitive items nearby. There is a body here that has Eldritch Rune in its stock.

- Gather the thing and return to the past room. Close to the case with the priest there is a control center - connect with it.

- Pick the choice to put the rune in a free space.

- You can quickly put your hand on the control center or complete an Arcana Check to intently inspect it.

- The first choice includes an Insight and Ilithid Check. Effective culmination of the checks will open the unit with Shadowheart. You can now welcome the priest to your party(or on the other hand, decline) and she will help you during the following clashes of the Preface.

In the event that you've bombed the Check and can't rehash it or you would rather not free Shadowheart presently, you'll meet her by and by during Act 1 in Congested Remains.

Prisoners from the remaining pods

In a similar room there is a subsequent control center controlling the units with residual detainees. The control center has 3 fastens and squeezing them make various impacts:

- Squeezing the left button (1) makes no difference.

- Squeezing the center button (2) will free certain individuals from the units. They will be heavily influenced by Psyche Flayers and will go after the group. The battle against these NPCs is easy, however there aren't any exceptional profits for it (you'll get a pitiful 1 encounter point).

- Squeezing the right button (3) will prompt the death of those in the cases.

How to enter Overgrown Ruins

On this page of our Baldur's Gate 3 aide, we show different approaches to getting to the Moist Sepulcher which is the inside of Congested Vestiges. Investigating this prison is one of the first assignment you get during Act 1 of the campaign. We depict 4 potential approaches to entering Damp Sepulcher.

Map of all entrances to Overgrown Ruins

The Overgrown Ruins are located to the north of the beach and to the east of the Nautiloid ship ruins. Consult the above map to view 4 main entrances to the underground part of the ruins. These are:

- **The beach door** - Entrance 1 on our map.

- The Chapel door - Entrance 2 on our map.

- Hatch east of the ruins - Entrance 3 on our map.

- Hole in Chapel floor (initially not accessible) - Entrance 4 on our map.

Entrance 1 - Beach

- Begin by arriving at Congested Destroys quick travel point. It is experienced soon after beginning Demonstration 1 and leaving north. Around here, you might experience Shadowheart on the off chance that you haven't freed her from her case during Preamble (assuming you enlisted her there, she will awaken on the ocean front close to the hero).

- This way to the vestiges is locked and going after them won't assist with anything. You should have Hoodlums Instruments and furthermore pick a legend with created Skillful deception for this errand. The ideal possibility for this is Astarion, who can be enrolled west from the vestiges and crashed carrier.

- The entryway drives directly to Wet Sepulcher.

Entrance 2 - Chapel

- The remnants of a Chapel are north from the quick travel point yet to contact them, you really want to come nearer from the west. In a similar area, you'll experience a gathering of thieves, and you can:

- Assault the crooks. We suggest astonishing the rivals so the group will land a couple of strikes beyond turn request. You can likewise drop a balancing object on the foes (favoring this in the Entry 4 portrayal).

- Persuade the thieves to leave. You can play out this through a couple Expertise Checks (Influence, Terrorizing, Trickiness, or Warrior check). Pick the Check that the drove legend has a ton of focuses in.

- After the fight or fruitful influence, arrive at the northern entryway of the demolished Chapel. Communicating with the entryway will start a discussion with a thief on the opposite side of it. You can:

- Pass an Expertise Check (of course Execution and Misdirection are accessible) Effective passing of the check will cause the watchman to open the entryway.

- Use Cheats Apparatuses - fruitful passing of the connected check will open the entryway.

- When inside the chapel, you will have to overcome the watchman. Additionally, in the Chapel's cellar there is one more gathering of thieves.

- Presently you can zero in on tracking down the mystery switch (screen capture) - it is taken cover behind the sculpture lit by daylight, to find it you want to finish a Discernment check. Pulling the switch will open a pathway which prompts Moist Tomb.

Entrance 3 - Hatch

- For this entry you need to follow the way east from the Chapel ruins that follows the edge of the precipice. En route you'll need to descend to a lower level.

- At long last you ought to arrive at a hatch displayed in the screen capture above. The hatch is locked - you really want to utilize Hoodlums Devices and effectively complete a Check.

- The hatch, presently open, will permit you to get to Dank Crypt.

Entrance 4 - Hole in the chapel's ruins

- This the main access to the Crypt that isn't noticeable from the very begininng. Arrive at the remains of the chapel that we portrayed for Entry 2.

- You can see a draping stone block over the thieves - we mark it in the screen capture above. Utilize any went assault to raise a ruckus around town.

- The struck block will separate and tumble down killing the two thieves and make an enormous opening in the floor.

- Rout all excess thieves nearby and after the effective fight, communicate with the opening. This is one more conceivable access to the Dank Crypt.

Chest near the Owlbear Nest

On this page of our Baldurs Gate 3 aide, we tell the best way to open a Plated Chest situated in one of the side passages of Owlbear Nest. Opening the chest requires the fruition of a little riddle including finding and perusing a request sheet and underneath we supply a total answer for the issue.

Location of the Chest and Selune's shrine

- The Plated Chest and Selune's Place of worship are objects that can be found in Owlbear Nest. This is a discretionary area from Act 1 of the game.

- The principal access to the Nest is situated in a woods west from Druid Forest and upper east from Cursed Town - we show it in the screen capture above.

- After entering the Nest, don't follow the primary street prompting the Owlbear, yet all at once go west.

- You'll experience a chest (we show it in screen capture above). Opening the chest customarily will mean getting serious harm. The chest is gotten with enchantment and lockpicks won't help here.

Finding the prayer sheet

- You really want to leap to a rack close to the sanctum - pick bounce from extra activities and the opposite side of the gap as the arrival spot.

- Pick the party part with most elevated Insight and look at the region behind the hallowed place.

- Fruitful fulfillment of a Discernment check will uncover a Selunite Petitioning heaven Sheet. Press RMB and decide to get it.

Reading the prayer sheet

- Get back to the plated chest and spot the legend who has the sheet near it.

- Open the stock and decide to peruse the items in the sheet, which is a request. Assuming you were adequately close to the chest the otherworldly atmosphere will be dissipated. You can now open the chest securely.

Contents of the chest

The chest contains:

- Idol of Selune;

- Moondrop Pendant;

- Selunite Rite;

- Bloodstone;

- Silver Necklace.

- Additional note - if you are traveling with Shadowheart, the cleric may warn you against plundering the chest and will oppose the action.

- You can solve this in two ways - **either send the cleric back to camp** before opening the chest or **complete one of Skill Checks** (Insight, Intimidation, Persuasion) to convince her to back down.

Stone slabs with runes - Emerald Grove

This page of our manual for Baldur's Gate 3 contains an answer for the stone rune chunks puzzle. You'll track down it in one of the offices of the Emerald Woods. Settling the riddle opens a secret vault.

Reaching the runic statue in the Enclave Library

- Emerald Woods is one of the areas tracked down in the Druid Forest. You'll find the entry in the focal piece of the town, close to the sculpture around which the druids have accumulated. Visiting this region is essential for the primary mission Eliminate the Parasite.

- Go to the adjoining Druids' Chambers and converse with Nettie. During the discussion, let her in on about the fledgling in your mind. Nettie will request that you follow her and open the mysterious passage to the Area Library.

- Finish the discussion in any capacity - we've portrayed it in additional detail on the Nettie and the cure page.

- You ought to ultimately end up in the library with a stone sculpture and four rune platforms (presented above), with the way to the Emerald Woods actually open.

- There are three runes around the sculpture. The fourth one, Rune of the Wolf, is missing, and you'll require it to finish the journey.

How to get the missing Rune of the Wolf?

- The missing rune is held by Rath, a NPC in the principal room of the Emerald Forest (presented previously).

- One method for getting it is to pickpocket him. Save the game and pick your trickiest person, like Astarion. Enter covertness, sit tight briefly (for instance, while the wolf is leaving) and pickpocket him. Remove the rune from Rath's pocket. Quickly get away from the druid, as he can in any case see the robbery and confront you. Hang tight for him to complete his hunt.

- The subsequent way is by a wide margin the most obviously terrible one, as it requires killing everybody in Emerald Forest. This could be a truly challenging fight and it will keep you out of certain missions. After the fight, you should track down Rath's body.

- Assuming that you're experiencing difficulty surprising Rath, you can utilize an intangibility elixir. You can buy one from Auntie Ethel.

- The third way is to find and safeguard Halsin. As an update, he's being kept locked down at the Troll Camp. We've depicted how to free him on the Halsin page in the Partychapter.

- Subsequent to getting back to the Emerald Woods, converse with Rath. He'll compensate you with the rune.

On the off chance that you've taken it from him in advance, he'll see it's gone, however will not blame you for burglary.

Placing the Rune of the Wolf in the pedestal

- Take the rune to the Area Library. Connect with the Unfilled Attachment presented previously.

- The consolidate things window will spring up. Open the stock and addition the Rune of the Wolf into the vacant space to one side. Then, click Consolidate.

- The platform with the Rune of the Wolf is currently prepared. Click on it to enact it.

- Do likewise with the leftover three platforms - the ones holding the Rune of the Hawk, Rune of the Bear and Rune of the Elk.

- Initiating every one of the four runes will bring down the sculpture and reveal winding steps.

Exploring the Hidden Vault

Your compensation for the journey is all the plunder in the Secret Vault. The main things here are:

- An intriguing (blue) two-gave weapon - Distress. It has an extraordinary weapon activity, Pitiful Lash, which arrangements harm and pulls foes closer.

- A remarkable (green) Robe of Summer. It awards protection from Cold harm.

- Different excellent elixirs, toxic substances and parchments - check the cases that aren't set apart by holding down the ALT key.

The door to the witch's hideout

This page of the Baldurs Gate 3 game aide contains an answer for the riddle with the contorted way to the witch's safe-house situated underneath the Teahouse. Our walkthrough guide depicts two fundamental strategies for managing the entryway obstructing admittance to the following region of the safe-house.

Location of the witch's hideout

The witch's hideaway is connected to the Teahouse mission, which includes meeting Auntie Ethel in her lodge. The Teahouse is situated in the southwest piece of the principal map.

During this experience, it turns out Ethel is a witch and you really want to safeguard Mayrina held by Auntie.

Contorted Entryway is situated in the first Office of the witch's sanctuary. You can contact them by cooperating with the chimney in Ethel's lodge - the flares will be doused and a mysterious passage will be uncovered.

How do you open the gnarled door?

- The choice of utilizing a cheat's instruments won't deal with enormous entryways. You can't open them that way, regardless of whether you utilize the administrations of a prepared rebel hoodlum.

- The first way is to connect with the entryway and begin a "discussion" with them. During this succession, you need to pass an Arcana ability test. Assuming you pass it (model in picture), the hero will discover that the entryway is a deception. In the event that you bomb the test, you can stack the last save record and rehash the test, ideally as a person with an exceptionally evolved knowledge capacity.

- Turn the camera so you can see the way behind the entryway. Click in it and the entire group will stroll through the entryway deception.

- The subsequent way is suggested provided that you bomb the Arcana test and, in spite of conceivable further endeavors, you neglect to finish it effectively. Investigate the Whispering Covers lying on the table. You should simply to make one of your characters put on the veil, and the rest will actually want to continue.

- You can wear the cover similarly as some other headgear. There are two vital elements related with it:

- The veil permits you to pass through a contorted entryway. Act similarly as in the first choice, so turn the camera and snap on the way behind the entryway.

- When the veil is placed on, there is a gamble that the colleague will fall heavily influenced by the witch. A shot in the dark is acted in each round. On the off chance that you prevail with regards to safeguarding, you keep control of the legend, and assuming you bomb the roll, the legend will turn on his buddies. The best strategy is to save the game before each veil is placed on, going through the deception as fast as could be expected, and eliminating the cover subsequent to being on the opposite side.

Moon

On this page of our manual for Baldur's Gate 3 you'll figure out how to settle the moon puzzle.

While crossing the Broke Sanctum (got to from the Troll Camp), you can run into turning circles on the lower level, representing the phases of the moon. Tackling this puzzle opens the way into the Underdark.

Intended solution

Position **yourself so that the lit disc is at the top**. Next, click on the discs in this order to rotate them:

- 1x left disc,

- 1x upper disc,

- 1x lower disc,

- 1x right disc,

- 2x bottom disc,

- 2x upper disc,

- 2x right disc,

- 1x upper disc,

- 1x right disc.

It should be noted this sequence will only work if you haven't tried solving this puzzle before. If you have, load a previous save and try again.

Lockpicking the way forward

You can likewise utilize a lockpick (Discernment check expected) to pull a switch concealed somewhere down here, behind the stone seat, as presented previously. This likewise opens the way to the Underdark.

Necromancer's Book and traps

This page of the Baldurs Gate 3 aide portrays how to take the Magician's Book from the lab in the cellar securely. Safeguarded by strong snares can rapidly kill a legend attempting to take the book.

As an update, the Magician's Book is tracked down in the Sorcerer's cellar. The structure you want to investigate is situated in the southeast piece of Scourged Town. You really want to find the hatch prompting the cellar and afterward offer the right responses while conversing with the mirror.

You'll get to the Sorcerer's lab. The Sorcery of Thay is put away in the eastern part and the way to the room with this ancient rarity is expected to be opened, utilizing the cheat's apparatuses.

Try not to attempt to take the book immediately. It lies on a strain plate, the arrival of which will set off the snares:

- The entryway will not far behind the legend.

- Fire traps are set off, causing extreme fire harm.

To securely eliminate the Magician's Book, you should put another item on the tension plate. For instance, you can find one more book in the lab and move it towards the ancient rarity room (hold down the Left Mouse Button and move it to somewhere else).

Place another book (or one more object of comparable size) on a tension plate close to the Warlock's book. You can securely get The Sorcery of Thay and leave the press-plate room with it.

Nettie and the antidote

This page of Baldurs Gate 3 game aide responds to the subject of how to get a counteractant and fix a harmed legend. Recuperating a controlled person might demonstrate essential after Nettie deceives and harms the hero, forcing a strong pessimistic status on him.

As an update, you meet Nettie in Druid Woods as a feature of the Druid Student mission. You can ask Nettie for help disposing of the parasite. After you tell her the subtleties of the legend's medical issue, she'll welcome you to the following room.

Nettie offers a cure. Assuming you pass the test effectively, you can decide prior to taking the fix that it is really a toxin. In such a circumstance, you can attempt to safeguard yourself calmly from taking the toxic substance by passing the influence test.

Assuming you consume the toxic substance, Nettie will illuminate you regarding this reality and make sense of why she acted along these lines. A solid negative status will be put on the person - At Death's Entryway. It obstructs the hero's all's capacities (primary insights). Besides, this impact deteriorates with each rest.

The cure permits you to dive into the toxic substance. You can obtain get it in more than one way:

The first choice is to get Nettie to give you the remedy by passing a skillcheck (for example influence, terrorizing or duplicity).

The subsequent choice is to overcome Nettie in battle and afterward search her carcass - track down the remedy.

The third choice is to surprise Nettie and utilize the pickpocket choice. On the off chance that you pass the ability test accurately, you can remove the counteractant from her pocket without being distinguished.

It is quite significant that Nettie, subsequent to harming the hero, won't allow him to leave the room naturally. There is an answer for this issue - you can find and open the mystery chamber displayed in the picture, which includes passing through noxious exhaust. The leave prompts an underground passage under the Druid Forest.

Toll House Basement secret room

In the game Baldurs Gate 3, you can visit the Assessment Collector's Structure (Toll House) from The Risen Street area. In our aide we clarify how for get to the basement of the structure with paladins drove by Anders, as well as how to open the entryways in the basement and how to get to the mystery room by settling the riddle. We likewise arranged the most important plunder to be tracked down in the mystery room.

Location of the Tax Collector's Building (Toll House)

- In act 1 of BG3, you can visit the Risen Street district. In its eastern part you'll find the duty collector's house (Toll House).

- Inside the structure is a gathering of paladins under the order of Anders. Naturally, they are not antagonistic towards the group. From the discussion with Anders, you could figure out that they are chasing after the Tiefling in Karlas and this is essential for the journey Chase the Devil.

Where is the key to the basement?

- Before you go down to the basement, you ought to get the Duty Collector's Critical.

- Go to the south of the structure. The key is lying close to the way near where Karl stows away. Utilize the choice to feature objects nearby - hold the ALT key. This will permit to find a tiny item without any problem.

Examination of the first part of the basement

- Get back to the structure and the room with Anders. Here there is a hatch prompting the basement. You can utilize it without battling with the paladins.

- You go over a vault entryway, which requires the utilization of a key got before. You'll open admittance to another piece of the basement.

- Here, you should be cautious due to the snares - these are fundamentally round grates on the floor. Pick the person that is best at remembering them (fruitful discernment tests). You can keep away from or incapacitate the snares.

How to open the secret room?

- You can see the mystery room by moving the camera - the image shows it.

- The mystery room in the basement apparently has no entry entryways. You need to cause the kickoff of the mysterious passage.

- There are 2 stone seats in the basement. You need to isolate 2 characters from the remainder of the group - this is finished by hauling their symbols and separating them from the chain. We portrayed this in more detail on the page How to partition the group?.

- Every one of the 2 characters should sit in a different seat - we checked them in the image. The right activity will prompt the bringing down of the stone passage.

Rewards for solving the riddle

Leave 2 characters on the seats, in light of the fact that after they get up, the passage will close in the future. Delegate again a person equipped for distinguishing and incapacitating snares to investigate the mystery room (among others. long board on the floor).

In the mystery room there is a ton of weapons and different hardware (feature them with the ALT key). The most significant are:

- Great Axe 1

- Gloves of Heroism - they offer a bonus to defense rolls based on strength.

The Hidden Harpers Chest

The secret Harper's Cache and the scuffed rock prompting it is one of the first secrets you'll experience in Baldur's Gate 3. However a piece confusing, the riddle will compensate you with some special treasure which should prove to be useful in the early game.

How to move the scuffed rock?

To arrive at the cache, go to the shore you've started the game on. The suspicious stone is on a small rough bluff you can easily arrive at by going south from the runic circle by one of the fundamental roads at Roadside Cliffs. You'll have to leap to the precipice.

As you approach the edge, your party will make a programmed Nature check. The DC is low, so it's reasonable no less than one of them will pass. In the event that they don't, you'll have to stack your most ongoing save and attempt once more.

Passing the test will allow you to collaborate with the scuffed stone. You really want high Strength to move it. Assuming that your characters are generally not strong enough, you could enroll Karlach the Brute. You'll find out about her on this page. Left click on the stone, hold down the button and move it.

Under the rock is a small chest, concealing some useful treasure and the Harper's Mapwith clues on the best way to arrive at the cache.

How to reach the Harper's Cache?

Perusing the instruction makes a marker show up on your guide, showing the treasure. Follow the way toward the north until you arrive at a small rough edge.

Hop up there and go uphill. After some time you'll spot a wooden structure denoting the cache. There are several barrels scattered around the campsite, and there's a small chest on the wooden stage. Make sure to steal from the skeleton on the ground, as it holds a jewelry, conceding its wearer access to a useful cantrip.

Ornate Mirror

Passing through the gateway behind the Ornate Mirror is one of the actions you really want to act to access the mage's lab in depths underneath Scourged Town taken over by Goblins. The research facility hides a strong curio, a book called Sorcery of Thay - to look further into the book, visit a committed page of our aide.

When connected, the Mirror will ask you a series of questions. Right answers will open access to additional rooms. Mistaken answers, be that as it may, will outrage the mirror, enacting a snare.

How to answer the questions of the Ornate Mirror?

After approaching the mirror, the object will ask a series of questions to the player. This is how the answers should look like:

- Question about the name - either answer honestly or use an option related to your race. Both will take you to the next question.

- Question about allegiance - introduce yourself to the mirror as an ally.

- Question about allegiance to Szass Tam - say that he is a foul lich and deserves thousands of deaths.

- Question about uses of balsam ointment - answer that it is used to clean wounds.

- The question about what the hero would like to see - an accepted answer is a spell that will free the hero from the parasite.

If you choose the following answers, the Mirror will recognize you as an ally of its master and allow you to access the laboratory.

Any incorrect answer will activate a trap - from the inside of the mirror, a metallic levitating sphere will appear, giving the party a taste of steam of fire. What's worse, the trap will also destroy nearby coffins from which aggressive undead will emerge. The undead are strong in numbers, which makes the eventual battle against them very difficult, so it is better to avoid this scenario.

Alternative methods of getting through the mirror

Offering right responses is not by any means the only choice to access the entrance behind the mirror. Almost any legend can attempt to scare the mirror. This will result in a Terrorizing roll. In the event that successful, the mirror will help scared and let you through. Notwithstanding, bombing the roll will enact the snare.

Some classes might approach elective methods of solving the issue of the Mirror. A brute, for instance, can endeavor to shatter the Mirror with a stone. On the off chance that the associated Strength roll was successful, the mirror will be destroyed, and the party can proceed.

How to get to the House of Hope

You can get to the House of Hope in BG3 through the entry on the second floor of the Devil's Expense. In this aide, we clear up how for play out a custom with a pentagram and how to open an entrance to Raphael's house. You'll also figure out how to stay away from the expense for Helsik and make an agreement with her.

How to enter the House of Hope?

You'll meet Raphaela in act 3 at Sharess' Caress in Rivington. The devil will offer you a settlement, in return for your promise to bring the crown, he will also give you the Obscure Mallet. Contingent upon whether you concur or refuse, you'll open a quest connected with sneaking into Raphael's house.

On the off chance that you have aligned with the Githyanki, you'll also meet Kith'rak Voss at the stairs in Sharess' Caress.

Subsequent to conversing with Raphael, return to the first floor of the structure and converse with Korilla, who will be standing at the counter. Persuade her to let you know how to get to the devil's house. She will educate you concerning someone in particular who assisted Gortash with sneaking into the House of Hope.

Go to the Devil's Expense in the Lower City and converse with Helsik. At the point when you advise her that you need to get to Raphael's house, the lady will offer assistance for an expense. You can make a capacity check to diminish the sum, or play out one more check and make an arrangement with her in which you'll need to steal the Gauntlets of Goliath Strength for her.

How to perform the Halsik's ritual?

At the point when you get the book and items expected to play out the custom, go to the second floor of the Devil's Expense. Halsik will eliminate the snare before the entryway by the stairs and you'll have the option to investigate the whole structure.

To open the entrance to the House of Hope, put the items from Halsik's pocket in their legitimate places:

- Put the skull on the star point close to the special stepped area.

- Place the coin in a circle to one side of the skull.

- Put the incense in a circle on the opposite side from the skull.

- Put the jewel in the circle on the left side of the incense.

- Place the Fiendish Marble in an enormous circle in the focal point of the pentagram.

At the point when every one of the items set in the pentagram light up, a gateway prompting Raphael's house will open.

You can also track down all items from Halsik in cupboards and chests in Devil's Charge. So, you don't need to make an arrangement with her to play out the custom and get into the House of Hope. Be that as it may, without her assistance you will not dispose of the snare before the entryway on the second floor.

We advise taking an extended rest prior to going into the House of Hope. Raphael is quite possibly of the most troublesome boss in the whole game.

ABOUT THE AUTHOR

Much thanks to you for perusing this Baldur's Gate 3 guide! I have endeavored to welcome you the most extensive guide on Baldur's Gate 3 that exists, and that implies the guide will be written in a special manner.

www.ingramcontent.com/pod-product-compliance
Lightning Source LLC
La Vergne TN
LVHW051436050326
832903LV00030BD/3111